THE TAMING OF NEW YORK'S WASHINGTON SQUARE

The Taming of New York's Washington Square

A Wild Civility

Erich Goode

NEW YORK UNIVERSITY PRESS

New York

NEW YORK UNIVERSITY PRESS
New York
www.nyupress.org

All photographs taken by and courtesy of Erich Goode.

Library of Congress Cataloging-in-Publication Data
Names: Goode, Erich, author.
Title: The taming of New York's Washington Square : a wild civility / Erich Goode.
Description: New York : New York University Press, [2018] |
Includes bibliographical references and index.
Identifiers: LCCN 2018021039| ISBN 9781479878574 (cl : alk. paper) |
ISBN 9781479898213 (pb : alk. paper)
Subjects: LCSH: Washington Square (New York, N.Y.) | City and town life—New York
(State)—New York. | Social control—New York (State)—New York City. | Deviant
behavior—New York (State)—New York. | New York (N.Y.)—Social life and customs—
21st century. | New York (N.Y.)—Social conditions—21st century.
Classification: LCC F128.65.W3 G66 2018 | DDC 974.7—dc23
LC record available at https://lccn.loc.gov/2018021039

CONTENTS

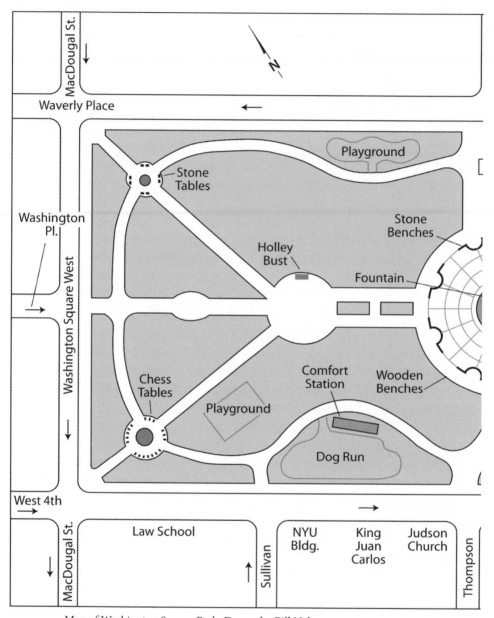

Map of Washington Square Park. Drawn by Bill Nelson.

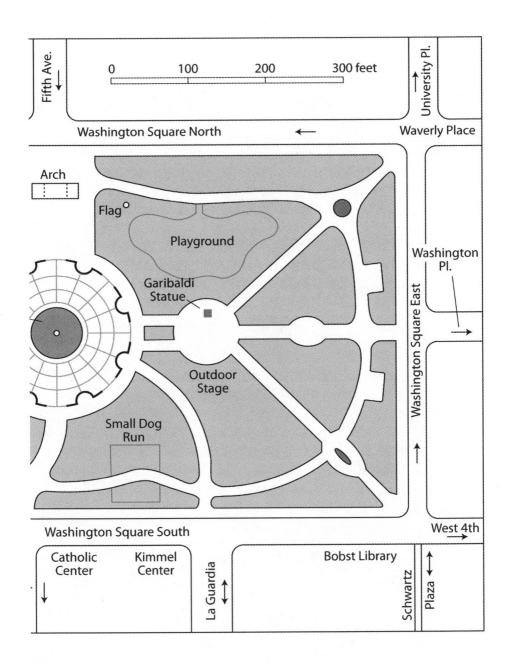

"You finish your book yet?" a middle-aged man teased me as I strolled through the northwest quadrant of the park.

I smiled as best I could and replied, "Working on it. Ninety percent done. I've got a few last-minute details I gotta take care of." I had no idea I'd be pressured into a time schedule by the very people I was studying. Hey, I thought, I'm a researcher. I'm supposed to be invisible! "I'll have the book done later this spring," I added, not unduly optimistically, I hoped. "Maybe June. I'll send the manuscript to the publisher in June."

"I'll be looking for my face on the book cover," the man retorted.

"So will I," was my response. "These things take time," I added.

Indeed they do.

A man is standing outside of New York University's Bobst Library, across the street from Washington Square Park. He seems to be biracial, is about forty, wears a Christian cross, and is holding up a large sign with black and red lettering that reads, on one side, "Racist Israel!" and on the other, "Google It!!! Israel Trains the N.Y.P.D." He yells to his audience, "This is a message to the non-Jews; there's no hope for the Jews. Israel is a racist state—it only allows Jews to emigrate." He crosses the street and walks into the park holding up the sign, ostentatiously displaying it to each party walking by or sitting on a bench. I have a sight-line on him and follow him for about twenty or thirty feet. Everybody gives him a wide berth. People in the NYU community know about the guy but consider him a crank, a crack-pot, a regrettable fool who can be ignored.

A fight breaks out in the dry fountain, but the would-be pugilists are too drunk to land real punches. A Park Enforcement Patrol (PEP) officer tells a guitarist to unplug his amplifier; though he complies, when the PEP leaves, the young musician makes a fist, explaining to a friend how mad he becomes when he's told he can't do something. One busker grabs the props of another—oranges he had been juggling—and hurls them toward some nearby trees, shoves him aside, commands the stage for himself, and begins his own act. A seeming protester holds up signs and loudly and pleadingly proclaims the virtues of farting. A would-be golfer grabs a club and whacks a rubber ball toward a crowd of people, hitting a woman in the leg; he retrieves the ball without apologizing. Someone who's clearly mentally disordered delivers an incoherent, biblical-sounding oration, first to one man, then to a woman, then to a couple, all of whom withdraw from his unwelcome presence and disordered blather; he approaches me, and, after a few minutes of cheerfully smiling and nodding, I do the same as well. A man sneaks off into a copse of bushes and urinates. Skateboarders zoom this way and that, weaving through streams of pedestrians at top speed. Three homeless gents sneak into the park after midnight and lie down on the grass; two NYPD follow them and eject them. Two guys blow up a fuck doll and explain how to have sex with it.

I'm with Phillip, a friend, under the Arch, and we're talking with Bob, an attractive, dark-skinned, athletic-looking man who's approaching forty. We watch a voluptuous young woman with honey-colored skin and a beautiful, curly, blonde confection of a hair-do on top of her head, wearing a summery, yellow-and-white dress, walk by, crossing Washington Square North. Suddenly, Bob bolts, runs across the street, catches up with the woman, and begins speaking with her on the sidewalk along Fifth Avenue. Dumbfounded, Phillip and I look at one another, then watch Bob chatting with the woman. After several minutes, he trudges back to us, looking downcast.

I ask him, "What'd you say?"

Bob responds, "I said, 'That's a nice dress you're wearing.'"

I ask, "What did *she* say?"

He tells us, "She said, 'Thank you.'"

I ask, "And then what?"

Bob replies, "Then I said she was pretty."

"*Then* what happened?"

"She kept walking," Bob tells us, sadly. Phillip and I look at one another and burst out laughing. We slap palms and hook fingers. "She's a *fine* lookin' woman," I say.

"Yes, she is," says Phillip. Our companion's face expresses abject humiliation; he was spurned, demeaned, and mortified, and doesn't like the way it feels.

To our right, there's a guy kneeling on the ground wearing a grey Kabuki wig and a fierce Kabuki mask. He has taped a canvas to the ground and propped up a red silk bag in front of it, and in front of the bag, a small sign that reads, "Contributions Welcome from those of you who Watch my Performance." He takes several sticks of black chalk out of a smaller bag and furiously attacks the canvas with curved strokes. People walk by and glance at his activity and his artwork; when he completes the picture, he has gathered fifteen or twenty onlookers. The subject is a kneeling woman dressed in tatters with a terrified look on her face; at the top of the painting, a dozen singleton eyes stare harshly and disapprovingly at her.

I scan the horizon. Behind us, there's a white gymnast—upside-down, standing on her hands, her legs leaning against the Arch; to our right, there's the Kabuki guy, who's Japanese; facing him, halfway toward the fountain, there's a bubble man, who's large and black; running toward us there are six or eight small children, who are white, South Asian, black, and East Asian, squealing and running after the bubble man and popping his bubbles; to our left, at the entry to the pathway that heads to the Garibaldi circle, there's a group of Sikhs wearing turbans and distributing rose water to passersby. I say to my friend, who's African American, "Man, there's a lot of diversity in the park."

He says, "Yeah, diversity and tolerance. That's what I love about it."

And yet, there are limits to both diversity and tolerance; Washington Square is neither dangerous nor out of control. It is not a place where anything goes. "Why do you come here?" I ask Jimmy, a white, seventy-eight-year-old Bronx resident. "There are lots of nice New York parks closer. Why come to Washington Square?"

"I like it here," he responded. "There's nothing like this place. Central Park? Forget about it. Tompkins Square? Belligerent drunks, guys on the needle nodding off. Here, it's peaceful. Nothing bad happens here." But Jimmy does grumble about the skateboarders, the homeless, the noise-makers, the drunks, and the schizophrenics.

And therein resides the nub of my inquiry: How do all these people, with their tumultuously different notions of right and wrong, what they consider good or bad, acceptable or reprehensible, get along in this limited space? How do people who visit a public space that's known for celebrating diversity and nonconformity react when they observe someone engaging in behavior of which they disapprove? What constitutes a meaningful, relevant reaction to a supposedly wrongful act in a public setting? What constitutes deviance in an unconventional setting? Most sociologists define "deviance" as behavior, expressed beliefs, or mental or physical conditions that violate a social norm or a value held by members of a group, category, collectivity, or social circle (an "audience") who regard the violation as wrongful, unacceptable, or offensive, which tends to cause them to punish, express disapproval, avoid, and/or condemn the violators. Deviance is a matter of degree, from mild unconventionality to capital crime. It is also mostly contextual—acceptable here, unacceptable there. And it is negatively reacted to in different ways by different audiences. Classic or "high consensus" cases of deviance include illicit drug dealing, homelessness, schizophrenia, murder, rape, and robbery. Here, in the pages of this book, we'll be meeting denizens and visitors of Washington Square Park, some of whom engage in what others regard as wrongful behavior. Yet, here we are, in an extremely tolerant and diverse setting; what do park-goers *do* when they encounter behavior that draws censure elsewhere? How do they react? What do they say to one another about what they've seen and heard? What does it take for someone to engage in behavior that's so offensive and considered so wrongful even to people here for them to react in a negative, punishing fashion?

In a study of unconventional behavior that takes place in a public place, the sociologist seeks to uncover social and cultural *tendencies* rather than lay out the minute particulars of specific instances of unique or marginal phenomena. Looking at the social life of Washington Square Park, my *mind* fixes on the generic, yet my *eye* and *ear* fix on the particular. Here, I offer multiple anecdotes to document and dramatize the heart and soul of Washington Square—to illuminate its culture and social structure. I have done some counting as well, and that likewise seems to offer reasonable evidence that authenticates the presence and influence of *certain kinds* of ongoing conditions and dynamics. Statistics offer one way of showing how things are, and so does anecdotal evidence. Stories? *True* stories? They ornament and demonstrate generalities. Well told, they are fun. Even statistical tables convey a certain charm, and they can pack a great deal of information into just a few lines.

I'm something of an agnostic when it comes to sociological cause and effect. I'm not entirely sure *why* people do unconventional things—for most behaviors, multiple explanations make sense—but I do know that observers and onlookers, whom interactionist sociologists call "audiences," frequently react in certain ways to behaviors they consider untoward. Instead of attempting to explain why people engage in unacceptable behavior, here, I'm more interested in what sociologist Edwin Lemert called the "social penalties, rejection, and segregation" to which these others, these audiences, frequently subject putative wrongdoers (1951, p. 22). I pay attention to audiences and their responses—or nonresponses—rather than attempt to answer the more global, and much tougher, "Why?" question. My focus seems more grounded to me, and what I observe, more amenable to the kind of enquiry to which I am sympathetic.

As I conceptualize the matter, Washington Square is a book—a *text*—that demands to be read but expects no singular interpretation. Some readings of this text *make a lot more sense* than others—to the park visitor, the reader, and the social science researcher.

This book constitutes my reading of Washington Square Park.

1

The People in the Square

A white borzoi wearing a Mets vest leaps over the barrier at the fountain in the center of Washington Square Park and trots down the steps into the pool, then laps up some water as he's wading. A middle-aged man, clearly the dog's owner, wearing a black jacket and black pants and a blue-and-white baseball cap, walks toward the fountain, leash in hand. The canine runs up the stairs, hops back over the wall, and heads for the Arch, then curves around and runs onto the adjacent grass and begins romping past startled couples on towels and a barking German shepherd on a leash; his owner walks toward him and the two play for a while. He takes off again, running to an open garbage can south of the fountain, yanking out and eating a few tasty morsels. As his owner approaches him, a woman, visibly annoyed, begins admonishing the man.

"Don't you know there's an ordinance against unleashed dogs in Washington Square? It's the *law*," she says sternly, with emphatic concern. He nods and says he knows. She stiffly walks past him, her face a mask of barely suppressed anger. By this time, the dog has attracted a crowd of a dozen people, myself included, who pet and softly coo to him.

The owner proudly tells a woman who's petting his dog that it has appeared on TV and in commercials. "Here," he says. "Let me give you my card."

"The *dog* has a business card?" the woman asks, expressing surprise. Putting the card in her pocketbook, she shouts, "Oh, *please* take a picture of me with your dog!" She hands her cell phone to the owner, who complies with the request. I ask the man for his business card; though it is not the *borzoi's* business card, it does feature a photograph of the dog's *eye*: Dr. Emil William Chynn, the owner, is an eye surgeon, and he has just violated a park ordinance against unleashed dogs, presumably so that he can attract the attention of potential customers. But no one there—save one, the woman who complained—was distressed that such an elegant, graceful, friendly canine was running around off-leash in the park. Informal social control, such as it was, proved too feeble to squelch such a delicious infraction of park rules.

I'm sitting with a friend on a bench in the Holley Plaza; across from us, diagonally, perhaps thirty feet away, there's an older gentleman with a goatee and a fairly large belly sitting on a bench, his head back, sunning himself. His eyes are closed, and he's shirtless, wearing only a pair of white shorts—no socks, no shoes. About ten minutes after we notice him, he begins putting on his shirt and socks and shoes, and less than a minute later, an NYPD (New York Police Department) officer wheeling a bike approaches him. The officer stops and begins talking with him. My companion and I are too far away to hear what they're saying, so we speculate.

As the man's talking, he's scowling and forcefully gesticulating. I say to my friend, "I think the cop saw him without a shirt and he's telling the guy he could get a citation and he's arguing with the cop about it. He obviously doesn't like the ordinance. Look at his body language, look at the expression on his face." We wait a while as they continue talking. "If I went over there right now and tried to interview them, they'd tell me to get lost, but if I wait till the cop leaves, the man would talk to me." Within a couple of minutes, the cop wheels the bike away and my friend says, "Go, talk to him."

The goateed man begins walking toward the fountain. I say goodbye to my friend, cross the circle, follow the man, and catch up with him about twenty feet ahead. "Hey, man, did that cop tell you to put a shirt on?"

He says, "Nah, we were talkin' about the fuckin' *noise* machine over there." He motions toward a young man near the fountain who's banging on a metal plate and four overturned white plastic buckets he uses as drums. "Look at that guy," the goateed man says. "It's like *Groundhog Day*—the same shit over and over again. Listen to him."

I say, "Well, this is a live-and-let-live atmosphere, isn't it? What can you do about it?"

He says, "You can *stab* him, but then you'd have to go to jail," and walks off.

I shake my head, chuckle, walk back to Holley Plaza, and resume my seat on the bench. The drummer's still doing his clamorous thing near the fountain, and it can be heard for more than a hundred feet in any direction. A man sitting on the bench next to me stands up and asks one of the two PEP (Park Enforcement Patrol) officers walking by if they can get the drummer to stop. The PEP replies that there is no ordinance that prohibits him from drumming; it's a violation of the law only if he uses amplification—*then* they can make him stop. "Wait a minute," says the guy. "What about the drummers yesterday? You guys asked *them* to stop and they left."

The PEP replies, "That's in a different category—that's two or more drummers, and *that's* prohibited. I can't stop *this* guy from drumming, he's just one guy."

So the man again objects, "But he's playing four or five drums." The PEP says, "That's allowed. The number of drums *he* plays doesn't matter." The PEP officers go off and the man on the bench is visibly annoyed. He's joined by two other annoyed guys, including the goateed man, who has just returned. They discuss the matter, commiserating with one another. "You hear it all day long," one says.

"I hear it in my apartment," says another.

"That woman over there asked him to quiet down and he said he would, but he just kept on doing it," says the third.

The goateed man suggests, "We could all just sit down right opposite him and *stare* at him. Bill is gonna do it, Harry's gonna do it, and *I'm* gonna do it. But if we *do* it, we'll get thrown out of the park." One of them says he's leaving and as he does, the goateed guy says, "Go kick the bucket." Nobody laughs at his joke.

As matters later revealed themselves to me, shirtlessness is allowed—in principle, to both men and women. And the clamorous drummer? Local representatives appealed to a sergeant in the park rangers and managed to have the rude, cacophonous percussionist banned from Washington Square.

Some existential actualities become conceptual and cultural *things*; they are phenomena that are real to us as recognizable entities that possess a life of their own. Big "things" attract a great deal of attention; little ones invite the disparaging question, frequently raised by comedian John Oliver, "Why is this a thing?" Washington Square Park is a "thing" that both comprises a physical, material area and most definitely deserves to be called *a place*, which constitutes, as sociologist Lyn Lofland tells us, a space that is, individually or collectively, "known about"; it is, for regulars, tourists, one-time visitors, and nonvisitors alike, a "familiarized locale," a "memorialized locale." Such places are *especially meaningful spaces* that are "rich in association and steeped in sentiment" (Lofland, 1984, p. 64; her italics). Thus expressed, explains sociologist Michael Ian Borer, a space "is only a place if it has culture makers—human beings—to create it, use it, live with it, live through it, and consider it significant" (2006, p. 175). Yet, in spite of being a phenomenological and sociological actuality—a *thing*—sociologists have neglected to give this storied place, Washington Square Park, its due. Here, in this study, I attempt to rectify that neglect.

Not all producers of culture go along with the neglect. Filmmakers have set their movies in Washington Square; Henry James wrote about the affluent, gilded, and flawed residents who once lived along Washington Square North, its northern border; André Kertész photographed its charisma and mystery, and Weegee, some of its eccentric, nonconformist visitors; tourist guides insist that travelers who come to New York from virtually every point on the globe visit this spot; and during the 1950s and 1960s, the fountain area of the park attracted folk singers, including Woodie Guthrie, Bob Dylan, Joan Baez—and, oddly enough, Ed Koch—as well as poets, including Allen Ginsberg, which made it the focal point not only for the space but for the surrounding community as well. Historians, both amateur and academic, have chronicled its past, its idiosyncrasies, and its importance, while countless artists have memorialized its charm. In *November, Washington Square*, Edward Hopper captured Judson Church, along with lower buildings to its immediate left, and to the right, a sector of the park's fountain, circa 1890. In his 1917 etching, *Arch Conspirators*, John French Sloan captured a drunken Marcel Duchamp, along with five of his confederates, on top of the Arch, declaring a "free and independent Republic of Washington Square." F. Luis Mora portrayed the 1907 meeting of Mark Twain and Robert Louis Stevenson on a bench in the park, and in 1989, James Rizzi graphically demonstrated that "Washington Ain't No Square Park." Off and on between 1904 and 1934, William Glackens—one of the founders of the "Ashcan school" of art, known for portraying quotidian scenes of New York street life—rented studios and apartments across the street from the square, and, looking out of his window, painted numerous canvases depicting the park and its visitors. And today, New York University makes this park its campus—the proverbial college quad.

What is this "thing" that Washington Square Park constitutes? What is the space's sociological significance? And what does that tell us about deviance and social control?

I'm sitting on a bench just west of the fountain with Nachman and Etti, two Israeli friends. "Think about it," I said. "In Washington Square, there's the balloon man, the pigeon woman, two pigeon men, the squirrel woman, the squirrel man, the woman with the plush pigeon statues, Tic and Tac, the acrobatic tumblers, you've got Colin Huggins, the pianist, you've got the guy who writes quotes from the Constitution with chalk in the area around the fountain, you've got the sand painter. I mean, the list goes on and on." I ask Etti if there's anything like Washington Square in Jerusalem. She shakes her head. "The ultra-Orthodox wouldn't accept it. Not even in Tel Aviv."

Since Etti and Nachman have lived in London, I conjecture, "Maybe Hyde Park is the closest thing to it."

"Not Hyde Park either," Etti replies. "There's much more diversity here. There's no comparison. Washington Square is completely unique. There's nothing like it anywhere in the world."

Washington Square: A Historical Introduction

The physical space on which Washington Square Park sits began its relationship with humans in a close-by Lenape village. It's not difficult to imagine the Lenape (also called the Delaware Indians) tramping through the space's then-marshy, woodsy terrain and fishing in Minetta Brook, which flowed within its borders. In 1625, the Dutch founded New Amsterdam at the tip of Manhattan Island and captured the lands north of the settlement. Peter (or Petrus) Stuyvesant owned and operated a sixty-two-acre farm (in Dutch, "*bouwerij*," or "bowery") just east and a bit north of what is now the park and deeded some of its land to freed slaves, but the Anglo-Dutch Wars (1664–1674), culminating in the Treaty of Westminster (1674), permitted the British to wrest New Amsterdam from Dutch hands. English municipal ordinances prohibited persons of African descent from owning property and so, by 1716, the authorities seized the real estate deeded to the former slaves and their descendants (Folpe, 2002, p. 54). After the American Revolution, the Common Council of New York purchased the southern portion of the land, turning it into a potter's field or burial ground for impoverished souls, but the council closed that down in 1825; the remains of twenty thousand bodies still rest underground. Contrary to legend, and despite an actual historical hanging—in 1820, of one Rose Butler, a slave accused of burning her master's house to the ground—from a gallows, in a spot somewhere between the current Arch and the fountain, no one was ever hanged from the property's now-three-hundred-plus-year-old elm, which nonetheless came to be nicknamed the "hanging elm" or the "hanging tree" (Miller, 1990, p. 54). In 1826, New York City bought the pauper's graveyard, leveled it, and created a military parade ground out of it; unfortunately, the "weight of the horse-drawn cannons proved too much for the rotting coffins underneath" (p. 54), and so, the spot had to be relandscaped.

During the 1830s, developers began building a row of grand homes for affluent families on the north side of the parade grounds, with gardens, stables, and carriage houses. Washington Square North became the most fashionable address in town. In the United States during the nineteenth century, decisions to build urban parks were made largely by the members of the wealthiest stratum of each city. They originally visualized parks as their own domain, where they could promenade and display their finery to one another. Historically, the elites have characteristically designed and built urban parks as institutions to serve or favor their own class interests, whether directly or indirectly, either for their own enjoyment or as a noblesse oblige means of pleasing the masses in order to better govern or control them. Toward the latter part of the century, the affluent class came to realize that city parks could draw the ever-burgeoning working masses away from taverns and ale houses and cultivate them to a more healthful, moral, and righteous way of life (Rosenzweig and Blackmar, 1992). In the nineteenth century, planners and designers intended public parks as an explicit means of social control, part of "the processes that tend to counteract deviant tendencies" (Taylor, 1999, p. 422).

All cities must solve the problem of a continuous supply of clean water. After several fires in the late 1700s and the early 1800s destroyed much of the city's infrastructure, the City of New York built an aqueduct of iron pipes stretching from the Croton Reservoir, over forty miles away, to Bryant Park, then called Reservoir Square. New York's Common Council proposed a similar structure for Washington Square; its original fountain, one hundred feet across, was built in 1852. Another fountain with a smaller basin and absent its original iron railing replaced it in 1871; henceforth, commented one social historian more than a century later, it would remain "the gravitational center of Washington Square" (Folpe, 2002, pp. 38, 102, 114, 157). Clearly, the presence of the fountain disrupted the park's utility as a parade ground, and so, that same year, the newly formed New York City Department of Parks chartered the parade ground as a public park—Washington Square Park—landscaping it for that purpose, laying down curved rather than straight footpaths, a sloping rather than flat terrain. We can delineate the history of Washington Square's acreage as follows: 1600s, Lenape woodlands; 1600s to 1716, Dutch and African American–cultivated farmland; 1797 to 1825, a potter's field, or burial ground for the indigent; 1826–1871, military parade grounds; 1871 to the present, a municipal park. In 1895, a permanent seventy-two-foot marble arch, modeled after the Arc de Triòmphe in Paris, was built to replace an earlier temporary wood-and-plaster version, which commemorated George Washington's military and civilian achievements.

In 1990, at the Museum of the City of New York, curator Jan Seidler Ramirez mounted the exhibition *Within Bohemia's Borders*, which documented the colonization of Greenwich Village by bohemian artists, a lure that stretches as far back as the immediate post–Civil War era. The community quickly became a "cradle of counterculture," a "district of difference," a "haven for nonconformists" (Ramirez, 1990, pp. 1, 3); almost inevitably, its denizens routinely hung out in Washington Square Park. By the early 1920s, the Village had acquired a reputation as an interesting, unconventional, artsy place to visit, and so, as a result, tourists began to be attracted to the place, often conveyed in tour buses that turned around on a roadway just north of the fountain. Eventually, some residents "feared the honky-tonk aspects of becoming a tourist mecca" (L.S. Harris, 2003, p. 210). As a result of New York's growing population and subsequent housing boom, builders began tearing down some of the low structures at the southern end of Fifth Avenue and built taller apartment buildings in their place—a trend that culminated, in 1927, with the grand twenty-seven-story skyscraper at One Fifth Avenue, which looms over the park. Afterwards, the Village—and the square—would never be the same; in 1951, One Fifth acquired a sibling—the twenty-story address, Two Fifth Avenue—whose lobby once featured a transparent plastic tube through which water from the Square's Minetta Brook flowed (Miller, 1990, p. 55). Sadly—according to the amateur historian at the building's front desk whom I consulted on the matter—management ordered the tube disassembled in 2012.

The Great Depression plunged the art world—indeed, much of the nation as a whole—into an abyss. As a means of selling artwork directly to its appreciators, the Artists' Aid Committee organized outdoor exhibits—some of them on the sidewalks adjoining or in Washington Square—that proved to be successful and profitable. But these exhibits made it clear to all who attended them that the park was in dire need of upgrading; its lawns had turned brown, its trees were "withering," its fountain leaked, the walkways were cracked and dangerous, litter was strewn throughout the park, and vandalism and panhandling were common (Folpe, 2002, pp. 278, 279).

Robert Moses, commissioner of New York City's Department of Parks between 1934 and 1960, proposed a thorough renovation of the park. But as far back as the thirties, Moses also intended to cut a major highway *through* the park (Folpe, 2002, pp. 10, 280) to connect it with lower Manhattan and Wall Street, as well as build a more southerly, raised east-west expressway that would seriously disrupt the neighborhood immediately south of Houston Street (a neighborhood that is now referred to as SoHo). The controversy lasted until 1958, when progressive forces defeated the Moses plan; the highway was not built, the park was spared, and even the Fifth Avenue bus turnaround was closed in 1959. *Ad seriatim*, the various schemes of Robert Moses, each involving substantial traffic flow through or directly around (or under, or over) Washington Square, were rejected by Village activists. Eventually, the community triumphed over the multiple proposals of planners and politicians who favored cars over the integrity of neighborhoods; the city settled on a plan to keep north-south vehicular traffic to a minimum *and* to close the square itself to all traffic except for emergency and police vehicles, preserving the space, in the words of Norman Vincent Peale, "as an island of quietness in this hectic city" (Folpe, 2002, p. 305). The defeat of the various Moses schemes, the killing of the highway plans that were to cut through a settled neighborhood, with cars as their centerpiece, all of this proved to be the death knell of wholesale urban clearance for American cities.

In contrast, New York University has been successful in acquiring most of the properties adjacent to the park, and, in the process of such acquisition, roiling activist Villagers and park denizens alike, who threw one protest after another into the university's path. NYU has had a Washington Square presence since the university's founding in 1831, as we saw, decades before the square's institutionalization as a municipal park. The early 1830s launched a construction boomlet on Washington Square North, where some of the grandest and most fashionable homes in the City at the time were built. By this time, the die had been cast establishing the symbiotic relationship between the university and the square, but the coming-of-age period of NYU's development has only been during the past generation or two, an era in which the university has risen enormously in prestige, endowment, budget, and the success of its alumni. For many students and their parents, the combination of the reputation of the school, along with the quality of its instruction, the luster of its faculty (thirty-seven Nobel laureates, thirty Pulitzer Prize winners, thirty Academy Award awardees), and its Washington Square location, makes it—according to the *Princeton Review*—one of the nation's "Top Dream Colleges." And, since most of the NYU buildings are large, are minimally landscaped, and offer insufficient sitting spaces, as I said, the institution's students use the park as their campus, the proverbial college quad—an ideal spot to kick back, socialize, gossip, and picnic. Remarkably, students report few untoward incidents with the minority of the park's sketchy characters, including the marijuana sellers and the homeless men; their experiences in the park seem to be overwhelmingly positive.

On its way to transforming itself from a somewhat dingy, low-prestige, but large commuter school to an illustrious, world-class, wealthy, and highly ranked university with a great deal of economic, political, and municipal clout, NYU won most of these battles. But with respect to space, the university is "bursting at its seams" (Bernard, 2011). "NYU 2031/NYU in NYC," NYU's long-range plan for growth, aims, according to its public relations office, "to be a thoughtful, comprehensive, city-wide vision for thinking about how to keep the University moving forward academically while respecting the communities and the city in which we make our home."

According to an April 4, 2012, memorandum from Lynne Brown, the senior vice president for university relations and public affairs, several NYU committees had identified a lack of space and "inadequate facilities" as seriously problematic for the university, "imperiling" the reputation of the school and its ability to recruit faculty. While the university's facilities are scattered around the City, "experience has taught us that most faculty and students prefer to be located near our Washington Square core." The university needs six million square feet of additional space, of which, according to the NYU 2031 plan, 1.5 to 2.2 million square feet are planned to be located around Washington Square Park. According to the university's representatives, acquiring this space remains at the center of the conflict. And perhaps central to the conflict is the fact that the superblocks on which these properties sit are home to several pieces of parkland, which ecologically minded interest groups intended to preserve. Opponents of the university's expansionist strategy want NYU to become a great university *without* having the university buy up substantial properties around the square; that may not be possible.

Washington Square Today

The latest, six-year-long municipal renovation was contentious. Finally completed in 2014, it cost $30.6 million—mostly in public monies. The project included centering the fountain to a clean line-of-sight perspective through the Arch, up Fifth Avenue, to the Empire State Building and midtown, and down Thompson Street to the "Freedom Tower" (One World)—the replacement for the ill-fated World Trade Center towers—and the Wall Street area; hiring off-duty police officers; constructing granite benches, which heat up and retain heat at higher temperatures, rendering them unsittable (Anderson, 2012); covering the asphalt mounds in the southwest corner and installing a playground covered with an Astroturf-type material; building a new "comfort station" or restroom; creating a small and a big dog run to ensure that the big ones don't bully the smaller ones; and installing a *pétanque* court, lampposts, and iron fences encompassing the park (Gregory, 2014). As the renovation progressed, I heard multiple complaints about it from park-goers; when it was completed, virtually everyone I talked to said they thought it had been a good idea. Perhaps the controversy over the construction of Bobst Library proved most notably controversial. Announced in 1964 but not completed until 1973, the remarkable-looking yet hulking, fortress-like, twelve-story red sandstone structure designed by distinguished architect Philip Johnson that the university built across the street from the southeast side of the park seems out of place in its environment and casts a shadow over much of the square. The controversy over its construction has long been settled, and it now looks over a stretch of parkland that is as peaceful yet as lively as any comparable space could be in the middle of a bustling neighborhood in the largest city in America. Today, the park, by common consensus, is a more pleasant place to visit than it was before the renovation.

The fountain is surrounded by a circular walkway and double-circumnavigated by the infamous eight black stone benches—"infamous" because of their tendency to heat up during periods of hot weather—as well as dozens of wooden benches. Three large and two smaller footpaths branch off the circle. Hundreds of trees and shrubs adorn its grounds, in addition to several acres of grass (a great deal of it worn to the ground through constant human use) and numerous flora, which is dug up in the fall and replanted in the spring. At the southwest corner, there are eighteen built-in, inlaid chess tables and, in the north-west corner, eight larger, non-chess tables.

By my count, there are 454 four-person wooden benches in the common areas of the park (40 of them in the fountain circle); they are 88 inches wide and 14 inches deep, divided in two by an iron armrest, thereby creating two two-person benches 44 inches wide. In addition, as I said, there are eight granite benches 33 inches wide, shaped like a semi-circle in the middle (13 paces long) with a "stem" at each end (6.5 paces long), providing roughly 420 feet of sitting space. They are wide enough to accommodate one person on each side; irregularly arranged and completely filled, they could fit 600 sitters. Two-person benches are also provided in the dog runs, playgrounds, and chess area, as well as two nook circlets at the eastern side of the park. All the common benches can reasonably accommodate more than three thousand visitors, and those in the more specialized areas, perhaps another three hundred. (In the playgrounds, of course, the children rarely sit; they're too busy playing.) There's also the fountain wall or barrier, as well as steps leading into the fountain pool, popular sitting spots for park-goers, the steps leading to the performance area, and those at the plinth of the Garibaldi statue and the Holley bust. And of course, there's the grass, spotty as it is. In addition, many people in the central fountain area stand and mill around, and a substantial number are in purposeful motion, walking through the park.

While Washington Square Park is a patchwork structure, with seemingly accidental bits and pieces built or renovated over the course of more than a century and a half, it nonetheless satisfies the hankerings of a substantially broad constituency, drawn from a multiplicity of neighborhoods and suburbs, not to mention tourists from almost everywhere, as well as NYU students. The visitors to this plot of turf virtually define diversity; for its size, socially, it is one of the most heterogeneous and variegated spaces on the planet—a far cry from the park's surrounding neighborhood, which is predominantly white and comparatively affluent. I began wondering about how the park's extremely diverse visitors get along with one another, whether and to what extent visitors reach a consensus about what constitutes wrongdoing there, and what sorts of behavior, to those visitors, violate park rules or the local normative order. In short, what's considered deviant or wrongful in Washington Square Park, and how do park-goers judge and react to it?

The Motliest Assortment

"There are many reasons to disparage Washington Square Park," intones a popular tourist guidebook, published only months before 9/11. "It attracts the motliest assortment of characters of any open space in Manhattan—drug dealers, street performers, runaway teens, aging hippies, NYU students, bridge-and-tunnel teenyboppers, and the all-too-ubiquitous homeless—all up to God knows what. Many people who do not belong to these groups therefore shun the park as unsavory." And yet, in spite of its "varied and well-documented shortcomings, people still flock to this open space. Despite the presence of all the unsavory characters, it remains a fairly safe place" (Morrone, 2002, p. 76). Certain *kinds* of deviance—the "unsavory" nature of the space, and the "unsavory" characters it attracts—may even offer more savory characters an *inducement* to visit Washington Square.

As we saw, sociologists define deviance as behavior, beliefs, and characteristics that violate society's, or a collectivity's, norms, the violation of which tends to attract negative reactions from audiences. Such negative reactions include punishment, condemnation, criticism, denigration, condescension, stigma, pity, contempt, and scorn. Perhaps the most common reaction to someone doing or saying something or looking a certain way is the withdrawal of sociability—walking away from the person in question. Deviance is a matter of degree. The *stronger* the negative reaction and the *greater* the number of audiences that react this way—and the *more sizable and influential* the audiences are—the more likely it is that the violator will attract negative reactions or labeling, and the more certain sociologists feel that they have an instance of deviance on their hands. Not all members of a given audience will react in the same way; usually—even within a specific society or social circle—reactions to such violations vary. And of course, the very parties whom the mainstream, the majority, define as deviant have acted and do act on their own definition of deviance; after all, some deviants—whom some sociologists refer to as "folk devils" (Cohen, 1972)—fight back (McRobbie, 1994). The sociologist's "deviance" heavily overlaps with the humanist's and literary scholar's "alterity." There are alterities of race, class, gender, nationality, politics, religion, cognitive beliefs, sexuality, physical condition, and behavior. Deviance is a form of otherness, but, with several important twists, covering the spectrum from mild to extreme, it shifts around according to the designee and the audience in question; it is an interactional, micro *and* a structural, macro concept, as well as a routine, mundane notion, woven into our everyday lives. The contextual part is basic. What's *deviant* depends on the audience making the effective judgment and reacting to what *its members* consider wrongdoing.

I'm interested in what constitutes deviance or putative wrongdoing in this very unconventional milieu: how parties in this space define it, and what park visitors and the agents of formal social control *do* when they encounter what they consider an instance of it. Even in a "society of saints, a perfect cloister of individuals," explained Emile Durkheim, one of sociology's pioneers, crime *as we know it* will not exist, "but faults which appear venial to the layman will create there the same scandal that the ordinary offense does in the ordinary consciousness" (1895/1938, pp. 68, 69). Washington Square Park is no "society of saints," but its collective definition of deviance is not what it is in mainstream America. But what is this Washington Square Park "definition of deviance"? Here, I'd like to offer a kaleidoscope or mosaic of observations of behavior and verbal articulations of attitudes by park-goers that operationalize or manifest several *overlapping* definitions.

In the park, extremely diverse aggregates of people get along reasonably well in a fairly confined space; I'd like to explore the question of how this works. Several unarmed, green-uniformed Parks Enforcement Patrol (PEP) officers walk through Washington Square on an irregular schedule between six in the morning and midnight, less frequently, the NYPD patrols the park, and, very occasionally, as I've seen, New York University Public Safety personnel make an appearance; in addition, nine surveillance cameras keep an electronic eye on locations around the park. But there's vastly more to the picture than agents of formal social control.

The PEP and the surveillance cameras aside, the most effective social control is informal or interpersonal in nature, activated as much by the park's visitors and denizens as by its salaried agents. Every day, many people engage in infractions of the rules explicitly spelled out by the signs posted at several entrances to the park, yet the agents empowered to enforce these rules do not enforce them to the full extent of their powers. As I have observed in the moments following one feeble fracas among indigents, law enforcement does spring into action when a certain line is crossed. Moreover, any socio-ecological space encompasses a diversity of audiences—social circles or collectivities who evaluate behavior in disparate ways. And yet, through it all, there's a method to this seeming madness.

Jane Jacobs remains one of our most influential observers of city life; her concept "eyes upon the street," the cornerstone of her insightful volume *The Death and Life of Great American Cities*—a classic after more than a half-century since its publication, in the early 1960s—informs the perspective of virtually all criminologists who study urban street crime. She argued that neighbors are the most effective force in inhibiting predatory crime and the fear that it engenders (1961, pp. 45–46, 71); but urban life has morphed considerably since she wrote; perhaps she overstressed the role of informal social control and underplayed the role the police play. In Washington Square Park, we do see eyes on the fountain, eyes on the walkways, eyes on the grass, and eyes on the benches—all exercised, for the most part, not only by local residents but by outside park visitors as well. Clearly, this is an unusual urban space; the noteworthy verity about this piece of real estate is that the ratio of small deviancies and petty offenses to serious crime is enormous, probably substantially greater than in most other places. And since the square's clientele is diverse and largely cosmopolitan, intervention is hardly ever activated for trivial, lifestyle behaviors. But behavior in the square hews to sociological patterning and so, it is both similar to as well as different from deviance and social control elsewhere.

We see several exceptions to the rule of eyes upon the street, the first brought about by the mobility of pedestrians and the second by the permeability of outdoor spaces. Looking at social control in its myriad manifestations, we see that park folk *frequently* exercise social control over parties who exhibit mental disorders, but usually in a specific and particular way: They ignore or walk away from mentally unbalanced individuals. The disordered are, in any case, relatively impervious to the usual forms of social control. In what are probably the three most important works bearing on the approach I've adopted here—Jane Jacobs, *The Death and Life of Great American Cities* (1961), Howard S. Becker, *Outsiders: Studies in the Sociology of Deviance* (1963), and William H. Whyte, *The Social Life of Small Urban Spaces* (1980)—Jacobs didn't discuss them (1961) and Howard Becker (1963, pp. 5–6) downplayed the "mental disease" and "medical metaphor" dimension of deviance, but William H. Whyte did include them among the categories of humanity ("odd people") that local management and business interests regarded as "undesirables" (1980, p. 64) and continually shooed away from their establishments.

We *do* see, and quite frequently, Parks Enforcement Patrol intervention in response to behavior that interferes with the rights of others—as we saw in the case of sound amplification, smoking, both cigarettes and marijuana, drinking, and, though only occasionally, skateboarding. But informally, when "eyes upon the square" sense that certain parties have seriously trampled on public civility, habitués often spring into action. What goes on in Washington Square Park seems a living critique of Kelling and Wilson's well-known "broken windows" theory (1982): If it ain't serious, park denizens seem to say, don't interfere, and if the PEP or the NYPD act against it, it's probably because it is detrimental to the rest of us. But, of course, it's not quite that simple.

In the square, more so than in most places, there's a substantial gray area between eccentricity, oddity, or *mild* deviance, on the one hand, and harmful—or mentally disordered, even deranged—behavior, on the other. Moreover, as with the annoyance ordinances, there are rules and regulations that are *legally* sanctionable but not socially or morally condemned; and, in a like fashion, there are behaviors that are commonly considered inappropriate but do not elicit formal social control of any kind. Moreover, there are classes of behavior that are explicitly prohibited by park ordinances but are acceptable elsewhere—riding a bicycle, for instance, or a skateboard, or feeding squirrels and pigeons. Here, I grapple with these basic, everyday but seemingly paradoxical Washington Square regulations and social realities.

At the micro level, a variety of audiences react to an array of putatively wrongful behavior in distinctive ways. First, the park-going public exercises informal social control, usually by a withdrawal of sociability and occasionally by means of something stronger, say, a reprimand, as when the woman chastised Dr. Chynn for letting his borzoi off-leash. In addition, the weaponless PEP issue a warning and, less commonly, a summons or citation calling for a fine in the case of a violation of a formal park ordinance, and they are empowered to make an arrest when needed. And third, when an alleged crime has been committed, the NYPD has the power to apprehend and take a suspect into custody. But many, perhaps most, violations are informal, not addressed by any New York City Park ordinances; their violation offends the ordinary person's notion of how others should act, and these others respond by refusing to interact with normative violators; that is, as I've said, they walk away from them.

The Squirrel Whisperer

I'm sitting with a friend on a park bench in the Garibaldi Plaza. Emily, thin, perhaps in her sixties, wearing jeans, a dark pullover, and a floppy hat, leans over the bench to my left and begins softly, affectionately talking to the squirrels, by name and gender. She holds a black handbag out of which she pulls a white, translucent plastic tub that contains peanuts and hazelnuts. "Come on, Blackie," she admonishes one. "Don't be so shy." She knocks a nut against the top board of the wooden bench. The squirrel she addresses cautiously climbs up on the bench and accepts the nut. I say to her, "I'm very interested in people who violate the rules of the park. Isn't feeding the squirrels a violation of park ordinances?"

"I like doing this," Emily tells me, "and I don't care what the Parks Commissioner says. I help the squirrels. Sometimes the babies fall out of trees and injure themselves. I've rescued forty-one squirrels." She takes a batch of color photographs out of her bag. "This is what they look like when they're tiny." I shuffle through them and hand them to my friend. They're hairless and helpless and their eyes aren't opened yet. "Usually this young, they fill my hand. He was so small." She shows me a picture of a grown squirrel. "This is what he looks like now. He's five-and-a-half." She says she's happy to be doing this—feeding and taking care of the squirrels in the park. "I was forty-nine when I started this," she tells us. "Then I got this," pointing to a scar that runs from the nape of her neck to down below the line of her pullover between her breasts. "I was in a coma in the hospital for a month. After my recovery, I decided that I wanted to retire. My pension isn't very good—I was a bureaucrat in the city administration—but now I get to do what I want to do. I've been doing this for ten years." She hands me a business card, on which she refers to herself as the "Squirrel Whisperer."

I ask if she has ever been cited by the police for feeding the squirrels.

"Oh, sure, lots of times."

"So, what do they do when they see you feeding the squirrels?"

"They give me a ticket."

"What happens then?"

"I go downtown and appear in court."

"Do you pay the ticket?"

"No, the judge just laughs and tears up the ticket and lets me go."

A blondish, bearded man who appears to be in his fifties is sitting on a bench just off the Holley Plaza near the walkway that leads to Washington Place; his bike rests against the bench. A small flock of pigeons surrounds him. He holds up his right hand and a pigeon hops on. He strokes its back and coos to it. One bird settles on his head. A park ranger shouts out to a teenager skateboarding by, "Excuse me, sir, no skateboarding." The boy picks up the skateboard and walks away, carrying the board. A PEP shouts a greeting to the pigeon man and he says hello to her, then she walks toward the fountain. I go over and say hello to the pigeon man. "Hey," I say, "this is interesting to me, but isn't feeding pigeons illegal?"

"You have to know how to do it. The other guy who comes here, he feeds them by throwing birdseed on the ground. You can get a ticket for that. I feed them by hand. That's not illegal."

I walk away, chuckling and again shaking my head. As it turns out, there are *two* pigeon men, who devote a considerable portion of their day to their chosen activity.

The people who frequent the cosmopolitan urban square, say Suzanne and Henry Lennard, "encounter others who are different from themselves. Their co-presence . . . may generate a rethinking and re-evaluation of assumptions on which unfavorable or prejudiced reactions are based" (2008, p. 33). On such a cue, the sociologist begins thinking about how much difference is too much. Perhaps observing *extremely* different others generates a feeling of otherness, distance, or estrangement from them. Washington Square is a magnet for eccentrics, weirdos, street people, outpatients, the homeless—people who would be very much out of place, not to mention unwanted and unwelcome, in most public locales around the country. Nearly everywhere else, many of these people would stand out; they would attract stares, become the objects of curiosity, and the most extreme of them would be avoided, shunned, isolated, stigmatized—considered or rendered *deviant*.

Washington Square also attracts a broad spectrum of more-or-less respectable visitors with an enormous heterogeneity of motives, as we saw, ranging from nearby residents, locals, and tourists, as well as New York University students and professors, to the indigent, the homeless, the beggars, the urinators. I find the physical mingle, mesh, and tang of radically different social worlds, mentalities, and sensibilities fascinating, sometimes intoxicating. It is true that park regulars acknowledge degrees of eccentricity, but the dial has been tuned radically in the direction of greater tolerance and acceptance—toward a "live and let live" approach to divergence from the mainstream. In a very real sense, such mixing and mingling offers a glimpse of the global future, when virtually everyone will encounter lots of people very different from themselves.

And yet, here's a point worth repeating more than once: In all the tumultuous diversity we observe in Washington Square—among the performers of almost every conceivable stripe, the genuinely mentally disordered, both medicated and unmedicated, and the not-quite disordered, the eccentrics, the homeless men (and a few homeless women), the haranguers and ranters and screamers, the incoherent speechifiers, the marijuana sellers, the oddballs and kooks, the can-and-bottle collectors, the urinators—within and amongst this quasi-circus atmosphere, we should keep in mind a fundamental fact: Families come here. Parents and caretakers push strollers and bring small children, who play in the central fountain area or in one of the park's three playgrounds. Parents throw birthday parties in the park. Elderly folks spend a great deal of time in the park, sometimes in wheelchairs, occasionally pushed by a guardian. People walk their dogs here. Dates meet at the fountain and embrace. Washington Square is a very *safe* park; serious crime is exceedingly rare here. As we saw, New York University administers most of the footage facing the square, and this neighborhood is among the most affluent in New York City. (In fact, the residents of Greenwich Village, among over three hundred identifiable neighborhoods in the City, earn the nineteenth-highest income.) In many ways, the square is a conventional, family-oriented space—though with many more than occasional twists.

William H. Whyte argues that good (or "felicitous") spaces generate what he refers to as "triangulation": a kind of "multiplier effect" that establishes social bonds between and among very different kinds of visitors. Such an outcome cannot and should not be coldly calculated or socially engineered, Whyte argues; it is serendipitous, a "happy accident" that occurs under the right circumstances (1980, pp. 94–101). Washington Square's fountain represents an accident of history, but it is a huge draw, and it does generate meaningful social mingling, linkages among diverse people. (As a matter of fact, the original fountain measured one hundred feet across, which, visually at least, created a kind of huge chasm of empty space.) The acts and performances, most of them pretty much spontaneous from day to day, draw crowds and reactions, which give rise, for the most part, to camaraderie and good cheer. Certainly the substantial presence of females, in comparison with some other public spaces, is both consequence and cause of the gregariousness of the park's visitors. Likewise, the substantial racial and ethnic diversity of park visitors, again, generates multiple bonds and connections that might otherwise not exist. Moreover, conventional park-goers continually encounter unconventional ones and so have to draw and redraw the lines of what's acceptable and what's deviant, thereby creating and recreating nodules across social spectrums that aren't nurtured in more traditional spaces. Chances are, the park is not quite what Michel Foucault had in mind when he developed the notion of the *heterotopia*, which I discuss in chapter 7, but it is as close to it as most of us are likely to come.

Eyes on the Street, Undesirables in the Square?

In 1952, Jane Jacobs began writing for *Architectural Forum*, mainly on the topic of urban planning. In 1956, she gave a talk at Harvard University, the text of which was read by William H. Whyte, at that time an editor at *Fortune* magazine, who invited her to contribute a piece for that publication. The result was "Downtown Is for People," one of the most influential articles on public behavior ever published (1958). The central propositions of this article addressed the importance of "eyes upon the street"—an arresting phrase—and how *feet* are attracted to the street. The article, and the author's book, now considered a classic in urban studies, *The Death and Life of Great American Cities* (1961), challenged the dominant working ideology of the urban planners who largely ignored the human equation.

Jacobs emphasized that, rather than allowing developers to bulldoze working-class "slums," the community grassroots should be left alone to pursue their own collective destiny. People will naturally gravitate out onto the street if the attractions are sufficient and the streets are safe. Few predators are foolish enough to rob, rape, or kill under the watchful eye of the community; and when urban centers are safe enough to walk through, people are attracted to them, to their hustle and bustle, and when the variety and selection of retail stores and the appeal of their entertainment draw and retain these people's patronage, cities will be healthy. They may be shabby, disorderly, and unruly, Jacobs says, but such urban cores are "magnetic," filled with "gaiety," "wonder," and "cheerful hurly-burly," which makes people want to come and linger.

Generating this magnetism should be the crux of the problem for city planners; not all cities possess such charm. How to engender an atmosphere of "urbanity and exuberance" (1958, p. 134)? What virtually all urban residents want is *other* feet on the street; what administrators often fail to do is to attract people *to* those streets. Planners should not be shunting the population off to the suburbs or through ersatz, park-like, open-space residential areas where no one mills or mingles; the city's center should be "dense and concentrated," teeming with street life and action. Streets should be enjoyed on foot, with retail display windows at eye level, offering a "variety and contrast" of merchandise. Downtowns that have been "created by everybody" will have "something for everybody." Above all, Jacobs says, a city should be "fun" (p. 236). And, she would add, they should be safe as well. The modernists pride-fully pointed to the clean, wholesome environments they produced, and the fact that they successfully separated work environments from habi-tation, and habitation from retail establishments—in effect, they sought to sweep people *off* the streets, *out of* public transportation vehicles, forcing everyone to conduct all their social life indoors or in spaces they themselves meticulously designed and constructed.

Our understanding of the dynamics of the notion of eyes and feet on the street is sharpened when we address contrasting perspectives. In Howard Becker's *Outsiders*—like the Jacobs volume, also considered a classic sociological work—the focus of attention is on *non-victim devi-ance.* Significantly, Becker did not discuss the social control of violent behavior, such as rape, robbery, and murder, because their criminaliza-tion is nonproblematic: Such acts are universally considered wrongs in and of themselves—*mala in se*—and are illegal everywhere. Instead, his examples of unconventional or nonnormative behavior focused on the possession, sale, and use of marijuana, as well as on being a dance musi-cian (1963, 1973).

The contrast between Becker and Jacobs is instructive. During the 1950s, when sociologist Howard Becker formulated his ideas on toler-able but deviant behavior, as we saw, Jane Jacobs began promulgating her complementary view of social control: that the presence of com-munity members on the street tends to discourage criminal behavior.

Jacobs regarded "eyes upon the street" as an unmixed blessing that produced nothing but positive results for the community; her theory was that spontaneous neighborhood surveillance enables a community to observe and discourage the behavior of suspicious, threatening, and potentially dangerous characters. When residents are out on the street or looking out of their windows, they deter crime, and when crime is deterred, people emerge from their sanctuaries and make the streets lively and interesting. It is important to note that, as urban sociologists Mitchell Duneier and Harvey Molotch have pointed out, Jacobs, writing in the fifties and early sixties, did not discuss homelessness, begging, or racial tension, possibly because "racial segregation and well-policed skid row areas then kept the marginal more at bay" (1999, p. 1266). Now they don't, and that's worth taking a look at.

Here's the contrast between the "deviance" perspective of Howard Becker and the "community" perspective of Jane Jacobs, and it's at the nub of my concerns here. In Jacobs's day, a community's members were likely to have disapproved of alternate lifestyles, such as two gay men or two lesbians holding hands or hugging. Or interracial dating. Or the very presence of African Americans, or Asians and Asian Americans. Or simply people who were from outside the community. Moreover, it's not clear in any public setting who, exactly, constitutes "the community." The residents of a given neighborhood may split along ideological and moral lines, with some expressing tolerant, laissez-faire attitudes and other reacting hostilely to outsider or unconventional proclivities. Responding to the feeling of being menaced by outsiders need not be expressed by an entire community; all it takes is a few. The Southern Poverty Law Center reports that, even today, gay people remain the minority that is "most targeted by hate crimes." The taunting, harassing, beating, and even torturing of gay men—occasionally leading to their suicide—has not disappeared in American society; far from it (Potok, 2010). Perhaps some of the members of the communities in which these gay people were abused were opposed to such ill treatment; why didn't they stop that abuse? In short, the "eyes" of the neighborhood may be as cruel and intolerant as beneficent. Gay people are entirely welcome in Washington Square, but that's not true everywhere in the United States, or for that matter, the rest of the world.

As the "eyes upon the street" tendency plays itself out in real life, it represents a serious dilemma, since it can work in both directions. Concerned citizens become protectors against predation, or they may be meddlesome busybodies, depending on the behavior in question. Multiple crimes—rape, assault, robbery, and murder, for instance—are violent, predatory, harmful; they have real victims. With them, watchful residents would do well to ensure that, by looking out for them, their communities do not become dangerous and lawless. But many other "eyes upon the street" address behavioral variants that are not crimes and do not have real victims, yet some members of the community try to stamp them out, too. We must consider the "broken windows" hypothesis. It argues that when the community tolerates minor offenses, miscreants are emboldened to commit more serious wrongdoing, perhaps even felonies. *Death and Life* concentrated on the predatory behavior that goes unmentioned in Becker's *Outsiders*; she focused on victimization versus public safety. In contrast, Becker focused on victimless violations and offenses, which Jacobs ignored. Jane Jacobs, as respected as her work remains, harbors a bias that epitomizes a very serious oversight, and it has produced, in my opinion, a slanted, selective analysis. Most scholars today believe that the community should *not* cast surveillance-like "eyes upon the street" for harmless lifestyle deviancies. Jacobs did not address the matter.

But Jacobs did argue that the community *can* and *should* spring into action when the well-being of its members is threatened—indeed, their very presence on the street reduces the likelihood that the community will be menaced by wrongful and exploitative criminal acts. (Jacobs did not acknowledge that challenging wrongful, predatory behavior often takes a great deal of courage.) Contrastingly, Howard Becker favored nonintervention in acts of moral or lifestyle misbehavior, and, in turn, ignored predatory crime. Yet, almost ironically, Jacobs and Becker arrived at precisely the same conclusions about urban planning, slum clearance, and the creation of the monstrous planned "model cities" proposed and built by futuristic utopians such as Le Corbusier and Oscar Niemeyer, and for the same reasons: Both Jacobs and Becker believed that these modernistic schemes will produce urban vacuums where no one is looking out for or protecting local residents.

When "we confront the problems of slums and urban renewal," wrote Becker with his coauthor, Irving Louis Horowitz, "we send for the planner and the bulldozer. But the lives of urban residents are not determined by the number or the newness of buildings." Urban planners who seek to clear cities of slums, ghettos, and other supposedly blighted neighborhoods ignore the all-important relationships that spring up informally between and among residents—which slum clearance would disrupt and destroy. These supposed solutions to supposed slums define such neighborhoods by "impersonal criteria" such a density, physical deterioration, and per capita income, adhering to a "rationalistic vision" that is unconnected to real people's lives and how they live them. Their conception of structures and cities ignores the mechanisms "through which the mutual desires, claims, and threats of interested parties can sort themselves out and allow a *modus vivendi*, if one exists, to uncover itself" (Becker and Horowitz, 1970, p. 19).

In a like fashion, Jacobs argued that the urban planning schemes that prevailed in the 1950s—and that continued to exert an influence on "slum clearance" and municipal renewal for decades afterwards—would produce an urban environment that would be "spacious, parklike, and uncrowded." These planning schemes will make urban spaces "clean, impressive, and monumental"; such spaces will have "all the attributes of a well-kept, dignified cemetery." Every one of these developments looks like every other one; none manifests a "hint of individuality or whim or surprise, no hint that here is a city with a tradition and a flavor all its own." These projects, Jacobs added, "will not revitalize downtown; they will deaden it. . . . They banish the street" (1958, pp. 133, 134). Both Becker and Jacobs opposed the kind of urban renewal and slum clearance that prevailed in the fifties and sixties because these schemes left the most essential element out of the equation—the social relations that arise and develop among members of communities and neighborhoods in unplanned, endogenous cities. In the cities designed and built by modernist architects, this human element is left out of the equation; they have residents walking—or driving—across vast expanses of vacant, hollow green space, unconnected to the socket of energy that all cities should provide: other people.

Clearly, as I mentioned, in addition to her strengths, Jacobs exhibited theoretical flaws. She believed that population *density* guaranteed *diversity*, but manifestly, it does not. Only the affluent can now live in the Greenwich Village that Jacobs once used as a model for her theories. It has become too expensive for the modest wage earner, and its residents are far from diverse; the people who live there are not only affluent but racially skewed. Her perspective turned out to be as much elitist and exclusionary as it was populist and democratic, and her "eyes upon the street" notion, useful as it is, applies more to small, neighborly communities than it does to large, postindustrial, postmodern ones.

In a satisfactory space such as a park, a more or less safe and stable public order represents one of the intentions of its designers and satisfies the hankering of most visitors. And some parks are so attractive and congenial that they magnetize a diverse and interesting clientele and hence, synergize the park-goers' experience above and beyond its formal features. Yet, as William H. ("Holly") Whyte explained in *The Social Life of Small Urban Spaces* (1980), attractive urban spaces may also entice "undesirables" or disreputable parties as well (pp. 60–65). Virtually none of the undesirables in Whyte's study, he assured us, were dope dealers, muggers, or truly dangerous people. Nearly all of them were "the most harmless of the city's marginal people," the people who collect their stuff in bags and carts (the "bag" men and women), the winos and derelicts, the homeless and indigent, the mentally disordered, "who act strangely in public," even hippies, "teenagers, older people, street musicians, vendors of all kinds" (p. 60).

Again, such people have gotten a bum rap, Whyte explained, and are not really a problem. What *was* terrible was the "measures taken to combat them" (1980, p. 60), notably, the restrictions, the signs ("no eating, no sitting"), the iron spikes or studs jutting out of walls and barriers or from the floor in nooks or niches or under tunnels to keep people off, or tubular or slanted benches that no one can sleep on, and the actions of the guards and police, who shoo the impecunious away. "The best way to handle the undesirables is to make a place attractive to everyone else" (p. 63). Exclusionist tendencies tend to cut down on the complexity of the visitors' encounters and also keep out a major compass of the civil and well-behaved. In contrast, Whyte stated, inclusivity attracts a broad diversity of the public, hence dilutes the undesirables so that their problematic behavior becomes less of a problem.

In a number of crucial respects, Washington Square is very different from Whyte's small urban plazas, which are dependent on a lunch crowd and go dead after six in the evening. The square is much bigger than these plazas and less dependent on lunchtime or local visitors; its attractiveness and liveliness draw a broad spectrum of people from all over, for longer periods, and for more reasons. Though weekdays tend to be active as well, Saturday and Sunday represent the highlight of the week for the park, and on warm summer nights, visitors hold the equivalent of an enormous party; none of this prevails in Whyte's outdoor spaces. Holly Whyte, a gracious and genteel observer of the urban drama, tended to err on the side of the better angels of human nature. Still, his observations on seating, the undesirables, exclusionist tendencies, the importance of the private-public and indoor-outdoor dimensions, sight-lines, entrances, safety, water, trees, and food remain valid, very possibly, for urban spaces everywhere. And sittable benches: there are *lots* of them in Washington Square.

All in all, in our contemporary fragmented society, the "eyes upon the street" that Jacobs tells us would exercise protective social control may actually produce any number of consequences—some of them far from benign—and sometimes an urban space's "undesirables" are not quite as benign as Whyte's almost-cuddly winos and derelicts (or, for that matter, Jacobs's juvenile delinquents). Likewise, Becker's "outsider" perspective lulls us into thinking that nothing is deviant but naming and responding to it as such—and technically, from a labeling/constructionist perspective, that is true. Still, terrible things occasionally happen to good and decent people, and some among us are truly terrible people who do truly terrible things to others. As historically consequential as *Death and Life*, *The Social Life*, and *Outsiders* are to our understanding of transgressive urban street behavior, I'd like to take a fresh look at how the participants in public deviance and social control dance this gavotte.

Washington Square at Night

For most of human history, the shroud of darkness rendered familiar public surroundings fearful and dreadful; fire offered an inefficient and potentially dangerous solution. Nighttime constituted a "frontier" that, in the reckoning of time, only fairly recently became effectively "colonized" by lighting (Melbin, 1987). Illumination through artificial means represents one of humanity's greatest accomplishments. Bringing light into darkness encouraged a panoply of nighttime activities, including economic enterprises—among them, as it pertains to deviance and its control, the public serving of alcohol. Still, artificial illumination is, by its very nature, limited, and humans who venture out beyond the reach of lighting remain at greater risk of criminal victimization—or may themselves be up to no good—than is true during the day. Men staggering out into the night under the weight of drunkenness provide us with a cliché that reminds us of the misleading protection of partial lighting.

"Under the cover of darkness"—the phrase conveys the notion of stealth, treachery, if not deviance and crime. Gallup polls indicate that, in spite of the decline in the crime rate over the past quarter-century, nearly four in ten Americans still fear walking alone at night; this fear is greater for women (50%) than for men (22%) and for less affluent individuals (48%) than those with higher incomes (23%). "Crime varies more by hour of day than by any other predictor we know" (Felson and Poulsen, 2003, p. 595). According to the Department of Justice, violent crime rises sharply after six o'clock, reaches a peak at midnight, falls to a low between five and six in the morning, then rises again thereafter. Hence, our fear of nighttime crime is far from unfounded. Night life represents a realm of risk and danger—as well as experimentation and possible adventure. William Hogarth, an eighteenth-century artist, executed a series of etchings devoted to the subject of activities that take place during different times of the day. His *Night* (1738) depicts all manner of deviant, criminal, and disorderly activities: Pubs and bordellos line the street; a stagecoach has been overturned and set on fire; a woman tosses the contents of a chamber pot onto the head of a man on the street; mischievous children squat under a balcony and play with fire; tenants skip out from their landlord without paying him; a barber-surgeon cuts a customer (blood stains his apron, and pots of blood sit on the barber's windowsill); a man holds a sword to the throat of a woman, who has one tucked under her arm. Hogarth seems to be saying that the cover of darkness encourages such unruly and dangerous activities.

Gustave Le Bon (1841–1931), an intellectual and dilettantish French social psychologist, argued that the crowd accords the individual a measure of anonymity, which, in turn, renders perpetrators who engage in untoward behavior more immunity from surveillance and seizure (1960). Night serves the same function as Le Bon's crowd: It offers the cloak of darkness and hence, anonymity. But at night, one may become victim as easily as victimizer. Still, several factors limit the intriguing potential of the shroud of darkness to illuminate deviance and crime specifically as it pertains to Washington Square Park. We already know that serious crime is rare in the park, and that the space is closed from midnight to 6:00 a.m. Moreover, during the summer, it doesn't get dark in New York until 9:00 p.m., which limits the hours of possible mischief there. In addition, there is a lot of lighting, and the police are vigilant about overnight sleeping. At the same time, as NYPD detective James Alberici says, in his account following chapter 4, during the day, the square is like Mayberry (a fictional peaceful, low-crime television community) and Bangkok at night—not lawless or unsafe, but wild and interesting. Wherein lies this wildness?

Murray Melbin, in *Night as Frontier*, explains that the nighttime "seems to harbor a different culture" from that which prevails during the day. It is "a little Bohemia of artists and poets and literati, along with street people, homeless persons, carousers, [drug] pushers, pimps, and prostitutes." Nighttime accords a certain measure of "freedom and safety for nonconformists and marginal persons. After-dark society bespeaks a tolerant milieu" (1987, p. 60). But the square is already fairly unconventional during the day; how is it different at night? And though the square is illuminated at night, sundown draws out a different cast of characters. Not being the virtually omnipresent sun, lamps are limited in their penetration.

During a half-dozen evenings during pleasant weather, I have walked into and around the fountain circle and throughout the park. One Wednesday in mid-June, employees begin breaking down and stacking folding chairs and taking down the movie screen in front of the Arch. The Marine Corps Band has just completed a selection of musical numbers and screened a military-themed film. Just south of the fountain, a sax, bass, and percussion trio is playing Hall and Oates's "She's a Man-Eater." Later, they play the hauntingly beautiful "Equinox" by John Coltrane. To their left, a man juggles Indian clubs. To his left, an Asian man in an orange jumpsuit vigorously practices karate moves. Under a lamp-post, the Marcel Marceau look-alike—no whiteface, however—named Edgar ("Eddie") Rodriguez engages in an animated discussion with a man who has just watched his routine; the man begins giggling. A tall, thin young man briskly walks around the fountain a dozen times hold-ing a baby in a Snugli. Someone has set up a small screen and a bright light at the south edge of the fountain barrier; perhaps three dozen peo-ple are watching the monitor on which plays a video that has just been filmed in the park. In the small crowd, I notice a six-foot-tall person, probably a transvestite, wearing a white suit, a fake fur jacket, a black hat, and pink heels.

The fringe walkways, dark and shadowy nearly everywhere, are thinly occupied. I circle back around and sit on the fountain barrier a while. The fountain is on, a slight breeze carries a fine, mist-like spray to the faces of the visitors on its receiving side, and I contemplate Melbin's char-acterization of the night crowd as unconventional, which now seems to me a bit glib, more literary than empirical, perhaps more a Paris movie set than actual Manhattan real estate. What I see is the usual off-beat, tolerant milieu, indeed, but they're not exactly marginal—we're standing a few dozen feet from one of the best law schools in the country, and a bit further from one of its better business schools. A touch bohemian, perhaps, following Melbin's characterization? Let's follow the square's characters and determine for ourselves. There's at least one poet—a thirty-ish white man wearing Southeast Asian garb and a conical straw hat who stands on a fountain stanchion wearing a sign around his neck that reads, "Ask Me for a Poem"; an artist or two, at work right here, as well as through the day; and as we saw, drug pushers—marijuana, yes, heroin and cocaine, decidedly not. The homeless make their appearance, most assuredly. But no prostitutes or pimps. Literati? Will professors do? There are dozens of them all around the park. And of course, their students as well—lots and lots of undergraduates. For my money, all this adds up to Melbin's "a touch bohemian."

On another evening, as I'm walking at night through the Garibaldi Plaza toward the fountain circle, the sound that greets me resembles that of a stupendous cocktail party of conventioneers attending a huge conference in a large midwestern hotel; the volume of *talk* is like a tidal wave of sound. There are twice as many people here as there were last week; I'm not sure why: 180 on the stone benches (half of them women), and 40 sitting on the fountain barrier or on the steps inside. The poem guy is there, as are a troupe of Indian club jugglers. Three guys who, like me, look like they spent much of their young adult years in the sixties, are playing and singing "Rocky Mountain High" surrounded by an appreciative crowd of about thirty, appearing to be mostly NYU students, who applaud when the song is sung. To my right, there's a cluster of half a dozen Asian Americans in their early twenties, again, no doubt, students at NYU. One man gets up, walks over to the crowd surrounding the singers, checks out the action, and walks back. "Who's singing?" a young woman in his circle asks him.

"A bunch of old, white people," he replies. She giggles.

I look around the circle and realize that this is a very coupled-up space, so I do a full 360 around the immediate benches and count the aggregates and units sitting on them. There are fifteen singletons, thirty-six heterosocial or male-female dyads, twenty homosocial or homophilic (more female-female than male-male) dyads, twelve triads, and four units larger than triads. A predominantly sociable and mainly coupled-up space indeed. Following William H. Whyte's characterization (1980, p. 18), as we'll see shortly in more detail, the presence of a huge number of women here tells us that this is a very safe and, from the point of view of crime as well as in spite of its social oddities, a fairly conventional place. Watching the co-occupation of this space by NYU students with mostly upper-middle-class backgrounds, whose parents will spend roughly a quarter of a million dollars for their four-year education, cheek-by-jowl with park denizens who occupy the bottom of the socioeconomic barrel is an enlightening experience. A man in a tattered black pullover and pants, and a bulging knitted cap protecting his 'fro, shuffles by me and stops to stare at two young, blonde women talking earnestly with one another. "You got anything for me?" the man inquires. Without hesitation, one of the women hands him an aluminum-foil container wrapped in a clear plastic bag. "What is it?" he asks.

"You'll like it," she says. "It's good. It's for you."

He accepts it, holds it, and stares at it, almost paralyzed. Finally, wordlessly, he shuffles off and stops in front of another gathering about twenty feet away. What is it about this space that encourages denizens from such disparate worlds to more or less amicably comingle and interact? Whatever it is, I love this place.

Who wouldn't?

* * *

Interview with Lee, a Washington Square Pundit

I met Lee, who's in his fifties, in the park; at the time I talked to him, he played chess competitively at the tables in the southwest corner of the park. Here, Lee articulates his theories of deviance, crime, and social control in New York City and in the square. I've changed the names, identities, and signifiers of his referents, as the phrase goes, to protect the guilty.

ERICH: You OK? [I ask him because his face registers distress.]

LEE: I'm OK, it's just that, one guy over here was smoking crack and the Parks Department can't do anything about it. That's why my face looks like that. These people get dangerous when they do stuff like that. I don't want to see it. You can't dispute the substance abuse problem. When people get involved with drugs, they start stealing to support their habit. These dudes here, they smoke crack, they steal to get it. The Parks Department, they're incapable of doing anything about it. Wherever there's a concentration of dope, robbery goes up, property values go down. People are fearful. The people in the community know that and they stay away.

Remember when Benjamin Ward was commissioner [1984–1989], then Guiliani came in [elected in 1993 and 1997, in office, 1994–2001]? [I nod.] They pushed the crack to the East Side, to Bleecker, to Fourth Avenue. It's a dope den now. There was a big raid. They use a porno shop on Sixth Avenue to smoke crack. The police know about it but they can't do a goddamn thing about it. In the morning, it spins out into the park. Why isn't the law enforced? Civil rights. It ties the police's hands. Some cops just turn their eyes away. They don't want to do the paperwork. They want to concentrate on the bigger crimes. [Lee takes a tube of Dermasil out of his backpack.] You see this tube? It comes from shoplifting. I got it from a booster. The cops know the culprit. We have a system of theft and the cops have to ignore it. The

thieves get away with it. Some of these acts of theft, they're an inside
job. You walk into a CVS, a Duane Reade—they are targets. Anybody
will tell you—somebody walks in, they walk out with a full shopping
cart. How can they get away with it? Because the guard is in on it.
They've got liners in the bag, they slip the stuff into the bag, inside
the liner. The security guard gets a kickback. This tube here is living
proof. I bought it from a fence for two dollars. This is a twenty-dollar
tube, that's what it costs in the store. It's a system that is put in place
and nothing is done about it. This is a factual issue. Somebody's
boosting. This tube was boosted. Silent Sam's—you know the place?

ERICH: Yes.

LEE: They sell high-quality drugs there. But the community doesn't
complain about it. They complain about vandalism. Robbery, that
starts with the drug abuser. People here, in the park, they'll tell you
they smoke crack. You can see it. Those guys hanging out here. It's a
cat-and-mouse game. You can close down the business, but it starts
right up again. The newsstand guy, they couldn't make a living because the crack abusers would steal off him. But he installed cameras.
The bookstore was a haven for crack dealing and they busted him
down. The liquor store on Sixth Avenue—they contribute to that
[substance abuse] too. This guy who walked in [he nods in the direction of a man who walked by], he's a king-pin for selling high-quality
weed. [Lee looks at the man quietly for a couple of minutes.]

This guy right here [he nods in the direction of another guy on a
nearby bench], he's an illegal alien. Algerian. He has no papers. He
sells to NYU students; they smoke weed, they drop out. He's contrib-
uting to that. These are things going on. I'm talking about hydro-
ponic weed. Powerful stuff. [He looks around at the men nearby.] I
ask some of the guys here, "Why you smokin' crack? What are you
doin' aggressively smokin'?"

Right here, inside [the Park], there's no robbery. If a guy tried to
rob somebody, the weed dealers, the crack dealers, they're going to
beat the crap out of him. Outside—outside the park—it can happen.
Not here. See this? [He shows me an item from the "Police Blotter"
files: "Bungled Park Theft."] That's one of the things that goes down.
You understand this guy is setting up shop right here. Right now. I
can take his picture, but he can't do anything about it. I got four big

sons. [He laughs.] I threatened to call immigration. People know you here. They treat you individually. It's the neighborhood. It's the back yard. This guy, the Algerian guy, he's very violent. This thing is wide open. Look over there. That guy's smoking a joint right now. Some of the people here, they go 'round and instigate stuff. Their brains has turned to jelly. "You're not going to shut me down," they tell the cops. They arrest him, they go to court, they get off.

Look at that guy over there. He smokes five vials of crack a day. What's the difference—crack or high-quality weed? You smoke five sticks of weed a day, you can smoke five vials of crack. You can't cover that up. The glass pipes—the smoke shops sell them. What are they for? All these bodegas, all these Muslim shops. They sell stuff that is illegal, that supports illegal industries. This is a 100 percent factual issue. It's dangerous. It's like a time bomb. When it's warm, sometimes regular people can't get a table. They say, you can't play in this space. It's a source of income, but then it all gets wiped out, they spend all their money and it's gone. When it gets cold, things get harder, it gets harder to make money, and a hungry man is an angry man. I try to get away from that. I kind of withdraw from that. These guys, they're not storing their nuts away. Today, when it's cold, not too many people come through. Sometimes people are ready for a rumble. So, you get in a confrontation and you got to back down. I made thirty dollars yesterday and some guy said to me, oh, you're so competitive, you taking all the customers. You understand what I'm saying? Today, nobody's coming through. You can sit here for three–four hours and not get a game.

ERICH: What would these guys [the chess players] do to somebody here if they did something they thought was seriously wrong?

LEE: Before, they'd speak out against the wrong. They'd step up and call the Man. Presently, now, the game has changed. These people would keep quiet. Maybe one or two would speak out. The majority would tolerate it. This is not a rebel society. There's a lot of intimidation. What I'm talking about is S-A-F-E-T-Y. If you stay around, you will be accepted by the community. You will find what I'm saying corroborated.

There are some people around here who are very aggressive. They're not normal. They have violent outbursts. There was this guy, he grabbed an old lady's pocketbook, and the guys around here beat the crap out of him. He was out of control. If somebody does something wrong, the community's going to step in. That really does happen. Around here, you're playing live chess with your body.

There used to be a guy here—he was a legend. He used to knock people out—walk up to some guy and knock him out. He used to be an enforcer. He'd say [menacingly], "You smokin' crack?" And he'd knock you down. Even though he was a criminal, he wouldn't put up with it. That was four–five years ago. If he was active today, there wouldn't be any crack smoking, there wouldn't be any dope. [He looks around at the other tables.] I'm a marked man. I know what some people do to make their money. There are certain people I won't talk about because I've known them for years. Some guys here are violent. Tell you the truth, in this environment, these guys are all criminals. Dope fiends. They play chess but they don't get much money for it. Two dollars, five dollars. They don't support themselves this way. Ninety-nine percent of the chess players are criminals. Ex-cons. You can spot the crack users—they speeding. The dope users, they slow down, but the ones who use crack—they're speeding.

ERICH: What about you?

LEE: I'm from the street. I can rumble and tumble. Bottom line—within the criminal element you got to protect yourself.

ERICH: Have you ever been arrested?

LEE: I was arrested for marijuana and crack. My last arrest was in 2009. I haven't been bothered since then. The cops were judging a book by its cover. This cop followed my wife [who is white] into the lobby of our building. Those cops didn't know my family. It was just a bad cop. They kicked him off the force. They found out he was a dirty cop. The cop who arrested me told the people here [at the chess tables in the park] that I was a snitch. They wanted me to be a stool pigeon; I said no. The cops here will feed you to the dogs.

White people support legalizing the drugs—they can afford it. They're the ones who can buy it. A black person can't buy a nickel bag of weed, we can't afford it. There are black people who are crack users but they are a small minority. Before, white people moved out of the cities and into the suburbs. Then they were hit with a big tax bite out there so they started moving back into the inner cities and they pushed black people out. Bodega owners are criminals. You take the food stamps and buy them and beat the system. You buy Similac with the food stamps in Pathmark, D'Agostino, then go to the bodegas with twenty cans of milk. That's where the income comes. Then they cash in their food stamps to buy drugs.

ERICH: Everything you've said is interesting. I really appreciate your talking to me.

2

Public Space

A film crew assembles at the Holley Plaza just west of the fountain circle. About thirty people begin milling around, checking equipment, preparing for a shoot, wielding four very large, professional-looking cameras, opening metal boxes of film equipment, and holding a couple of boom mikes. Two crowd control guys station themselves to keep the foot traffic in the park moving. "Go over this way, so I can do my job." Patterns reveal themselves here, and the more one watches, the clearer these patterns become. We also begin to see that seated people likewise display identifiable patterns of aggregation, together or apart. Strangers don't sit next to one another when empty, two-person spaces are available nearby; an adult rarely sits on another's lap, and so on.

The observer of sociability in the square is willy-nilly challenged to understand this flow of human bodies in motion, as well as the positionality of parties at rest, in this patch of space visitors occupy. Orderly as it seems, it's quite possible that the patterning of aggregation and apartness offers clues to the volume and dynamics of deviance, crime, and social control in the public space. What happens when the patterns are violated? To the extent that behavior that defies informally evolved rules regarding unit structuring, park-goers will regard the violator as uncivil—and deviant—and will respond accordingly. In short, clustering and gathering offer yet another realm in which deviance is committed and social control exercised.

"Spatial coordination" applies to the more or less synchronized movement and aggregation of people on the micro scale—down to the level of the self-placement of a single individual—as well as the view from above, the aerial shot or the big picture, encompassing, as it does, both large-scale crowds as well as the singletons, dyads, and triads within public spaces. The occupation of spaces in urban settings fosters two contrary human tendencies. Such environments are, by their very nature, public, which means that the visitor's behavior is visible to others and, to that extent, is accountable and hence constrained. Considering this factor alone, *public* behavior tends to be more civil and normative than private behavior. But, paradoxically, this coming together of strangers in an urban setting may offer the possibility of having the opposite effect as well—that is, of straying from the conventional norms of society, or of one's own community: Being anonymous lends to the individual actor a measure of freedom that interacting in more private and familiar spaces with intimates doesn't.

These seemingly contradictory qualities of accountability and anonymity do not *dictate* that users engage in any particular behavior in public, but crowds, that is, this copresence of a substantial number of strangers, *potentiate* certain kinds of behavior while making others less likely. Human aggregation also increases the likelihood of many forms of deviant behavior, including exploitation *of* and *by* strangers. Still, Washington Square is a lot smaller and more community oriented than, say, Times Square, though a lot less communal, more animated, and a lot less orderly than a small, private, gated community (Low, 2003).

During the late nineteenth and early twentieth centuries, commentators emphasized the irrational, barbaric, and frequently violent side of crowds, in a perspective called "mass psychology," which culminated in the extremely influential but misguided volume, *The Crowd*, by the French writer Gustave Le Bon, originally published in 1895 (1960). To counteract the theory, promulgated by Le Bon and his ilk, that humans became uncivilized and barbarous in gatherings and collectivities, a number of American sociologists, including Ralph Turner, Lewis Killian, Clark McPhail, and David Miller, argued that crowd behavior obeys most of the same principles that prevail in everyday life. For the most part, they emphasized the heterogeneity of the mentality and social characteristics of crowds and the lack of compulsion in their behavior; the rationality of the norms governing behavior in the physical settings within which crowds assemble; the cues that influence human congregation and dispersal; the importance of family, friends, and organizational ties; and the occasional partial redefinition of conventional norms in the light of novel circumstances (Turner and Killian, 1987; McPhail, 1991; Miller, 2014).

Common sense dictates that pleasant weather brings out crowds to Washington Square Park, most of their numbers gathering in the central fountain area, usually standing and milling, walking from an entrance to an exit, or sitting; in this case, common sense is correct. Popular performers bring assemblies together in a more compact formation. But the majority of the visitors in the square at a given time are *not* in interacting crowds as such; their assembly tends to be most often in the form of micro units—that is, singletons, dyads, triads, and triads-plus; their primary bonds are within these capsules, not with the crowd as a whole. Hence, in considering deviance and social control in a public space such as Washington Square, we should think about the dynamics of both compact collectivities (such as an audience watching a movie or a concert, a protest, a demonstration, a strike, a Times Square New Year's gathering, in which the assembled attend to and respond to the same cues) and more dispersed collectivities (gossip and rumor, fad and fashion, urban legends, collective delusions, in which same-cue responses tend to be dissipated by intervening forces). But it's also important to note that the very factor that modern social theorists of collective behavior minimize—mental disorder—plays a significant role in a substantial proportion of the deviance enacted and reacted to in Washington Square Park.

The scattering of park-goers around Washington Square might seem to display more qualities in common with what sociologists refer to as "diffuse collectivity" than with the crowd, in that gaps and spaces separate their numbers and hence, they do not directly influence one another. But consider the fact that if we enter Washington Square on a warm day on a weekend in the afternoon, we will see *crowds* of people in certain spots, nearly always in the fountain circle, sometimes, in other spots, surrounding a performer. Competition for bench space in the central area is sometimes energetic; often more people will be standing than sitting, and often, virtually as soon as a bench-sitting couple gets up, another pair takes their place.

Moreover, certain performers will draw audiences numbering in the hundreds, again, occasioning dynamics that demand an explanation. Even smaller gatherings reflect crowd dynamics in miniature—and yet, members of crowds seem more or less civil to one another. In addition, the factors that *make* for crowd behavior also operate in such a way that, *in the absence of the influence of such factors*, crowds will *fail* to coalesce. Typically, there is no single *focus of interest* among the people in a park as a whole—although in Washington Square, again, the fountain represents its centerpiece—and hence, there is no coalescence of bodies in the same space at the same time. Yet, the crowd offers a benchmark against which we can compare and contrast the more diffuse congeries within Washington Square. At times, the square is crowded; at other times, very few people show up. Something—or some *things*—bring them there, and some factors keep them away. In this chapter, I'd like to identify some of these patterns of assembly as well as circumstances that minimize coming together. In addition, we have to keep in mind the fact that a substantial sector of the people who are in the park at any given point in time are *passers-through*—they are traversing the park from one point outside the park to another. What brings all this movement and gathering into focus? And what do the dynamics of collective behavior and crowd behavior tell us about deviance and social control?

Temporality and Seasonality

Every urban space attracts visitors and denizens in ways that are both different from and similar to the way other spaces do. And though Washington Square may be "completely unique, nothing like it anywhere in the world," it is also similar to other spaces in that it follows certain rules of congregation. Some of the factors that influence patterning include season of the year, day of the week, and hour of the day. In other words, there is a time-linked *ebb and flow* of social life. In his classic monograph, *Suicide*, Emile Durkheim documented that the frequency of suicide is related to time, day, and season (1897/1951, pp. 104–22). From every place he gathered data, Durkheim found that the suicide rate of the population was highest in the spring and summer and lowest in the winter and fall. None of this, he argued, is related to the impact of the weather on the human organism but rather to *the intensity of social life* during the warmer seasons. Everything picks up during good weather and during days with a longer stretch of daylight, as measured by travel and economic activity. Economic activity—for example, in the form of the number of passengers traveling and the amount of money spent on travel—is greatest in the summer and least in winter. In a parallel fashion, Durkheim argued, in pleasant weather, interaction of all kinds increases; people do everything more—including, ironically, kill themselves.

As with the seasons, so it is with days of the week. Durkheim's prede-
cessor, André-Michel Guerry, found that the share of the total number
of suicides in France for the weekdays of Monday, Tuesday, Wednesday,
and Thursday averages 15.37 percent per day; by Friday, it begins to dip,
to 13.74 percent; for Saturday, it is 11.19 percent; and for Sunday, 13.57
(Durkheim, 1897/1951, p. 118). In a similar fashion, time of day influences participation in activities of all kinds, including rates of suicide.
The daytime, as opposed to nighttime, "favors suicide because this is
the time of most active existence, when human relations cross and re-
cross, when social life is most intense" (p. 117). Again, keep in mind that
the "active existence" to which Durkheim specifically referred is self-
obliteration. Durkheim was interested only secondarily in suicide and
primarily in social behavior; he argued that economic—and by extension, social—activity is greatest during the week and least on weekends.
Far from being *asocial* behavior, suicide, he argued, is a particular *form*
of social activity. The fact that it represents a termination of all sociability for those persons who end their lives is not the point; what is important is that, according to Durkheim, suicide follows the same pattern as
conventional forms of social interaction. Is this true of routine sociability in Washington Square Park?

If park-going is a social activity, its temporality and patterning—its
ebb, flow, and structure—should likewise follow sociological lines and
obey sociological principles. As obliquely related as it might seem, Durkheim's analysis of suicide bears a particular but somewhat complex,
indeed, in some respects, contrary, relationship to visiting parks and
other such public spaces. Quite obviously, park-going is an enjoyable,
recreational activity; committing suicide manifests precisely the opposite
kind of behavior, presumably, the acknowledgment and denouement of a
miserable existence. But let's take Durkheim literally and regard visiting
a park, like suicide, as a social activity, subject to the rhythms and regu-
larities of everyday life. In 2008–2009, the Central Park Conservancy
conducted a study entitled *Report on the Public Use of Central Park*. The
research team, consisting of 275 volunteers and 75 Conservancy staff,
which "contributed more than 2,800 hours collecting survey data and
800 hours of data entry," counted 4,600 entrances into, and interviewed
3,300 people who were exiting, the park, and conducted 9,900 observational studies of visitors. The findings of its research report are extremely

detailed and systematic and its conclusions, reliable. Visits to Central Park, as common sense would dictate, take place *mainly* during the warmer seasons. Of the total of 36.5 million estimated visitations, over a third (35.6%) were made in summer, and roughly a quarter (27.6%) in the spring, another quarter (24.1%) in the fall, but only an eighth (12.6%) took place in the winter. For Durkheim's thesis, so far, so good.

An intuitively obvious, and banal, observation is that the weather influences behavior in public. In good weather, most people are stationary; more people sit or stand than walk through the park. In bad weather, more people walk through it than sit or stand. And clearly, good versus bad weather is a matter of degree—for example, a sprinkle or a downpour or cloudlessness. The Central Park Conservancy study of the use of that park estimated that when less than half an inch of rain falls on the City, only 60 percent of the average number of park-goers visit; when between half an inch and a full inch falls, only a third of this average show up; and when an inch or more falls, only 10 percent of the average come to the park. Count the number of people *sitting* on an outdoor public bench in the rain or voluntarily standing in place out in the open, then do the same thing when it's not raining.

I've done the counts and here's what I found. It's evident and there's no reason to belabor the point: Rain tends to discourage public activity and assembly. Late on a drizzly May morning with sixty-degree weather, I count a total of 103 people walking in the entire park, of whom 51 are carrying umbrellas. One apparently homeless man, the only person who's stationary in the park, is sleeping on a bench under a blanket. No one is walking a dog; two women are pushing strollers covered with a plastic roof. No one is sitting in the fountain area; in fact, no one is sitting in the park at all. By the afternoon, the rain has stopped; since water tends to pool on the stone benches around the fountain, only six people are sitting on them, while the wooden benches, under small trees and mostly dry, hold eighteen people. In contrast, on pleasant weekdays, I've counted two or three thousand in the park, and on weekends, a thousand more than that.

Another obvious weather-related factor that influences park attendance is temperature. In the Central Park research, mild winter temperatures boost attendance by 100,000 on weekend days and 27,000 on weekdays. But during the summer, temperatures of ninety degrees or more cut attendance by 12 percent. Far fewer people visit parks in cold weather, as we saw in the winter visitation statistics. On a warm, clear weekday late in April 2017, I attempted a rough nose count of all the visitors to Washington Square Park between 2:00 and 4:00 in the afternoon; I came up with a total of 2,870, about a third of them in the central fountain circle. In contrast, on one chilly, gusty, rainy November day, *no one*, except a small handful of drug sellers milling in the usual spot, was stationary in the park. No surprise here. Durkheim argued that the relationship between volume of social activity and volume of deviance (namely, suicide) is contingent in part on ecology, that is, social and physical location: The greater the number of people under consideration, the greater the amount of deviance. In the square, we have something of a case contrary to Durkheim's formulation: many people, but very little serious crime. Moreover, as with everyplace else, we also have many *minor* violations and very little felonious crime, and it's partly because behavior is very visible in the park. It's quite different from the well-known panopticon formulation of Jeremy Bentham and Michel Foucault, which dictates that the few (guards) view the many (the prisoners): In the park, many people view many *other* people, thereby exerting a measure of social control.

According to Durkheim's logic, *seasonality of normative breaches* (specifically, suicide) should follow seasonality of overall *activity*, and on this point, Durkheim was correct. The New York City Department of Parks and Recreation records the felonies that are reported to the police by seasonal quarters—that is, in the winter (January 1 to March 31), the spring (April 1 to June 30), the summer (July 1 to September 30), and the fall (October 1 to December 31). It follows that the greater the number of people who *use* New York City's parks, the greater the number of crimes that take place in them: more people, more crimes. Again, these are people who are spread out in different parks over a year's, or a season's, time. Is this always true? More people means more "eyes upon the park" and presumably, less crime. Perhaps; we'll see.

The number of felonious crimes reported to the NYPD for five categories—murder, rape, robbery, assault, and grand larceny—that took place in all New York City parks and playgrounds (excluding Central Park, which has its own precinct station) during 2015 faithfully follows use according to season. During the winter quarter, only 78 such felonies were reported, the lowest for the year for all quarters; during the spring quarter, when use of the city parks increases substantially, crime that takes place in them increases substantially as well, to 240. The use of New York's parks reaches a peak during the summer season, as does crime—383 of these felonies were reported to the police during the three summer months. Finally, there's a significant slackening off of crime, paralleling use, during the fall months, with 223 such felonies reported. As we'll see in the next chapter, with respect to felonies, Washington Square is *virtually* crime free, with only five grand larcenies reported to the police in 2015—with no murders, rapes, robberies, or aggravated assaults taking place at all. (Again, the sale of marijuana is a partial exception.) And once in a rare while, someone commits a genuine violent felony. On Friday, May 17, 2017, at 2:25 a.m., after the park was closed, on Washington Square North, near Fifth Avenue—across the street from the park—an NYU faculty member flagged down a Department of Safety Patrol vehicle and reported that he had just been robbed by two men who demanded his wallet and cell phone; he complied with the robbers' demand and was unharmed—by the FBI's definition, a robbery. On June 2, 2017, in the southwest corner of the park, at 5:00 in the morning, according to *dnainfo.com*, a man "may have shot himself in the left leg." The police believe the shooting was accidental. And in July 2017, near the chess tables, a man pressed his groin area against an unwilling woman's body. Clearly the park and the streets around it are not *immune* from violent crime.

But there's an almost obvious exception to this rule: There is the occasional Washington Square Park denizen who has committed serious felonies *elsewhere*, and here's a recent example. In February 2017, an NYPD sergeant-in-training—significantly, he's not named in the story—glanced at a "Wanted" poster on the wall at the Police Academy in Queens, and recognized a familiar face, one Sheldon ("Slim") Edmond, a suspect in a shooting committed the previous May. The suspect was, the cop realized, a homeless man who played chess at the tables in Washington Square Park. The officer, who had previously patrolled the area, called a former partner in the Sixth Precinct, its station located about six blocks from the park, who walked there and, on an unseasonably warm, spring-like day, arrested the suspect on the charge of marijuana possession. Then the police changed the charge to murder and malicious wounding, alleging that, during the previous May, in the Bronx, Edmond and his companion pulled up on two presumed drug sellers waiting for a red light and opened fire, killing one and wounding the other; the shooting, the police claim, had been drug related (Annese and Tracy, 2017).

But as we've seen, *minor* or petty offenses are common in the park, among them, solicitation for the purpose of the sale of marijuana, as well as violations of numerous minor ordinances, including (rarely) letting dogs off-leash, (fairly frequently) smoking cigarettes, and (very occasionally) the use of marijuana, feeding squirrels and pigeons, or (more commonly) wading in the fountain's pool, skateboarding and bicycle riding, and (hardly ever) urinating in the bushes—at least one of these violations is taking place during almost the entire time the park is open. But, because park visitations are substantially more numerous during spring and summer, these offenses are predictably greater during those seasons as well.

Here's a summary of the impact of the weather on Washington Square. Again, this is intuitively obvious, but it's a piece of the equation of park-going and hence, possibly, the tempo of offenses as well. When it rains or snows, especially heavily, very few, if any, people sit on the benches. (People do, of course, walk *through* the park at such times.) The temperature is closely correlated with the weather: The colder it is, the smaller the number of people there are in the park, but, as with Central Park, above ninety degrees, the frequency of park-going slackens off. Of course, in hot weather, children love playing in the park's fountain.

The weather equation is slightly off-kilter for snow, and for a particular reason. I go out to the park one January day; it's thirty-five degrees and snowing, though almost everywhere the snow falls, it melts. I spend ten to fifteen minutes walking through the entire park, along every walkway, from 2:05 to 2:20 p.m., but by 3:00, it has stopped snowing. There isn't a single person, sitting or standing, who is stationary in the park; everyone is perambulatory, except for three guys in the northwest corner, who are standing around, selling marijuana. As I walk through that corner, a man approaches me and says, "Weed, smoke, pot. I've got a special today. Very green." I say, "No thanks, man."

The major exception for the snow equation is, I'd say, intuitively obvious to any child. After a snowfall, the presence of the white stuff on the ground brings young children out to play and parents and caretakers to supervise. One January day drops six to eight inches on the ground. Roughly thirty people are in and around the fountain or standing next to or within a few feet of it; most are children with their parents, some are people taking pictures, either with cell phones or regular cameras. With the snow on the ground and almost no traffic on the roads that surround the park, it seems as if we are in an outdoor amphitheater, and you can clearly hear the sounds of the children squealing with pleasure as they play in the snow. Several parents and kids have built a snow ramp inside the fountain, from the top of the wall down to the floor of the fountain, and there are about six kids with plastic sleds, a couple of whom are, with their parents' assistance, sliding down the ramp. Several kids are lying on the ground, making snow angels. Someone has stuck a small, skinny fir tree upright in the center of the fountain. Dozens of people are walking their dogs; several have unleashed them. It's all very festive. In a heavy snowfall, the big city becomes a small town.

Commonsensically, and *contrary* to Durkheim's hypothesis, the most popular days for visitations to parks are Sundays (in the Central Park Conservancy study, 660,000 visits) and Saturdays (615,000 visits); in contrast, the typical weekday draws only 424,000 visitations. Obviously, a certain proportion of visitors come to the park on weekends because they work during the week, and are free on weekends. The same is true of attendance and patronage at theaters, movies, concerts, museums, bars, malls, and virtually any and all enjoyable, recreational activities. As we saw, in contrast, suicide is exempt from this contingency, and indeed, according to Durkheim's logic, is spurred on during the work week. With respect to time of day, in the Conservancy study, arrival at Central Park peaked between 2:00 and 4:00 in the afternoon; roughly one-fifth of visitors (21%) enter within this time frame. Just under a fifth arrive in the two hours just before as well as just after the peak—that is, between 12:00 and 2:00 p.m. (19%) and between 4:00 and 6:00 p.m. (19%). Only 6 percent of visits to Central Park begin before 8:00 a.m., and only 9 percent of visitors enter after 6:00 p.m.

Hence, though park visits are indeed temporally patterned during the day, not surprisingly, they follow very different lines from those that keep company with suicide and hence, call into question the iron-clad quality of Durkheim's sociological hypothesis. Though park-going is indeed sociable behavior, in many ways, it is a movement *away* from many of the activities that embody the tempo and pace of everyday life. It is a time to relax and contemplate, to step back and take a deep breath, withdraw from the demands of quotidian life. The larger the urban park, the higher the proportion of visitors who go to it for the purpose of being *in* it, and the lower the proportion of those who are simply traveling *through* it. Park-going peaks during weekends specifically because, during the week, to visit one, one must be exempt from one's workaday activities, even if only for lunch. Far from reflecting quotidian life, recreational activities, including park-going, tend to constitute a movement away from it.

My observation tells me that Bryant Park (located in Manhattan, between Fifth and Sixth avenues, between Fortieth and Forty-second streets), as well as the idyllic "vest-pocket" Greenacre Park, at Fifty-first Street between Second and Third Avenue (no dogs, no pictures, no frisbees allowed), visitations follow a less casual, more work-oriented, weekday schedule because of the abundance of business offices nearby. Of course, regarding Washington Square, some jobs and activities—particularly those associated with colleges and universities—do not fall within the modal nine-to-five routine either; most students don't have full-time jobs, some people don't work at all, and some people work within a short walk from the park. Again, taking Durkheim's cue, we should be alert to the possibility that deviant behavior is likewise influenced by the hourly, daily, weekly, or seasonal routines of social life.

Units and Groupings

Durkheim's overgeneralization aside, the way people aggregate themselves in public bears directly on their tendency to engage in—and, if victimization is involved, become victims of—criminal behavior. Moreover, certain arrangements of collectivities, aggregations, and units encourage milder forms of deviance. And deviance encompasses violations of the rules of aggregation themselves. Where do we want to focus our microscope?

The smallest human unit is the *singleton*—a single person, alone in public. The singleton is not, technically speaking, a *social* unit; it is a solitary individual. The dyad is a twosome; two people walking or sitting together in public, whether coed or unisex, constitute a dyad. The triad is a threesome, which can be made up of three men, three women, or mixed as to gender, and composed entirely of adults, or one or more children, or all children. Then there is what I call the "triad-plus," that is, four or more people together. To any observer of public settings, group aggregation is interesting because it is related in more or less predictable ways to normative violations. As a general rule, the greater the proportion of people in a given public space who are in singletons, the greater the likelihood of nonnormative behavior taking place there—both as an indicator and as a causative factor.

"Homophily" refers to social units whose members share the same relevant characteristics; "heterophily" refers to social units made up of people with different stipulated characteristics. Hence, a male-female unit—a male and female together—is heterophilous (or "heterosocial") with respect to gender. Sociologists and criminologists believe that, when it comes to gender, the more heterophilous the units in a given space or area, the lower the likelihood of crime and deviance. Likewise, a dyad made up of a black and white person—one in which a black person and a white person interact—is heterophilous with respect to race. Most sociologists would hypothesize that, other factors being equal, racial heterophily is both a manifestation of as well as an influence on harmonious relations between the races. The opposite of heterophilous is "homophilous," and the opposite of heterosocial is "homosocial." These terms are specific with respect to a particular stipulated characteristic, such as race and gender; they do not imply sexual orientation.

Thus, we can think of group aggregation as either a *dependent* or an *independent* variable. When a high proportion of singletons go about in public—especially where few or no women are present—this may be indicative of an anomic environment: Single men may be "lone wolf" predators, women may fear for their safety, and very few visitors frequent such a place, or the few social groups that do visit, scurry away from it to avoid being victimized. The predominance of singletons may *influence the likelihood* of deviance and/or may *be caused by* some third, anomie-like factor, which both causes single men to hang out in a particular space *and* causes further deviance as well. The Center for Problem-Oriented Policing (COPS) defines an "unsafe" urban park as a place in which "crime and disorder have become the norm," to the extent that locals and other potential visitors consider the park unsafe and avoid going there. The measurable indicators that tell them that they are in an unsafe park include substantial littering, the frequent presence of dog feces, routine drug and alcohol abuse, and the sight of public sex (Hilborn, 2009, p. 6). Risky parks are like neighborhood "hot spots"—a small number of locales where most harmful crime takes place and hence, where the police frequently intervene (Sherman, Gartin, and Buerger, 1989). Some parks are "crime generators" (Hilborn, 2009, p. 8); as a result of their layout, size, location, or the proclivities of nearby residents, a substantial volume of criminal acts is likely to occur in them.

The researcher, even the layperson, can determine which are the "bad" or "risky" parks by observing how quickly visitors pass through them without lingering, the number of drunken people who hang out there, the absence of females and the setting's domination by young males, the fact that mothers don't bring their children to play there, and the presence of empty beer bottles and cans as well as hypodermic syringes littering the grounds. These and other signs communicate to the potential visitor who is scanning the landscape that there's a certain risk of being beaten, robbed, or, in the case of women, raped; they are spaces to be avoided.

A safe urban park is one in which parents feel comfortable taking their children, where females visit as often as males, the elderly regularly visit, and workers have lunch and take breaks there (Hilborn, 2009, p. 5). The presence of social aggregates, especially if women and children are in the mix, taking their ease in a space both *indicates* that that space is relatively safe and constitutes a factor that *makes* it safer. Hence, the student of public behavior is likely to be rewarded by a consideration of how park visitors group themselves in the space under consideration. In his book *The Social Life of Small Urban Spaces*, as well as in his film of the same name (1979), William H. ("Holly") Whyte observed that the tendency of people in public to "form groups of various sizes is remarkably consistent" (1980, p. 121). Washington Square should be subject to the same generalizations as elsewhere.

In a dozen New York plazas, as well as specifically in Seagram's Plaza (in Manhattan, on Park Avenue, between Fifty-second and Fifty-third streets), where Whyte made most of his observations, and in Europe, Australia, Tokyo, and Manila, where associates made theirs, he notes that between 60 and 70 percent of people in *social* aggregates gather themselves into groups of two; about 20 percent, in groups of three; and between 12 and 19 percent, in aggregations of four or more (Whyte, 1980, p. 121). Whyte does not incorporate singletons into his tables, but he does mention that the "best-used plazas are stable, sociable places, with a higher proportion of couples than you find in less-used places, more people in groups, more people meeting, or exchanging goodbyes" (p. 17). In the five most-used plazas in New York that he studied, the proportion of people in social groups runs about 45 percent; in the five least-used ones, it's only 32 percent (p. 17).

On nine occasions between November 2015 and April 2017, during the afternoon, each of these observation sessions lasting several hours, I counted how people aggregate themselves in Washington Square Park. Categorizing units as singletons (people alone), dyads (twosomes), triads (threesomes), and triads-plus (four or more people together), I found that, according to Holly Whyte's formulation, Washington Square is a very sociable space indeed: Out of a total of roughly 4,500 *units*, 58 percent constitute singletons, and out of a total of about 7,000 *people* in these units, over six in ten (63%) are in *social* units, that is, in dyads, triads, or triads-plus; hence, less than four in ten of the *people* walking in, into, or out of the park (37%) are alone, that is, constitute singletons. In addition, roughly two-thirds of the people in *social* groupings are in dyads (64%). In other words, in Washington Square, the proportion of people in social units is substantially higher than in Whyte's safest plazas—63% versus 45% (1980, p. 17)—(see table 2.1), and so these spaces are, predictably, even safer. To emphasize the point, such sociable clustering is both indicative of and conduces to low levels of crime victimization, and such is the case of Washington Square Park.

Union Square, located in Manhattan, north of Fourteenth Street and south of Seventeenth Street, between Broadway and Park Avenue South, is an earthen platform held up and surrounded by a stone and concrete buttress that is flanked by wide sidewalks that host weekend markets. It is like Bryant Park in that it is ringed by office buildings. During lunch hour on weekdays (say, between 11:30 a.m. and 2:30 p.m.), as well as on market days, which are held on weekends, the sex ratio is fairly even. But during the morning and late afternoon, and especially into the evening, we see more males. At seven o'clock, most of the units I observed in

TABLE 2.1. Washington Square Park: Units and Groupings

Units	Number of Units	Percent of Units	Number of People in	Percent of People in
Singletons	2616	58	2616	37
Dyads	1453	32	2906	41
Triads	321	7	963	13
Triads-plus	148	3	653	9
Totals	4538	100	7138	100

Social Units Only

Units	Number of Units	Percent of Units	Number of People in	Percent of People in
Dyads	1453	76	2906	64
Triads	321	17	963	21
Triads-plus	148	8	653	14
Totals	1922	101	4522	99

Source: Nine observations, units and groupings entering into or exiting from Thompson Street entrance/exit and walking around in central fountain area, Washington Square Park, 2015–2017, afternoons, weekends and weekdays, during pleasant weather. (Percentages rounded off so that not all sums will add up to exactly 100 percent.)

Union Square were males in singletons, which gave the place a slightly anomic feel.

For Washington Square, as opposed to Union Square, singletons constitute a lower proportion of my people count (37%), and females made up 50 percent of its visitors, which, according to Whyte, is high for a public place, and hence, indicates that the square is likely to be a relatively safe space. The streets that configure Washington Square are entirely residential; in contrast, as I said, Union Square is ringed by office buildings, it harbors a major subway station, and the sidewalk that surrounds it sponsors a marketplace on weekends and so, generates more hustle and bustle than Washington Square and correspondingly, more anonymity and, to an extent, a more anomic atmosphere. And, as we'd predict, table 3.3 shows that violent crime, though rare in all of New York's parks, is more common in Union Square than in Washington Square.

But more generally, New York is an extremely *safe* large city. (During the seventies, when Whyte and his teams made their observations, the City was not nearly so safe.) During 2016, of the nation's thirty largest cities, only Seattle, Washington, and Honolulu, Hawaii, have a significantly lower homicide rate (2.4 and 1.5 versus 3.9 per 100,000 in the population). The increase in 2015–2016 for the country's twenty largest cities, taken as a whole, was 11 percent; from 2015 to 2016, the murder rate of the three cities that had 2015 rates *lower* than New York's (San Diego and San Jose, California, and Austin, Texas) actually increased, while New York's decreased, from 4.1 to 3.9. (Four large American cities—Detroit, St. Louis, New Orleans, and Baltimore—have rates ten times as high as these safe cities.) Much of the 2015–2016 increases in murder rates in large cities were both heroin- and gang-related; New York does not have a heroin problem that is as serious as other cities do, nor does it have gangs as violent or as dangerous. Chicago, with less than a third of the population of New York (2.7 versus 8.4 million) was the site of more than twice as many murders (732 versus 336); its homicide rate, which increased a third between 2015 and 2016, was almost seven times higher (Friedman, Grawert, and Cullen, 2017). Moreover, 78 percent of the city's criminal homicides were committed in a set of contiguous Chicago neighborhoods ("sub-Chicago") that constituted ten of the city's twenty-five police districts; "sub-Chicago's" 2016 homicide rate was 51.2 per 100,000—double that of Chicago's citywide rate. "Nowhere else in the country is there an area so large and so heavily populated with a murder rate this high" (Mangual, 2017). New York City does not harbor even remotely such a murderous swath of neighborhoods.

Thus, there are many reasons why Washington Square is an unusually safe public space—and one is that it is located in a city with a very low crime rate. True, murder is not crime in general—in fact, murder is an extremely rare event, relative to the other crimes—but violent crimes are what the public worries about most, especially murder. More generally, and more importantly, graphs of all the crimes in America's large cities between 1990 and 2016 reveal similar trajectories for *all* the Index Crimes (Friedman, Grawert, and Cullen, 2017). Murder is a *paradigmatic* crime, and where it is common, so are the other street crimes. Another reason for the square's relative safety and absence of violence is the neighborhood that surrounds it, that is, it is a lived-in, upper-middle-class community rather than a warren of offices. A third is conveyed in the analysis above: its high rate of *social* units, especially dyads. The fourth reason is conveyed by its substantial representation of women (roughly 50 percent), and fifth, the fact that so many males are in dyads *with* women (see table 6.1). And sixth, there is the fact that a substantial proportion of interracial socialization takes place in the park. True, these factors are both consequence and cause, but the threads of all of these relationships need to be unraveled and revealed.

Private, Parochial, and Public Spaces

Lyn Lofland (1998, pp. 10–12, 46–47) maps out what she refers to as a "trichotomous distinction" between urban social realms or "orders" of sociability: the private, the parochial, and the public. The *private* realm, Lofland tells us, is characterized by *"ties of intimacy among primary group members who are located within household and personal networks"*; the *parochial* realm or order is *"characterized by commonality among acquaintances and neighbors"* (p. 10; the emphasis is Lofland's)—the world of extended or more distant communities, the workplace, and associates; and the *public* realm is the world of strangers, of most streets and plazas and squares and parks. The public realm includes the places where, in an urban setting, one does not, and one's intimates do not, necessarily exercise dominion. Cities are, as Lofland argues, the most complex of settlements because they are the only settlement form that by its very nature contains all three realms or orders. It's important to emphasize that *realms are social and not physical territories* (Lofland, 1998, p. 11). It is not the fact that these realms are outside or inside that matters, in a yard or on the street, or one type of geography or another. This is a point that demands elaboration.

Washington Square is a *public* space in that one's behavior is on view by everyone assembled there. In principle, it could accommodate public, parochial, and intimate (or private) *behavior*—in other words, a *setting* for different kinds of sociality. Lofland is correct in that a given space (such as a street) is not *intrinsically* public, parochial, or private, but it is the "proportion or density" of certain kinds of relations that counts here. A deserted street may potentiate or permit certain kinds of behavior, deviant or otherwise, but a space that is large and open—and is observed by security cameras and distant, unseen spectators—can never be fully private. We may feel that others have no right to intrude into our intimate nuzzling or tête-à-tête, but in a public place such as Washington Square, onlookers are likely to intrude, at least visually, whether we like it or not. Certainly "public," "parochial," and "private" relations play themselves out in the midst of a public place, but any of these relations may be challenged by visitors, denizens, and agents of social control who have different ideas on the forms of sociality that ought to take place there. Still, *physicality matters*; certain realms of people are attracted to certain kinds of spaces and hence, certain kinds of sociality are *enabled* in these places.

For the purposes of our discussion, as it pertains to Greenwich Village and Washington Square, the parochial realm is useful as an abstract marker, a conceptual cell or box in the delineation of forms of sociality that, in effect, has largely been rendered obsolete. Gerald Suttles describes the parochialism that prevailed among boys and young men in the 1960s in the neighborhoods he studied in Chicago. He maintained that peer relations provided a moral basis for behavior, an ethos "that seemed calculated to reproduce . . . the importance of the vigilante group and the defended neighborhood" (1972, p. 223). The working-class male felt insecure about intrusions into his neighborhood. Territorial defense, Suttles argued, developed out of the inadequacies of formal institutions that failed to protect individual, local, and group rights. The peer group "barricaded its neighborhood according to local values and individual comportment." The boundaries of the neighborhood, Suttles explained, "form the outer perimeter for restricting social relations." Adults "cross ethnic boundaries to shop or go to work, while children do so running errands or attending school. Free time or recreation, however, should be spent within one's own ethnic section" (1968, pp. 225–26).

These norms, rules, and patterns vary according to degree and specificity, but all social and ethnic categories and socioeconomic strata in the slum at that time obeyed or followed them. Minerva Durham (2015) writes that during the seventies and into the eighties, Martin Scorsese's Greenwich Village "mean streets" did not welcome African Americans (and certainly not in the company of white women). None of this is true anymore. The defense-of-neighborhood violent incidents between the local Italian American residents and black males, by definition outsiders, once common, could not take place today. Over the years, too many former interlopers have settled into the neighborhood, most of them exceedingly cosmopolitan; too many residents and visitors did not grow up there, and Greenwich Village is no longer a parochial milieu, no longer an "urban village."

What we do see, and everywhere, including in Washington Square, is attempts to maintain what Lyn Lofland refers to as parochial "bubbles" (1998, p. 12), which are only *nominally* protected from infiltration by outsiders. A wedding party gathers in Washington Square; the bride is resplendent in her white gown, her maids of honor are crowded around her, and all are giggling as the groom and his ushers snap their pictures on cell phones. One usher asks a bystander to take the entire retinue's picture, and she does. The "bubble" is partially penetrated—by the bystander, taking the bridal party's picture—but it was at the request of one of the retinue that the bystander *not* be included in the picture; hence, in some sense, the bubble remains intact. Similarly, an organized youth group—each one wearing a green t-shirt and all being led by an adult chaperone holding up a cardboard paddle—walks through the park, but there are gaps in the assemblage; some bystanders "penetrate" the bubble by crossing the group to proceed to the other side, while others skirt around the group to observe the integrity of the bubble's boundaries. In large cities, parochial bubbles are eminently permeable.

Presumably, bubbles may also constrain a private interaction from the public, or even the parochial, realm. But it depends on the nature of the interaction taking place within a given bubble. A couple sitting on a bench in Washington Square, lost in one another's gaze, seems to have forgotten that they are in public; immediately surrounded but socially unconnected by a dozen people, they enjoy an intimate, passionate kiss. Before long, their kiss becomes a full-body embrace, with hands roaming over one another's face, neck, and chest. Finally, the woman, entangled in the man's arms, looks up, blinks, and giggles. Several parties surrounding them, including myself, are staring at their embrace. The man checks himself, looks around, and laughs. They adjust their clothing, stand up, and walk off, hand in hand. They imagined a perceptual bubble that wasn't there, engaged in an intimate act in a public realm *as if it were taking place in a private realm*; the intensity of the act was certain to attract attention and pop the bubble. The people surrounding them would have honored their bubble had their kisses been more measured and tethered. Their embrace became too interesting, too *conspicu-*

ous, to ignore. Even in an extremely broad-minded, latitudinous venue, the line is drawn somewhere, and, at a certain point, the couple realized that they had crossed it.

Behavior in Public

When we're aware of being observed, we become self-conscious about the judgment of our "audiences" and usually alter our behavior accordingly. We tend to refrain from picking our nose, knowing that when others see us doing it, they will consider us vulgar and gross. With a surveillance camera trained on them or a set of eyes watching their every move, potential shoplifters are more likely to refrain from stealing. It's not enough to know that people tend to adjust their behavior when they are in a public setting; we'd like to know the *degree* to which they do so, what they do *instead*, and *how* such public surveillance impacts on what people do. Indeed, taking others into account must be regarded as a variable rather than a constant.

Erving Goffman investigated the "micro order," that is, the intimate, face-to-face encounter. His forte was "the minute analysis of the social positioning of participants as they take heed of each other, address each other, move toward or away from each other, parade before each other, lay claims on each other, insulate themselves against each other and make a range of varied adjustments to each other" (Blumer, 1972, p. 50). The essence or crux of the Goffmanian problem is the nature and dynamics of social interaction. However, as Lyn Lofland points out (1998, p. 20n.), although two of Goffman's book contain "public" in their title—*Behavior in Public Places* (1963) and *Relations in Public* (1971)—they're really only loosely related to the sort of public settings I discuss here. For Goffman, public-ness is not the analytic variable. According to Herbert Blumer, who reviewed Goffman's latter volume, Goffman identifies the "field of public life" as the "realm of activity that is generated by face-to-face interaction and organized by norms of comingling—a domain." The "ground rules" of social interaction—or "norms of comingling"—within these and like settings are widely understood and taken for granted; they establish the public order (Blumer, 1972, p. 50). For the most part, Goffman's domain is *how* people adjust to the presence of others—that is, the forms and dynamics of their adjustments. Most of the social gatherings he examines are small; what he looks at is *points of contact* when people encounter one another, or even when an individual *visualizes* encountering others. Encounters between family members and a doctor who is treating one of them. How a woman in public adjusts her appearance so as to seem more attractive. Sizing up others one sees with respect to their potential dangerousness. Couples holding hands. A couple eating dinner at a restaurant. A customer-clerk interaction. People greeting one another. Face engagements. Situational improprieties. Goffman discusses tiny units *in* a public or a semipublic space. Though he does not addressed the matter specifically, his analyses nonetheless have a direct bearing on the behavior, including the interaction, that we look at here.

I'm looking at public behavior through a slightly wider-angle lens than Goffman did. My oyster encompasses micro, face-to-face encounters *within a context of* the surrounding park observers or onlookers. The latter influences the former, but sometimes in subtle, complex ways. This is not contextless behavior; indeed, the context *is* the park—indeed, the particular settings *within* the park. At the core of our interest here is *how* context influences behavior—or doesn't, according to the actors involved—and why the park community makes judgments in the ways that it does. The "park community" is not a monolith; it is composed of smaller units, some of whom congregate in particular spots within the park, and some of whom are more fluid, less fixed. Still, there is one overriding issue that undergirds context: the matter of civility. I'm interested in whether and to what extent all subunits within the park respect the rights of others, how they define and act upon the rules of civility. Since, as we'll see, most Washington Square visitors do not live in the surrounding neighborhood, we want to know if such rules express the feelings of the communities in which they live, how their members adjust their behavior according to their definition of such rules.

Informal Washington Park norms tend to manifest tolerance for the rights of others to express themselves, but sometimes an action violates the rights of others. To understand how tolerance and civility work in a public place, we have to expose ourselves to narratives of real-life behavior and real-life responses to that behavior and contemplate the implications of both. Civility is a construct, embodied and expressed within particular contexts. This particular context is a public park—an *urban* public park—but it does *not* embody the relevant qualities of *all* public places. Following along the lines of the Suttles-Lofland distinctions, a large park is not a bar, a house of worship, an athletic event, or even a street—which are also public places—the consideration of which reminds us that the public-private distinction is a spectrum, not an either-or proposition. The park is a particular *type* of public place with distinct qualities of its own. The complexities of the events I narrate here offer shading to our comprehension of the "public" aspect of public places—as well as help us qualify our understanding of the concept of deviance itself.

Streets and Squares

Streets and squares are both different from and similar to one another. One of the features that the two share is that, as compared with the interior of buildings, they are relatively accessible to virtually everyone; strangers to a neighborhood are *usually* able to both walk along the street *and* enter a square. (Roughly nine hundred of New York City's streets are privately owned; in chapter 7 we'll encounter a *park* that is privately owned.) Until just a few generations ago, many urban neighborhoods, even in Manhattan, were ethnic enclaves, and their residents intentionally made outsiders feel unwelcome.

Still and all, streets are more diverse and cosmopolitan than the interiors of buildings. Most people in cities do not customarily invite any and all strangers into their apartments, but streets outside these dwellings typically tolerate and may even welcome strangers. This tendency is even more emphatically the case of squares, plazas, and parks. In fact, in many locations in urban centers around the world, foreigners and other nonresidents are tourists and hence, likely to purchase merchandise in local retail establishments, and so, are decidedly welcome. But what makes open spaces such as squares, plazas, and parks different from streets is that most of them allow, and even encourage, visitors to remain for longer periods of time. According to Whyte's classic study of "small urban spaces," when an open space offers sitting spaces, it's more likely to attract lingerers; if there are fountains and trees, likewise, people will stay longer; and if food is to be had there, so much the better (1980, chapters 2, 3, and 4). In any case, most streets provide walkways for pedestrians, who tend to move on; in contrast, attractive open spaces such as squares and parks, with plentiful places to sit, invite pedestrians to bide their time, stay a while, chill, take a break—in a word, to *loiter*.

We typically see more specifically utilitarian perambulatory behavior on the street, and more optional or leisure and relaxation-type behavior in parks, squares, and other open settings—more lingering, tarrying, and hanging out. Though walls and steps to sit on have often traditionally accompanied squares, benches represent a fairly recent invention in European squares (Lennard and Lennard, 2008, p. 57)—judging from the Lennards' many photographs, they are as likely to be absent as to be present—though more common in Europe than in Asia, where, in principle, the grand squares "were intended to set apart royal or sacred buildings, to create a stage for the display of power" (p. 11). In Europe, movable chairs are often placed in squares to accommodate patrons of adjacent restaurants and cafés.

In the United States, benches are far more common in squares and parks than on the street and hence, in them, visitors are more likely to take the opportunity to relax, look around, meet others, socialize, talk about matters of mutual interest, and perhaps make merry. (Today, one may find seats or benches at bus stops, which, however, typically empty as soon as one's conveyance arrives.) As a result of this lingering and tarrying, entertainers and buskers frequently perform for persons so assembled in order to solicit donations from them. In populous areas, squares represent one of the major sites of human congregation. People gather, then separate; they meet, interact, then leave, either together or independently. They come together and do things in these open spaces that they are less likely to do elsewhere, including on streets. They meet and talk to particular people, or categories of people, with whom they socialize only in specific public locales, encounter mostly strangers—as opposed to mostly intimates—and reveal themselves in ways they might not with their friends.

All in all, streets typically lack the qualities that make many urban squares interesting. Yes, *for the most part*, streets are usually readily accessible to everyone, and, in most neighborhoods, they *more or less* welcome the stranger. But, again, they tend to be conduits rather than target or end-point locations, and most are automobile oriented rather than ambulatory, do not invite lingering, and rarely, except in the case of bus stops, provide much in the way of benches. The dynamics of sociability that apply to the street do not always reliably translate into the park.

Strangers in the Agora

Archaeological digs have turned up formerly open spaces in prehistoric settlements into which pathways once emptied. Such spaces, often centered by a well or a fountain, a statue or a monument, served as markets as well as locales for convening and gossiping, listening to music, being entertained, listening to oratory and announcements or local news; they were often bordered by a house of worship. In the Neolithic world, the square comprised the heart of a loose and far-flung, nascent community; it circumscribed a particular space within which local and nearby inhabitants carried on specific types of sociability. True to its prehistoric precedents, in the sixth century BCE, the city fathers of Athens laid out a square or public space they called the "agora." Inside the buildings that bordered it they located the seat of government where politicians enacted legislation, and outside, the space provided a locale for the public discussion of matters of importance. In the second century BCE, the Romans conquered Greece and built a forum in Athens, which served many of the same functions as the original agora. The Athenian agora, and the Roman forum, satisfied a range of functions for a broad sector of residents as well as visitors; the population of the entire city patronized this central space, and for many reasons. Over the centuries, multiple armies invaded the city, killed, captured, and scattered its inhabitants, and reduced the square and its circumscribed buildings to rubble. During peacetime, the residents returned and rebuilt its structures, but in the sixth century CE—some twelve hundred years after its origin—the Slavs invaded Athens, destroyed its agora, and the citizenry never rebuilt it (Camp and Mauzy, 2015).

One of sociology's earliest focuses of interest involved the impact of *urbanism* (a demographic variable) on *urbanization* (a cultural variable, and, presumably, the consequence of urbanism); indeed, it might be said that American sociology, which adapted the theories of European intellectuals, was born out of this concern. Over the course of historical time, sociologists of a century or more ago would have argued, cities brought about among their inhabitants a more cosmopolitan, universalistic proclivity, a tolerance for diversity. Among the earliest pioneering works along these lines, the 1887 tome by sociologist and social philosopher Ferdinand Tönnies, *Gemeinschaft und Gesellschaft* (first translated into English in 1957 as *Community and Society*), was perhaps most influential. Tönnies contrasted social relations in traditional rural society, most clearly exemplified by premodern institutions, especially the family, with the interaction characteristic of a rationalistic organization in modern society, most distinctly represented by the modern joint stock company. (Max Weber's *The City* not only appeared later, but it was structural and institutional in its approach rather than centered on the nature of social ties.) In *The Division of Labor in Society* (1893/1984), Emile Durkheim contrasted *mechanical* solidarity, which characterized social relations in relatively small, simple societies that were held together by the *homogeneity* or the similarity of members to one another, with those in larger, more complex societies that were based on *organic* solidarity, which depended on difference among parties and their *interdependence* on one another, that is, their functions were interlocking or mutually linked.

For hundreds of generations, humans in urban settlements have routinely carried on social relations with outsiders, or people who are significantly different from themselves; learning how it should be done, in a more or less civil fashion, represented one of humanity's half-dozen most important cultural accomplishments. Today's intellectuals are more likely to refer to the ancient agora as an open urban space wherein citizens had license to make speeches, but I'd like to emphasize its quality of attracting visitors (that is, strangers) who are personally unknown to locals—travelers, traders, exiles from their own society—which makes it necessary for societies to devise the means by which their members can interact with such outsiders. In a way, every time we step into a public space, we replicate ten thousand years of social evolution.

The smaller the community, the greater the likelihood that its residents know one another and hence, socialize with one another as intimates. *Almost by definition*, larger communities potentiate and effect sociality among strangers. True, even in cities, residents interact mainly with intimates, but the nature of their interaction and their relationship with the parties with whom they interact are considerably more varied than is true of members of smaller communities. Sociability that takes place among intimates is quite different from that which takes place among strangers; the coming together of and interaction between and among strangers fosters a distinctively different set of dynamics. Certain *types* of sociability tend to take place with people we don't know, and seem more appropriate in certain locales. Larger communities characteristically foster a diversity of public spaces, and both the public behavior and the social control that are exercised in each species of space cry out for sociological investigation.

The complexion and character of social interaction in public spaces is related to the size of the community in which people live. Eight decades ago, Louis Wirth famously pinpointed the quality that characterized the urban sensibility in the following words: "The juxtaposition of divergent personalities and modes of life" on which large cities are predicated, Wirth wrote, "tends to produce a relativistic personality and a sense of tolerance of differences," which in turn potentiate rationalism and "a secularization of life" (1938, p. 15). The city potentiates and facilitates a "degree of freedom" that cannot be found in the small town. The "indifference, anonymity, intellectualization, and cosmopolitanism of urban life" provides an "independence of action" that small-town life precludes. While residents of small towns may tolerate eccentricity, the big city rewards it (Karp et al., 2015, p. 122).

The urbanist might find some support in Karl Marx's supposed phrase, in *The Communist Manifesto* (1848), "the idiocy of rural life," which is, alas, a mistranslation. The phrase Marx actually used was the "isolation" (it's an example of the translator's "false friend"—in German, the relevant word is "idiotismus") of rural life, and it's an isolation from that very heterogeneity, energy, sophistication, and cosmopolitanism of the big city that puts urban dwellers into contact with people who are very different from themselves. Under freely chosen circumstances, such sociability has the effect of accepting diversity, valuing differences, and welcoming—at least, tolerating—contrasts. While size does potentiate neighborhood segregation based on income, wealth, ethnicity, and lifestyle—the larger the city, the more viable separate and distinctly different communities become—it also potentiates contact and comingling of members of distinctly different categories of humanity and hence, the possibility of empathetic understanding between and among one another. And, in larger communities, such comingling, I maintain, is likeliest in *public nodules*, such as marketplaces, stores, theaters and other places of entertainment, public transportation—and parks.

A quality that characterizes the city is *how welcome* strangers are. Lyn Lofland defines urban public spaces as those areas of the city to which "all persons have legal access" (1973, p. 19). Parties who control private spaces may legally restrict them in ways in which public space cannot be restricted. A private club "may deny access to all but its members and invited guests." A home owner or tenant "may deny access to the unwanted visitor," but a municipality "may not restrict entrance to a public street"—or a public park (pp. 19–20). And let's not forget the *gated community*, these "suburban fortresses" (Low, 2003) where, likewise, outsiders are not welcome at all unless a resident invites them. As Lofland explains, however, the line between a public and a private space "is a fluid one. Is a bar public if access is restricted to certain categories of age or sex or race? Is a park public if police systematically clear it of sleeping men? Is the sidewalk in front of a home public if the elderly resident of the house continually chases away the neighborhood children who try to play there?" (p. 20). Not all "public" spaces are truly *public*. Strangers, especially strangers with certain racial, ethnic, sexual, or age-related characteristics, may be made to feel unwelcome in a putatively public place by its entrenched denizens. Despite these definitional wrinkles and complications, we have a commonsensical but reasonably accurate notion of what the sociological observer means by the term "public space." We are likely to encounter strangers in a public space—locales to which people unknown to us have legal access. This has not always been the case, nor is this necessarily *socially* true.

The city is "a world of strangers," that is, a place to which people unknown to locals have access (Lofland, 1973, p. 18). Urban spaces have "made it possible to live with and relate to larger and larger numbers of other humans. In the city, the parochial tribalist died. In the city, the sophisticated cosmopolitan was born" (p. 23). In metropolitan communities, for the most part, we interact in public with people telegraphically, on the basis of a few superficial characteristics that are readily observable: age, sex, putative socioeconomic status, and race. Nearly all urbanites have learned that they should act in a more or less civil manner to strangers; incivility and rudeness are matters to be remarked on (Smith,

Phillips, and King, 2010). Many folks, it is true, avoid the vagrant, the indigent, and the homeless—they would say, for reasons of self-protection, but perhaps also to avoid ritual or actual contamination—just as many of us tend to avoid young, rowdy males, that is, as a source of potential trouble. In times past, in public, whites often avoided African Americans, especially males, and most especially young males. Today, this is less true, and it is particularly less true in cosmopolitan settings, such as Washington Square Park. In my estimation, civility is one of the great wonders of modernity; it puts into outward terms the feeling of empathy, and represents one of the factors that makes public interaction workable.

Most American cities are measurably racially segregated, but many large municipalities harbor at least one "cosmopolitan canopy" or "island of civility" where people very different from one another come together, mingle, and jostle side by side with mutual respect and a blasé attitude and demeanor about their differences. "The homeless, the mentally ill, the well-to-do, black homeboys, bicycle messengers, office workers, and businesspeople are all here," Elijah Anderson writes, describing such a setting in Philadelphia, "observing the show and, for the most part, not only getting along but thriving on one another's energy" (2011, p. 23). To a major extent, persons entering these canopies have agreed to a kind of pact of courteousness; likewise, for the most part, such spaces are subject to surveillance and hence, disruptive street people are excluded or discouraged from entering. Much of Anderson's canopy is administered by a multiplicity of commercial interests, as are other large cities' cognate establishments—Baltimore's Inner Harbor, San Antonio's River Walk, Seattle's Pike Place Market, and San Francisco's Fisherman's Wharf—which employ private security. These are POPS—privately owned public spaces. The principal reason for the construction and administration of the POPS is to earn a profit for its entrepreneurs and investors; hence, its primary relationship is between the consumer and the retail establishment and, ultimately, between the consumer and capital. If the POPS fails to earn a profit, it will go out of business. Truly publicly owned and operated spaces do not have to earn a profit—although in today's political climate, most municipalities do keep tabs on how popular a space is—and the primary relationship is between and among visitors.

Washington Square is a municipal park; it is administered by the New York City Department of Parks and Recreation. Formal social control comes from the uniformed presence of the PEP, or Parks Enforcement Patrol (New York City Special Patrolmen and New York State Peace Officers), the Urban Park Rangers, the NYPD, and, occasionally, the NYU Safety Patrol; informally, it is exercised by the presence of park visitors. The PEP carry a baton and handcuffs and can make a "warrantless arrest" and issue summonses and citations.

Stranger contact is, Lofland argues, "one of the great miracles of city life" (1973, p. 95). People learn to interact in a world of strangers; they learn to "code" one another, though outward appearances and primary characteristics are of less value in predicting potential behavior than they used to be. "We can live in the world of strangers only because we have ordered our cities such that it is possible to identify those personally unknown to us with some degree of accuracy" (p. 176). The city has created "a new kind of human being—the cosmopolitan—who was able, as his tribal ancestors were not, to relate to others in the new ways that city living made not only possible but necessary" (p. 177). In the city, we "know" most of the people with whom we interact, and we initially interact with them categorically as well, and hence are able to sustain "surface, fleeting, restricted" relationships with them (p. 178). In a pragmatic sense, urban dwellers are amateur urban ethnographers; they know, more or less, how to interact with one another, and they apply rules that predict how others are likely to act.

The public realm is, as Lyn Lofland argues in the subtitle of *The Public Realm*, "the city's quintessential social territory" (1998). Urban folk are not sensorally, culturally, or interactionally overloaded, not blasé to the point of indifference, and the "world of strangers" is not an asocial realm (Lofland, 1973). What happens in public *matters*; it manifests sociological forces in the same measure as religious ritual, courtship and marriage, and voting for a political candidate matter. The simple fact that so much social interaction in public takes place between and among strangers does not mean that it should not be the stuff of sociological investigation, but it is different in important ways from private interaction with intimates—and it is the sociologist's job to understand how and why it is different. Let's be clear about this point: *Most* of the people with whom residents of cities interact are not strangers; they are friends, neighbors, relatives, shopkeepers, clients, functionaries with whom they've dealt for a stretch of time. But "interact" is a matter of degree;

much superficial interaction—such as passing someone on the street—hardly constitutes interaction at all. And this is not Lofland's point, nor is it mine. The point is this: Cities are the places where strangers are most likely to meet and interact with locals frequently and comfortably. And over time, urbanites become more cosmopolitan in dealing with the people they don't know because they have been socialized into this perspective as a result of having had experiences relating to diverse sets of interacting parties. Moreover, there's a selection process going on here; it is the most cosmopolitan of the rural dwellers who migrate to cities in the first place—more for employment than anything else, but the more adventurous are more likely to migrate for that reason while the more traditional are more likely to stay put.

In *Behavior in Public Places*, Erving Goffman defines the locus of his subject matter as "any regions in a community freely accessible to members of that community" (1963, p. 9). But he immediately backtracks, as well he should. "There are many social settings that persons of certain status are forbidden to enter"—that is, they are not full-fledged members of the community in question; members of the community are motivated to avoid "contamination by undesirables" (p. 10). Rules of trespass—even in "open, unwalled public places"—dictate that certain categories of humanity be excluded from such places. This has always been the case, although far more so in the past than today. For instance, in Europe, during eras when the aristocracy held sway, commoners were excluded from many locales. In the ancient Middle East, certain quarters of cities remained off-limits at night to Christians, or Jews, or Muslims. In the United States, until recently, evening curfews made it illegal for juveniles to be unaccompanied by an adult on the street. Not too long ago, the authorities might have taken certain parties in for "questioning" who seem to embody one or more criminal stereotypes. And for much of the history of the United States, rules of exclusion stipulated that persons of African descent who were not slaves or servants were unwelcome in many neighborhoods. Where such rules exist, whether formal or informal, Goffman explains, "certain categories of persons may not be authorized to be present, and . . . should they be present, this in itself will constitute an improper act" (1963, pp. 10, 11). Restrictions on the movements of the members of particular categories of people in some areas of towns and cities have been applied for as long as human settlements have existed, and their relaxation and abolishment has been one of the more momentous developments in human history.

Though in the past, law and custom often limited the accessibility of the agora or central square to certain visitors, it was one of the few places in ancient cities where residents welcomed strangers and foreigners. Though the agora's accessibility to women and slaves was restricted in certain ways, such regulations did not represent a total ban: Both women and slaves could draw water from the agora's wells or springs, and slaves, both male and female—as well as females from less affluent families— often shopped at the marketplace. Moreover, the mobility of women anywhere outside the Athenian household varied from one historical period to another and so, in earlier times, more affluent and respectable women could walk through the agora on their way to the wells (Rotroff and Lamberton, 2006). During more recent history, most restrictions on the right of women's access to public spaces have been informal and cultural rather than strictly legal. Women have feared entering certain public spaces unaccompanied, especially at night, because of their physical vulnerability to attacks by men (Valentine, 1990)—an assumption that Lofland (1984, p. 13) argues needs to be better documented. A different sort of restriction, that which forbade foreign merchants in medieval English towns from selling their goods in certain markets, forced them to locate their shops in specific neighborhoods. "This separation of denizen from foreigner" was motivated "by the desire to capture the best trading areas for the native merchant" (Salusbury, 1948, pp. 56, 57). Such restrictive covenants prevented the social mingling of merchants with diverse backgrounds, thereby minimizing what native merchants could learn from foreigners, and perhaps, as a consequence, preventing them from becoming more cosmopolitan in their outlook.

Worldwide, most small towns have squares or open spaces where people congregate, but in them, the stranger may or may not be welcome. Likewise, even in large cities, in certain neighborhoods, the community casts a parochial shroud over public spaces. But the larger and more diverse the city, the greater the likelihood that the resident will encounter strangers—that is, people different from locals in important ways. Moreover, some particular open spaces or squares become known as places where strangers, people different in significant ways from locals, can betake themselves. Urban squares, plazas, and parks offer the sociologist an invitation to investigate and understand behavior in public places.

Lennard and Lennard (2008) find in the European square a democratizing and civilizing "genius" that generates and reinforces sociability and a sense of unity among a community's populace. After fire, language, agriculture, and the wheel, the city is probably the most influential human creation, and the market square, according to Lewis Mumford, the most important contribution of the city. But he also argues that the open-air market has disappeared from the European city, replaced by lines of shops in which display and commerce take place "behind glass windows," and every day "tended to be market day," affording the lady of the upper-middle-class house the opportunity "to dress up, to sally forth, to exhibit her own person" (1938, p. 99). The Lennards maintain that the attractive town square fosters civic engagement and philanthropy, or the love of humankind and the readiness to share the world with others, while the unattractive square, contrastingly, fosters "misanthropy" and the "tendency to shun others" (2008, pp. 17–18), where the few people who do frequent it are those whom many of us choose to shun—that is, the homeless and the alcoholic (p. 7). But the fact is, so-called undesirables likewise frequent desirable urban spaces—unless local agents of social control banish them (Beckett and Herbert, 2009)—which is one of the features of Washington Square that makes it so interesting to the sociologist of deviance. Indeed, desirable urban spaces that manage to attract and embrace so-called undesirables who are as accepting of the rights of others as those others are toward theirs have achieved a golden balance of harmony and creative conflict. We might also keep in mind, however, that during the rule of Fascist Italy and Nazi Germany, town and city squares provided the sites of speeches by officials and politicians—a fact that the Lennards do not mention. Hence, public squares clearly do not *inevitably* or *necessarily* foster democracy, humanism, or inclusivity.

Catchment Area

Squares, plazas, and parks vary with respect to their catchment area—the size of the domain from which their visitors are drawn. We may call this the "draw versus localization principle": To entice visitors from beyond the immediate neighborhood, a place needs attractive and appealing features, and the more desirable the place, the more effort people will invest in getting to it.

Propinquity matters, but so does the appeal of a place. Visitors to a charming, attractive place come from all over, though, as with everything else, they are more likely to come from some places than others. With respect to a park, square, or plaza, such attractions include benches, a fountain, a waterfall, a stream, ponds or lakes, a statue, grass, trees, flowers and other plantings, food stalls or carts, shops, a playground, lampposts, proper upkeep, and the absence of litter and crime. Perhaps most important of all, spaces are likely to attract more—and more diverse—visitors the more powerful their lure. Many squares consist of little more than a tiny rectangle or triangle of space accommodating a few benches and perhaps some bushes. The drawing power of most such open urban spaces is weak; most are simply a space that pedestrians or vehicles transect on their way to somewhere else. The few who do stay longer are from the immediate neighborhood.

Parks, as distinguished from squares and plazas, tend to be larger and more consciously designed for recreation and relaxation—but keep in mind, there's *some* pragmatic hustle and bustle as well, since many parks, including Washington Square, are conduits to someplace else; while there, the visitor tends to remain longer and engage in a wider range of activities in the space. New York City's Central Park, with its 843 acres, which holds a reservoir, small lakes, geological formations, the Great Lawn, Strawberry Fields, roadways, paths, restaurants, and a carousel, stands at the upper end of this spectrum. Its catchment area is huge—people routinely come from all over the City, and even from the suburbs, to enjoy its amenities—and, because of its attractions, it holds its visitors in its embrace for substantial stretches of time. Visitors from a wide area spend time in Bryant Park, in midtown Manhattan, located behind the New York Public Library's main branch, chiefly for a very specific and utilitarian reason: Many workers in offices and retail establishments nearby partake of lunch or take their coffee breaks in the park. Not even this was always true. Until the 1980s, very few people (aside from drug addicts and homeless men) entered this now-attractive, grassy, 9.6-acre urban space because it had acquired a deserved reputation for being unsafe; shrubbery and its elevation above the street made it difficult for passersby to monitor behavior within its borders and hence, a perfect place to commit a predatory crime; women rarely ventured there, even during the day (Zukin, 1995, p. 28). Following the ideas of Holly Whyte (1980), the Bryant Park Corporation renovated the park, reopening it in 1992, thereby creating one of the most popular open green spaces in the City (Weber, 1995)—establishing a model of "pacification by cappuccino" (Zukin, 1995, p. 28).

Times Square likewise verifies the rule of appeal versus propinquity; it is famous, interesting, vibrant, and engaging—and hence, sightseers arrive there from all points of the globe to visit. *Travel + Leisure* estimates that 41.9 million visitors enter Times Square a year—making it the most popular tourist spot in the United States. Though it is a much more car-oriented space than most squares, pedestrians come there either for the sake of tourism or to go to a nearby Broadway show. Recent additions to Times Square include pedestrian walkways or plazas, which help give it an on-foot feel. Planters accommodating saplings distributed around the square pass for the locale's nominal green space. Central Park is the country's second most popular destination, with forty million visitors.

An uncountable number of European, Latin American, and Asian squares and plazas encompass or border on handsome major sights that attract tourists and visitors from around the world—the Zócalo in Mexico City, Trafalgar Square in London, the Grand Place in Brussels, the Place de la Concorde in Paris, Piazza San Marco in Venice, St. Peter's Square in Vatican City, the area around the Trevi Fountain in Rome, the Piazza del Campo in Siena (which features a horse race, begun in the 1300s, in which each contestant is backed by the city's most prominent families), Red Square, near the colorful St. Basil's Cathedral (built in 1552) and the Kremlin (erected in the 1400s)—two of the most impressive architectural sites in the world—the area in front of Notre Dame Cathedral in Paris, which was completed in 1363, and Tiananmen Square in Beijing, the site of a pro-democracy demonstration massacre—in which as many as a thousand or more young people were gunned down—a quarter-century ago.

These public spaces represent only a few of the locales that host huge numbers of visitors from virtually everywhere; they are not primarily neighborhood spaces—they are in fact international in their appeal. Washington Square Park has no such nearby attractions and yet, it does

attract tourists—one frequently sees them taking out maps and looking around. More important for our interests: Most of these attractive
squares do not provide seating, though some are ringed by cafés and
restaurants, which do, and some have amphitheaters or fountains with
walls or balustrades, where visitors may sit. Some of these spaces—Red
Square and Tiananmen Square—are used primarily as military parade
grounds, some function primarily as market squares, and still others are
mainly drive-through in character; moreover, these categories are not
mutually exclusive. These spaces are heavily visited by tourists, though
many of them do not linger for extensive lengths of time.

A trio of researchers studying incivility in everyday life suggests that
the scope of much social science investigation on problematic or wrongful behavior is restricted to a catchment area that is defined as "within
a 15-minute walk of the respondent's home" (Smith, Phillips, and King,
2010, p. 5). They feel that a phenomenon such as incivility is likely to take
place on a far broader stage—in fact, in practically every public sphere
we might imagine: to and from work, in shops, driving one's car and taking public transportation, during sporting events, in bars and restaurant,
and so on. For the purposes of the present study, the fifteen-minute walk
is a useful gauge by which the interested observer can measure the moti-
vation of a potential visitor to reach a certain location. Attractive locales
hold a more powerful lure for outsiders—hence, the greater the effort
they will make to visit them. Extremely alluring places may demand
taking public transportation or driving to get there; visitors come from
neighborhoods *other than* the one in which the site is located in order to
enjoy *that* particular space. If substantial numbers of people are willing
to walk multiple blocks, or take public transportation, the place must
be highly appealing. I've interviewed visitors who regularly travel from
the Bronx and, in one case, even New Haven, Connecticut, to partake
of Washington Square's charms. Tourists put appealing places on their
itinerary when visiting a given city. Time and distance from the visitor's
place of residence to Washington Square is a rough, approximate measure of the park's appeal. More appealing places have a larger *catchment
area*; for less appealing ones, their catchment area is smaller.

If we look at different public spaces, especially parks, in this way, we
can compare the appeal of different public spaces to determine their
relative appeal. Of the sixty people in Washington Square I interviewed

about their residence, forty-six, or three-quarters (77%), lived in New York City. About a quarter (sixteen, or 27%) told me they lived in Green-wich Village or SoHo; nine (15%) lived in Brooklyn, six (10%) in upper Manhattan, six were tourists, and four (7%) lived in the Bronx; three were homeless, three lived in Queens, three in Chelsea, and three in New Jersey. The remainder were from lower Manhattan, Midtown, Rockland County, and Long Island. Washington Square Park is one of the most felicitous and *interesting* open spaces in the New York metropolitan area, and so, in this sense, it is a *city* park, not exclusively a neighborhood park. In addition, tourists often stop in on the park during their New York visitation, but the others nonetheless make a special effort to get there from where they live—and that is, for some, a substantial distance away. Any investigation of a space that is visited by a substantial number of outsiders should include a look at its charms.

New York City, Manhattan, Greenwich Village

New York is not only the largest city in the United States; it is also extremely compactly inhabited. People are packed together, with one exception, more than twice as densely there (27,000) as in all the country's other large cities—for instance, San Francisco (with a total population of 805,000 and a density of 17,200 per square mile), Boston (population, 645,000, density 13,300 per square mile), Chicago (2.7 mil-lion, 11,900 per square mile), and Philadelphia (1.5 million, 11,000 per square mile). This places New York City at the very top of the density index of the nation. And if Manhattan were an entire city, its density (nearly 70,000 per square mile) would be four times greater than the country's most crowded municipalities. Manhattan's density is largely due to the height of its apartment buildings, not to mention that rel-atively few of its blocks are vacant. Population density contributes to the crowded feel when residents take to the sidewalks. Parks represent a major exception to this tendency: They offer uninhabited spaces to teeming communities.

But Manhattan's packed-together quality carries with it a conglom-erate of associated features, all of which influence human sociability. American society harbors a distinctly car-oriented culture; in contrast, Manhattan offers the most perambulatory and the least car-oriented of any major diverse urban environment in America, including the other boroughs of the City. Drivers plunge into downtown Manhattan at their own peril; through virtually every street, a red light and perhaps a traffic jam lie in wait for them. And parking there is distinctly burdensome—or costly. These difficulties result in a paucity of automobile ownership. The population of New York County (Manhattan) registers fourteen passenger vehicles for every one hundred residents; Richmond County (Staten Island) registers fifty-three. Compare Manhattan with Los Angeles County, whose residents own sixty-one vehicles for every one hundred residents, and the United States as a whole, where there are eighty cars registered per hundred. Fortunately, the MTA, the New York Transit Authority, takes up most of the transportational slack.

A portion of our story here focuses on the ambulatory culture versus the car culture. One of the features that give our square its special flavor is that private passenger cars—including taxis—are prohibited from penetrating its borders. As we saw, Washington Square is most emphatically *not* a drive-through park. Unlike Manhattan, which is, in comparison with other municipalities, a walking environment, Washington Square specifically is currently pretty much an *entirely* on-foot setting, which offers the researcher an eye-level, perambulatory perspective on the relevant social action.

Washington Square Park is a municipal park administered by the New York City Department of Parks and Recreation, located in Greenwich Village, in the southern half of Manhattan Island. The New York Police Department's Sixth Precinct is made up of two subcommunities, Greenwich Village and the West Village; the precinct includes the two-thirds of a mile square area that stretches from Fourteenth Street to the north, with Houston Street at its southern border, Broadway to the east, and the Hudson River in the west. These two neighborhoods in this compass are slightly more densely populated than Manhattan generally (they are populated by 78,000 people per square mile), and substantially more than the City as a whole. Villagers, compared with New Yorkers as a whole, live in smaller households (an average of 1.7 people versus 2.7), in units that are less likely to be defined as "family" households (20% versus 46%). Though bisected by Sixth Avenue, the entire Sixth Precinct is coterminous with "the" Village, that is, these two demographically similar neighborhoods, Greenwich Village and the West Village.

According to the 2010 U.S. Census, the total population of Greenwich Village and the West Village was 66,880. Given its tolerance for diversity, the residents of the two Villages are not, by urban American—or even New York City—standards, especially diverse; in fact, the reverse is true. As I've pointed out, only 2 percent of the population of Village dwellers are African Americans—down from nearly 3 percent in 2000, though up from 1943 (0.8%); 78 percent is non-Hispanic white (also down, from 2000's 83 percent); 8 percent is Asian; and 6 percent, Hispanic. (The rest were classified by the census as "other," of mixed race, or "unknown.") These figures sharply contrast with the racial composition of Manhattan as a whole, which is 13 percent black, 48 percent non-Hispanic white, 11 percent Asian, and 25 percent Latino. The racial skew can be explained largely by the neighborhood's pricey real estate, not to mention the possible lingering effect of the historical practice of redlining. Baruch College's Weissman Center for International Business calculated Manhattan's per capita income at roughly $120,000 for 2013, more than two to three times that of the other boroughs—$51,000 for Staten Island, $50,000 for Queens, $42,000 for Brooklyn, and $32,000 for the Bronx. According to *Higley1000*, a website that tabulates statistics by neighborhood, eight out of ten of New York City's ten richest neighborhoods are in Manhattan. Greenwich Village ranks in nineteenth place, with a median household income of $248,322. (Greenwich, *Connecticut*, ranks at number one in the nation, with a household income of well over $600,000.) In short, the modal Village dweller is white, is substantially more affluent than most New Yorkers, is the resident of a very small household, and does not own a car.

These qualities—Manhattan's size, its population density, its relatively perambulatory quality, its racial and ethnic composition, its per capita affluence, the small size of its households—all exert an influence on the behavior that plays out in public generally, and in Washington Square specifically, though as much for the *reaction* of its park's visitors to behavior of certain sorts as to the behavior that that reaction engenders. The Village is a New York neighborhood with a particular disposition, though, yes, most of the park's visitors are not from the neighborhood. And, though its residents are better off financially, whiter, better educated, and more crowded than is true of the other neighborhoods in the City, at the same time, the Village manifests certain features that are *paradigmatically urban*, and that manifest themselves in ways that characterize city life in general. It is an attractive, desirable community that draws more visitors than is true of its sister neighborhoods. In fact, the same is true, in more exaggerated form, of its keystone park: "Washington Square is now more densely used, per square foot, than any other park in the city. . . . Neighbors in the vicinity have come to accept the Square's crowded, carnival-like atmosphere as a condition to be enjoyed, endured, or ignored" (Folpe, 2002, p. 310).

What was true a decade and a half ago applies with even more force today. There are numerous things to see and do in the Village, and residents of other neighborhoods *go there* to see and do those things. Its street and sidewalk traffic is, in comparison with most other neighborhoods, abundant, bustling, and vibrant. And, in spite of its elitist real estate prices, the residents of the neighborhood tend to welcome members of other communities onto its streets, into its commercial establishments, and to be embraced by its open public places—its parks, squares, and plazas. If the residents of the Village are not diverse, its visitors are, and the nature of the social relations that the mix, mingle, and conglomeration its drawing power stimulates constitutes a topic worth exploring. And what goes on in Washington Square, I maintain, is exemplary— something of a lodestar—of modern urban spaces generically. The chapters that follow explicate the charms and complexities of Washington Square Park. The public quality and accessibility of a space, along with the presence of a multitude of strangers, may potentiate behavior that is somewhat out of the ordinary, perhaps unconventional—even deviant. Even further, our park may be different from other large urban spaces in this respect. Washington Square may have a special "genius" that other, less popular spaces may lack.

* * *

Interview with Peter May, a Busker

Peter is sixty-four, stems from a New England Anglo-Saxon family, has a husky voice, and regularly plays rock, pop, and some folk songs at one of the walkways that leads into and out of Washington Square South, at Thompson Street. He's a busker—someone who performs in public for donations. Though he rarely attracts a stable, stationary crowd, Peter is a factor influencing the ambulatory flow of the park, its collective behavior; he lends a flavor to the space.

ERICH: How did you get into busking? What's your life story? What led up to you playing in Washington Square?

PETER: Since the age of thirteen, I played the guitar. I've been playing for more than fifty years. I played at weddings and dances and stuff. I loved it. I went to a trade school rather than a regular high school. At some point in my late teens, a buddy said, "Why don't you come to New York? Play there, you'll have good luck." I worked in a music store for a while, then I worked with vending machines. I lived in Hoboken for a period of time. I commuted. I walked from my job to the train station to return home, and one day, I lost my ticket. I had my guitar with me and I strolled around the streets of New York, familiarizing myself with my surroundings, and I wandered into Washington Square. And there were other musicians playing there. It was great. I joined them and played with them. At night, I was tired, everybody wandered off, and I found a spot on the grass, lay down, used my guitar as a pillow, and went to sleep. So, for a while, I played with the musicians who got together in the square and after that, I began playing solo for money. I started playing for a few clubs on Bleecker Street. Gerde's Folk City. Peculier Pub. Mills Tavern in Hoboken. Places like that. For a while, I opened for some big acts. Alice Cooper and the Scorpions. Kiss—we put out an album, "We're All Good—Except for Jerk-offs." I worked at a record store so I was exposed to all the stuff that was coming out. Now my only real gig is Eva's Health Food on Eighth Street, near Fifth, between eight and ten o'clock Saturdays. I tried to get a job on a cruise ship, but that didn't work out. Now I play here in the park. During the winter, when there's snow on the ground, I play on that marble platform over there.

ERICH: You play in the winter, when it's cold?

PETER: You gotta do what you gotta do. If I don't have money coming in, I can't pay the rent.

ERICH: Where do you live?

PETER: Well, right now, I'm renting a buddy's couch. In his basement. He has a place on Twenty-eighth Street. I rent it for $125 a week.

ERICH: Does all this get you down? How do you feel about what you're doing for a living?

PETER: If I feel crappy, I play. All the crap goes away. Playing makes me feel better. I see smiles on the faces of the people walking by who hear it. Once, I performed for a couple, "Don't Let Me Down," and he proposed marriage to the woman he was with. That made me feel good. I've played before cancer victims in a hospital. Making people happy makes me happy.

ERICH: How did your parents feel about you playing for pay?

PETER: It was OK with them. When I was practicing, I wasn't getting into trouble on the street.

ERICH: What about your wife? How did she feel about it?

PETER: My wife and kid, they knew that this is what I wanted to do.

ERICH: Excuse me for asking such a personal question, but how much money do you earn doing this?

PETER: Let me tell you a story. One day, a young woman came by, she knew some songs and she sounded pretty good, so I said to her, why don't we play together? I'll pay you a certain sum of money and you can sing with me. So, we did, and at some point, we took a break, and I put my guitar down and walked away, got a drink or took a leak or something and I came back and I saw her going through the can. I had rigged it up so it's not that easy to put your hand in there, and she was trying to take some money out. So, I don't like to advertise how much I have. No offense, you understand.

ERICH: No problem, no offense taken. OK, if you could turn the clock back and live your life over again, would you make the same career choice?

PETER: I like doing this. I'm my own boss. I had some paying jobs here and there, but I'm a year and three-fourths short of being eligible for Social Security. I've played for clubs around here but none of it turned into anything regular. I do enjoy it, but I'm sixty-four and I haven't even earned enough for retirement. I don't wish this kind of life on anyone.

3

Defining Deviance

On the eastern side of the fountain circle at the opening of the Holley Plaza walkway, sitting at the end of a stone bench, there's a quartet of vagrants—two of them have shopping carts crammed with junk—who have inaugurated a little party. They are drinking Heineken out of twenty-four-ounce cans, laughing, and speaking loudly, just as one would imagine four stereotypical drunken, homeless men would do. Their boom box, at their feet, is blasting hip-hop. "You think you a bad dude but you not!" one says. "Yeah, yeah, party like a rock star," says another. "I kissed my old lady goodbye. Then I jumped in the water," says a third.

"I never knew no God-damned Tom," says the fourth. "I never knew him, I never fucked him. You gonna say I fucked Carol? Yeah, I fucked her every which way to Sunday. Take off your glasses, you fool, lemme see your eyes. You gonna give me trouble with that? Sally? I never met her. You want me to say I had sex with a woman I never met?"

A tall, bearded, white man approaches them. "Hey, Fred, how ya doin'? Come on, my man, sit down," says one of the beer drinkers.

The man shakes his head. "Naw, I gotta go, I got things to do," Fred responds.

"Come on, my man, sit down." Fred shakes his head; the man sitting down pats the bench. "Sit down, sit down, we be talkin'." Again, Fred shakes his head. "Sit down, God-damnit! Git your ass down here!" Once again, Fred shakes his head, then he leaves—more accurately, he wanders off.

One of the men on the bench turns off his boom box, picks it up, slides it into his cart, and wheels the cart west through the Holley Plaza walkway toward the Washington Place exit. Another, also without saying goodbye, stands up and walks east into the fountain circle. Within two minutes, the four men who were so enthusiastically, convivially, and boozily socializing with one another have unceremoniously and word-

lessly scattered to the four corners of the park. While they were talking, other than looking askance at them, the park-goers in their vicinity
exercised no social control over their behavior whatsoever; indeed, it's
not clear what others could have done to exert such control. Clearly,
mainstream norms have a weak hold on these men, as does the social
glue that holds most primary groups together.

Just like refusing to join a group whose members are engaging in behavior of which one does not approve, *ignoring* someone who wants to
join the interactional orbit of one or more parties expresses censure of
that person and what he or she is doing. A middle-aged man whose general demeanor indicates mental disorder approaches two young, attractive, clearly upper-middle-class blonde women sitting on a stone bench
in the fountain circle, animatedly chatting with one another, and says to
them, "Hi, how y'all doing?" They ignore him; they say nothing and do
not even turn their faces toward him. He repeats the question and again,
he is interactionally shunned. "Mind if I join you?" For a third time, they
freeze him out. He finally gets the point and shuffles away, hopelessly
searching for a worthy social unit to join.

"One of the hallmarks of a great city," say Karp and his associates,
"is that it fosters a tolerance for differences in behavior and group lifestyle. Urbanites learn to cope with, adapt to, and often enjoy lifestyle
differences; they seem to have developed a sophistication about lifestyle
diversity. . . . The very notions of urbanity and cosmopolitanism are
caught up with . . . tolerance for a wide range of differences in behavior,
attitude, and beliefs" (Karp et al., 2015, p. 119). *At the same time*, some
behaviors, some lifestyles, practices, or beliefs, stretch beyond the pale
for nearly all relevant parties; very few sectors of the society accept, tolerate, or encourage them. Most of the mainstream, that is, more or less
conventional folk in the society, do not want to be in the company of
persons who engage in certain blatantly offensive nonnormative behaviors, such as the loud and crude talk and the overt, public beer guzzling
of our quartet here. (Unless, of course, they are on the same behavioral
and like-minded attitudinal wave length.) As I see the matter, deviance
is a universally applicable workhorse concept, both transhistorical and
transcultural. It is, at the same time, a matter of degree; the points along
a spectrum can be determined by audience reactions to a person's behavior, expressed beliefs, and appearance. The observer does not even

DEFINING DEVIANCE | 81

have to accept or agree with such rejection, only recognize that it tends to prevail.

Is Washington Square a petri dish of perversion, depravity, and crime? Is it "out of control"? Is serious deviance rampant in the park? From time to time, the media have highlighted serious wrongdoing in the park; for the most part, we can characterize their claims as journalistic hyperbole, a very small media panic in a small urban space. During 2011, concern about wrongdoing in the men's restroom produced articles such as "Sex, Drugs, and Indecent Exposure in Washington Sq. Park Bathroom" (Anonymous, 2011) and "Washington Sq. Bathroom Hours Cut amid Concerns of Sex, Drugs" (Swalec, 2011). Since the renovation of the comfort station and the shortening of its hours in 2014, the public has heard virtually nothing about men's room hanky-panky.

Another mini-panic bubbled up in August 2016 concerning a putative rash of illicit behavior in the park's northwest corner, which was captured in the storyline of the *New York Post* article "Crackheads, Bums, and Hookers Rule Washington Square Park" (Allan and Golding, 2016). The reporters described the park as "an open-air den—and the NYPD is doing nothing about it. As many as 20 strung-out vagrants have taken over several benches in the park's northwest corner, where they openly consume hard drugs, just steps from the children's playground." One neighbor walking his dog claimed to have seen a man injecting narcotics "into a vein in his neck as two cops sat in a cruiser about 15 feet away." The headline—and the substance of the article—were hyperbole, of course, and guilty of the use of strongly slanted pejoratives ("bums," "hookers"), not to mention the fact that solicitation for prostitution, according to my observations, is very rare in the park. Virtually no parent, neighbor, or anyone concerned with public safety wants risky and dangerous activities to take place in a family park, let alone so near a place where caretakers bring infants, toddlers, and preschool children.

A day after the *Post* story broke (August 5, 2016), Fox5 News repeated the story, generating no new details and simply reiterating what Allan and Golding had said; its headline read "Drugs, Homeless, Prostitutes in Washington Square Park." The park, the story ran, "appears to be harkening back to a much seedier time" in the city's history; drug dealers, addicts, and homeless men "have taken over several benches in the Park's northwest corner," Fox5 News reported, echoing, nearly word for word, the *New York Post*'s story; in fact, Fox's story *was* the *Post*'s story. On that same day, the *Post* ran a story bearing the headline, "Cops Finally Take on Washington Square Park Crackheads" (Allan, Gepner, and Massarella, 2016), which seemed to put a lid on one aspect of the problem. (I would like to thank Linda Massarella, a *Post* reporter, for her insights on this story.)

But I am a sociologist, not a reporter, and I try to understand how small events reveal ongoing conditions and dynamics. Hyperbole aside, what is clear is the following. Some Washington Square Park habitués use illicit substances; use tends to be confined to a small number of denizens, who are located in a small sector in the southwest and northwest corners of the park—true, located near a children's playground. Most of what these abusers take is marijuana, but, some park denizens have told me, a very few of them do smoke crack; in addition, park pundits have told me that the use of heroin is very nearly unknown. A few conventional park visitors use marijuana in the park. At any given time, between four and as many as ten or twelve marijuana sellers, all of them, to my knowledge, African American, patrol the area between the walkway leading from the fountain to the Holley Plaza, or in the plaza itself. If park visitors tell them that they are not interested in purchasing marijuana (I've done that), these entrepreneurs are easily discouraged. Knowing that they are being observed, their more-or-less conventional customers take their tiny stash and quickly scurry away from the locale.

As I've said, marijuana sale is common in the park, while crack use and sale are far less common; they do take place, but not openly, blatantly. And all of this untoward behavior nearly always takes place in a limited sector of the park. However, such statements do not provide raw material for a sensationalistic news story, while the exaggerations do. No, "crackheads, bums, and hookers" do not "rule" Washington Square Park, but yes, crack has been smoked there, though it has always been unusual. In any case, this story, presumably, has a happy ending.

We—audiences all—define or *constitute* what we regard as deviance by our negative reactions. That is, we *render judgments* regarding what we consider good or bad, right or wrong, acceptable and unacceptable, by responding in a negative fashion to that which we find distasteful. Likewise, sociologists argue that someone can violate the formal norms (mainly, the criminal law) as well as informal or interpersonal norms.

But here's a wrinkle in the deviance picture: *power*. The more powerful the individual, the collectivity, the social class, the greater the likelihood that it will be capable of institutionalizing or imposing its notion of right and wrong, whether *formally*, in the embodiment of the criminal law, or *informally*, in the give and take of day-to-day social interactions. In plain and simple terms, the poor are politically weak, vastly less capable of institutionalizing their notions of what's wicked into the criminal law. Unfair? Absolutely. But remember, deviance is not a hard, concrete reality like the laws of physics (and even the laws of physics seem fickle and variable under quantum conditions); it is defined by audiences, and varying audiences have differing degrees of power to get their way.

How does this definition play out in Washington Square? If no one there rejected or socially isolated these boisterous, beer-guzzling men, in what way did they engage in deviance? By drinking alcohol, they violated the park's rules, as they did with their blasting boom box, it's true, and, from the perspective of most park visitors, they exhibited unacceptably boorish behavior, also true, but what was *deviant* about what they did? Washington Square's denizens exhibit an extraordinarily broad degree of tolerance for behavior that audiences elsewhere would react to as wrongful, which is also true. But setting aside that fellow park-goers ignored them (and the fact that Fred refused to join them), how did park visitors *express* their disapproval of what they saw and heard this quartet do and say? We'll see momentarily.

A barefoot, goateed man, about forty, with long, stringy, gray and light-brown hair, dressed in black khakis tattered at the cuffs and an unbuttoned black shirt with long sleeves, wearing a key and several crosses around his neck, is leaning against the post of a chain barrier, jabbering. His voice is reedy and he has a slight Boston accent. "He's been talking to me for five hundred years about the star system," he says. "Now, God makes constellations. They all change. I told Gabriel, you see, God does all this. God said, 'Let there be heaven and Earth,' and He made the ocean. You can look right down into the Atlantic Ocean, thousands of feet, to the sand." He opens his arms wide, then walks over to and plants his foot on a bench, seemingly speaking to a couple, probably tourists, who are sitting on the adjacent bench. (They're studying a map, resolutely ignoring him.) After a minute or so, they get up and walk away; he walks slowly, almost casually, after them for about ten feet, toward the center of the park.

The babbling man stops, stretches out his arms again, then pushes his hands against a lamppost, leans against it, turns around, and sits on a bench next to a woman who seems to be caring for an elderly man who's asleep in a wheelchair; she's also resolutely ignoring his disquisition. "God rose up and brought forth the light and dark, the sun and moon, and stars and oceans. And it was all a muddy abyss. Then God made the fields and the valleys and streams and every living thing, the grass and the fruit, all that moved, and didn't move, on the Earth and in the water, everywhere, and it was truly a miracle." What the man said was grand indeed, though not very original, yet no one seems willing to become a member of his audience.

Another couple, appearing to be in their twenties, directly across the walkway from him, stands up and walks off. Again, he follows them for a few feet, then stops in front of a professionally dressed man in his twenties sitting on the bench who tries to ignore the jabbering man by staring at a book in his lap and turning the pages. The guy with the book looks up, smiles, nods, and pretends to agree with him. People are streaming by him as he babbles. "God blessed all of this, and then brought forth the angels, and all of it was good," he declares. He puts one foot on a bench, talking at the man, who continues to read. He gesticulates and, once again, opens his arms wide, presumably to make a point.

"But first, let me say something," the man intones. "In your case, the first order of business has to be what I told you before. After God made the oceans, and land, and green fields, and valleys, and the angels, including Michael, he created red apples. And *beaches*. I could put my toes in the sand in Jones Beach and everybody in the park, and all the students at NYU, would drop to their knees in amazement. It was the size of a *platinum quarter*. Now, as for my mission, I had *eight hundred and eighty-nine cars!*" He continues for some time along these incoherent lines, seemingly delivering a theological sermon whose point is likely to be understandable to no one—himself included.

The man trying to read the book gets up, stretches, and walks off. The blathering man comes over to me and sits down and begins his oration. I smile, look at him, pretend to seem sincere and interested, nod, and continue listening. There's no hint of menace or anger in his expression, and he occasionally laughs. I probably should have stayed longer, but his palaver becomes extremely tiresome and, after about ten or fifteen minutes, I too get up, smile, excuse myself, and walk off.

All who are more or less sane would regard what this man is saying as crazy talk; his blather manifests a type of mental disorder, a symptom of the malfunction of his brain. By extension, likewise, virtually all of us would acknowledge the man himself as *a* deviant by reacting to him accordingly, as we saw, by rejecting him socially. Virtually no one wants to be in the presence of such a man doing such a thing. I didn't want to, and the other park-goers he talked to before me didn't as well. Withdrawal of recognition and sociability—even more so, a withdrawal from the very *presence* of a person babbling in such a way—represents an audience's acknowledgment that it disapproves of, or doesn't want to have anything to do with, another, that is, the speaker, the actor and what he is doing, and would agree that he and the content of his blabber are socially unacceptable. He is, in the words of William H. Whyte, an "undesirable" (1980, pp. 60–65).

Deviance is my area of investigation, so I must satisfy myself with observing the *reactions* of others to this man's visibly and ostentatiously deranged public behavior, and that reaction is, to emphasize the point, the *withdrawal of sociability*. The man is in Washington Square Park because he's allowed to act out in this space, without being kicked out or dragged off and confined to a restrictive psychiatric facility. The interpersonal rebuff the mentally disordered babbler received in this public setting is undoubtedly generic. As Erving Goffman explains, "improper conduct in one situation can bespeak a general disenfranchisement in face-to-face interaction" (1963, p. 216). Some forms of deviance are *fungible*; they possess a generic quality in that they are regarded as inappropriate and improper just about everywhere. They need not, like our disordered, babbling friend here, be driven by a psychopathological condition—though it is the manifestations of his disordered mental condition that gave rise to his particular excommunication by observers.

It is true that the jabbering man is mentally disordered, but that's not the central issue. Mental disorder *is* a form of deviance, at least sociologically, but *most* forms of deviant behavior are enacted by people whom psychiatrists would *not* regard as mentally disordered. Much of the deviance that takes place in the park is lifestyle in nature, expressive more of eccentricity, unconventionality, and often a haphazard, disorganized, marginal way of life. Or it is behavior that others regard as too normatively wrongful. The babbling man represents an extreme point along the spectrum of mental disorder, resulting in his consequent social rejection, which manifestations of such disorder entail. Still, mostly, when we look at deviance, we see a universe of nonnormativity but more or less normal psychiatric functioning. Some of it is peculiar, and some is frivolous and impulsive, and some of it others see as just plain offensive.

The Mental Experiment

How do we know that an instance of behavior, the expression of a belief, or a given physical condition is sociologically deviant when we contemplate it? How can the sociologist *define* deviance in the situational absence of negative reactions by an audience to a specific act, the expression of a given belief, or a particular physical trait or condition? How can we talk about social control when it does not take place in many, and perhaps most, actual, concrete manifestations of the violation of norms? What about "secret deviance"—is an act deviant if no audience witnesses it? Or if unconventionality occurs in public and no audiences react—except for walking away or ignoring the transgressive party? This dilemma has plagued sociologists of deviance at least as far back as Howard S. Becker's *Outsiders* (1963, p. 20). Being fired from a job, getting slapped in the face, arrested, executed, being socially shunned and isolated, or insulted—in short, being reacted to in a negative fashion—all manifest the behavior and beliefs or characteristics that generate such reactions *as deviant*, or wrongful. Whatever elicits or touches off such reactions in others (particular "audiences") *qualifies* the act, belief, or trait *as* a form of deviance, at least in that setting.

But we need not define deviance solely and exclusively by actual, real-life, concrete reactions; all practicing members of a society know what behaviors are widely considered wrongful, and all of us are able to articulate what is likely to be done or should be done when certain audiences are face to face with such violations of the moral code. These judgments constitute an empirical evaluation of the behavior and its likely consequences to "audiences," including themselves, others they know, as well as the members of the society they don't know. One way of answering the question "What is deviant?" is to perform a mental or "thought" experiment. Imagine behavior being enacted or beliefs being expressed before many different and varied audiences and under a variety of settings and circumstances. Imagine a mother walking past a bathroom in her home and seeing her daughter smoking crack cocaine or shooting heroin into her arm. Imagine a father seeing his son sexually molesting a six-year-old boy. Or imagine watching your best friend robbing and then stabbing an elderly man. If we are perceptive, our mental experiments will sensitize us to what's deviant. Deviance is, of course a matter of degree, and most acts that audiences consider offensive are only mildly so. But when audiences put their judgment into negative reactions, whether in concrete behavior or in their own mental experiments, their reactions *embody* what's deviant—to them, of course.

In our mental experiment, someone enacts behavior, expresses a belief, bears or possesses an undesirable physical condition, and each is observed and evaluated by an array of audiences in an array of circumstances. Perhaps these audiences do not directly observe the person but hear about the behavior from eyewitnesses. What *makes* a given activity, belief, or condition deviant is that *a given audience* regards it as reprehensible and considers the actor, believer, or possessor as worthy of scorn, condemnation, or rebuff; were they to come face to face with him or her, they would express that scorn to this person—by acting in such a way that that scorn is known. (Again, keep in mind that power and influence enter the equation in that not everyone is allowed to express himself or herself freely.) The members of these audience could wear a scornful or sour look, stare the perpetrator down, look at him or her disapprovingly or walk away, tell others about what happened, discuss the event in a disparaging fashion. In these ways, certain parties or audiences express or feel *some form* of disapproval of the nonnormative interaction, even though it may not manifest itself in overt behavior in a particular instance.

Our thought experiment leads us to envision many potential audiences and settings. Imagine our quartet of boisterous, obstreperous Heineken guzzlers in a restaurant, in the lobby of a hotel or apartment building, or in the living room of most Americans. Now picture parents and children on the scene. Yes, deviance is contextually defined—and that's my point. These men were drinking in an arena where drinking is formally prohibited, they were playing amplified sound—also contrary to park rules—they spoke in a substantially louder voice than most people in the park find acceptable, indeed, in a manner that forced everyone around them to pay attention to *them*, and two of them trundled carts full of possessions—for most audiences, a sign of homelessness. Though they were in a public space, even here, our mental experiment would lead us to only one conclusion: Most of the other people in the park would not want to be in their company, would not gravitate toward their gathering, and would not want to associate with any of them even on a superficial basis—all signs of the lack of social acceptability of their behavior. Even a hard stare, a smirk, a frown, a whispered statement to one's companion constitutes a negative reaction to actions that one disapproves of.

What of our babbler, our ranter—our barefooted, goateed, mentally disordered man? Time and time again, he tried to make contact with one, then another audience, the members of which did not wish to be in his presence; one after another, they melted away. The self-removal of the man's audiences from the scene speaks volumes about how they felt about his acting out. The clangorous drummer in chapter 1 attracted a completely negative audience, one of whom not-so-secretly wished to *stab* him; the potential stabber was deterred from doing so, he himself admits, as a result of contemplating official intervention, *knowing* that his knife attack would be regarded as criminal (and deviant) and he would have to pay the consequences; one hopes that his conscience intervened as well.

When we witness actions that appear to violate norms or rules that are widely and strongly held, if we are observant enough, we usually see a negative reaction of some kind—but we may not. *In a particular context*, the behavior may not be regarded as wrongful, or may be considered wrongful but not reacted against in that context, but mentally placing that act in a variety of settings forces us to be aware of the extraordinarily *contingent* nature of social deviance. And it reminds us that social control, though it is the sociological cornerstone of deviance, is often weak, vacillating, or contingently expressed. Still, though reactions of audiences to disapproved-of behaviors may not be expressed in overt behavior in a particular instance, they may be *stored up* and articulated, perhaps later, in verbal form. The results of my survey, spelled out in table 3.1, exemplify how park-goers express their feelings to me, in an interview situation, about whether and to what extent they consider various behaviors wrongful.

There's a certain likelihood that audiences or publics will *evaluate* and *react negatively to* what someone does, says, or is. To the extent that these audiences feel that their notions of right and wrong have been violated and react in a negative or punishing fashion, sociologists sense that they have a case of deviance on their hands. Sociologists do *not* believe that deviance is *defined by* statistical unusualness, pathology, or dysfunction (Becker, 1963, pp. 4–8). The same goes for harm; most unconventional or nonnormative acts are not predatory, violent, damaging, or physically harmful in any way. The fact that a man wears a dress harms no one; being eccentric, weird, or a kook, eating with one's hands, or believing that extraterrestrials inhabit the earth is, from the perspective of damage to others, fairly innocuous. For the most part, negative judgments or reactions from so-called audiences flow from the transgression of a *norm*, a rule, an audience's sense of what's right or wrong, good or bad, desirable or undesirable, which is promulgated in and by the members of a society, or, at least as often, a smaller collectivity of some kind. What audiences regard as wrongful, undesirable, or unacceptable often manifests itself in a particular situation or *context*—the social or physical place where it appears: in public, in private, at work, in a house of worship, on a beach, in a bar or restaurant, in a classroom, in a crowd, on the street.

Sociologists of deviance "interrogate" the relevant audience; they direct attention to an audience whose members evaluate and react to behavior, beliefs, or conditions. Still, some conditions or behaviors, such as those of our talkative, mentally disordered friend, are so widely and strongly considered unacceptable that virtually everyone, everywhere, avoids the person and disapproves of his or her actions; in that case, the potential "audience" is virtually everybody, that is, the society at large. We all enact behavior, express beliefs, and bear certain negatively valued traits or characteristics that others—audiences—evaluate and react to. In sum, this is how contemporary sociologists define deviance: *violations of a norm that tend to generate negative reactions among designated audiences.* Washington Square is a public space, a type of locale whose denizens expect behaviors, and promulgate norms, that are somewhat different from those that tend to prevail in private. Moreover, a public setting permits *certain kinds* of nonnormative actions that would be unlikely to take place elsewhere.

Park Rules–Plus

Some laws and norms (though, as we just saw, not all) are *rational* in the sense that they tend to protect society and its constituent members from physical harm and lawless bedlam; the wanton, unjustified killing of an ingroup member offers an example here. On the other hand, many sociologists argue that deviance is not always protective; some of what's defined as nonnormative violates a prissy moralism that protects only the arbitrary standards of the pious and sanctimonious (Becker, 1963, chapter 8). Certainly, encouraging people to be decent and ethical toward one another is an end in itself, but some values that may be considered a good for one person (say, freedom) may result in a harm committed against another (exploitation).

Most of us can recognize the difference between those rules that serve a larger purpose—protecting a society or a substantial number of individuals from harm—and those that protect the morality of the few. Some rules are thinly disguised ruses to protect the interests of a particular faction of society—for instance, the very rich, or the religiously pious, or right-wing conservatives, or the politically correct and their supposed benefactors. Rules may protect a society's notions of right and wrong—for instance, Wahabist-dominated regions in Muslim societies dictate that women wear headdresses or prohibit women from driving. In contrast, drinking while driving is dangerous and kills people; it is criminalized everywhere. In a different vein, the connection between access to and use of pornography is not definitively causally related to men brutalizing women; in Western society, porn is accessible to anyone with an Internet connection. Drunk driving remains illegal largely because of its harmful consequences; pornography, once banned, is now freely available partly because, in all likelihood, it doesn't have the baleful consequences its opponents once attributed to it, and partly because the Internet makes virtually unlimited access to it unpreventable. Consider the fact that certain behaviors are condemned worldwide and throughout historical time, while others—such as divorce, gambling, homosexual relations, the use of contraceptives, alcohol consumption,

having an abortion, and interracial marriage—are deplored in some societies and during certain periods of history yet tolerated in others. The
Pew Research Center tracks attitudes about what is morally acceptable
and unacceptable, while the Gallup polls have followed them for generations; they give us a clear understanding of the immense cross-societal
variation in notions of right and wrong.

To address the deviance versus civility question, I constructed an
interview schedule and selected a convenience sample of sixty respondents in the park and asked them about whether they considered each
of twenty-two behaviors as wrong, or not wrong. Several of these questions speak to ordinances that are prohibited specifically *in public parks*
by the New York City Department of Parks and Recreation: feeding
squirrels, feeding pigeons, riding a bicycle, riding a skateboard, smoking cigarettes, smoking marijuana, allowing dogs off-leash, begging, littering, sleeping, and playing amplified music. I also asked about staring,
urinating in the bushes, appearing naked, talking to oneself, and having
sex and making out in public.

The answers the respondents gave to my questions about the wrongfulness of the hypothetical behaviors stemmed largely from support for
communality rather than from mere stiff-necked conventionality. In the
majority of respondents' views, allowing certain banned activities would
sabotage sociability in the park rather than weaken a conservative brand
of self-righteousness. Several questions addressed the issue of whether
young children should rightfully be exposed to certain sights that could
"corrupt the innocent." When children are brought into the picture, the
difference between pragmatism and morality becomes substantially
more complicated.

The value of communalism is expressed by the respondents con-
demning littering, staring, and public urination. The wrongfulness of
letting dogs off-leash attracted a slight though not the overwhelming
majority—though only 12 percent said it was not wrong, a quarter qualified their response, saying mainly that it depended on whether the dog
was big or small, vicious or good-natured, wild or well-behaved. The
respondents regarded the wrongfulness of riding a bike and a skateboard
in a less staunch fashion; a quarter didn't think it was wrong at all and a
quarter felt the matter depended on how skilled, fast, or wild the rider
was. Slightly less than half felt that smoking, whether marijuana or to-

bacco cigarettes, was wrong; those who didn't cited the fact that the park is an outdoor environment in which smoke readily dissipates, and as a result, it does not irritate the smoker's neighbors. Several critics of the naked man and sexual intercourse in the park cited the fact that these were sights to which children should not be exposed. Respondents were as critical of consuming alcohol in the park as of skateboarding, that is, not very; one suggested that the Gallic practice of picnics on the grass involving wine be allowed—a conception not all respondents shared. We see a continuum, from strong agreement that certain prohibited behavior be sanctioned to the feeling that the prohibition itself is unacceptable—and everything in between, that is, substantial disagreement about the acceptability of the ban.

Perhaps most interestingly, two activities that seem to be the most clear-cut examples of eccentricities, if not outright deviance—talking to oneself and a man wearing a dress—were deemed among the *least* wrongful of the list. Yet they represent behaviors that cause many, if not most, of us to shun or reject a hypothetical person as an intimate friend or even an acquaintance, and would probably lead to our warning our children against associating with an individual who engages in the act. (Recall our sociable but incoherent babbler.) Again, many disapproved actions pose no physical danger to others, and their unacceptability could easily be explained to small children—still, they are nonetheless likely to be regarded as the basis for classifying the actor as a deviant.

We can draw a more or less clear-cut line between drinking alcohol in the park and skateboarding; above that line, more respondents think the activity is wrong than consider it not wrong, while below that line, it is the reverse. Moreover, as the eye moves up the list in table 3.1, the weight of pragmatic arguments increasingly prevails; as the eyes move down, moralistic arguments tend to predominate. True, some respondents made practical-sounding arguments even for items in the bottom half: amplified music produces a din throughout the park; if the homeless sleep on the benches, there's not enough bench space for the regular park-going patron; the person who talks to himself may prove to be dangerous; and so on. No one enjoys visiting a garbage-strewn park, urine-soaked plants do stink, people who stare may be up to no good, bikes and skateboards can knock pedestrians down, hardly any nonsmoker wants to be forced to breathe cigarette smoke, and too much

TABLE 3.1. Washington Square Park Rules-Plus

Are the following wrong or not wrong?	Wrong	Not Wrong	Not Sure, Don't Know, It Depends	NA	Number
Littering	98	0	2	0	60
Couple Public Sex	88	2	8	2	60
Man Urinating	87	8	5	0	60
Man Naked	85	10	5	0	60
Staring	67	13	20	0	60
Dogs Off-Leash	57	12	25	7	60
Bicycle Riding	50	27	23	0	60
Marijuana Smoking	48	28	17	7	60
Cigarette Smoking	47	38	15	0	60
Drinking Alcohol	45	25	28	2	60
Skateboarding	45	27	28	0	60
Feeding Pigeons	43	45	12	0	60
Woman Topless	38	50	10	2	60
Amplified Music	37	37	27	0	60
Begging	30	38	30	2	60
Feeding Squirrels	23	68	8	0	60
Sleep Park Bench	22	50	25	3	60
Gays Making Out	17	53	28	2	60
Man Wearing Dress	12	82	5	2	60
Straights Making Out	7	63	30	0	60
Talking to Oneself	5	63	30	2	60
Interracial Couple	0	100	0	0	60

Note: Based on interviews of sixty interviewees in Washington Square Park, conducted by the author between November 2015 and June 2016. ("NA" means the respondent didn't answer the question or the respondent's answers were irrelevant to the matter I asked about.) Gender: male, 32; female, 28. Race/Ethnicity: white, 42; black, 11; East Asian, 3; Latino/a, 3; South Asian, 1. Percentages are rounded off.

alcohol consumed in a park is likely to lead to rowdiness. Some of the park rules address civility and its absence—rudeness—while others center on common courtesy. Even the matters of a couple having sex in the bushes and a man appearing naked appeal to a sense of pragmatism in that perpetrators force children to watch something their parents haven't chosen for them.

The modal park-goer tends to regard Washington Square as communal property. What harms the park harms me—and it harms you, the potential offender, as well. For the most part, park-goers adhere to that dictum and regard violators as miscreants who foul their own nest. Moreover, some respondents reasoned, a relaxation of specific rules may lead to anarchy—that is, the relaxation of all rules.

Public displays of affection (or PDA) are acts of intimacy between romantic partners, whether straight or gay, in a place where they are likely to be visible to others—the street, a restaurant, a park. To most people, "making out" includes kissing, nuzzling, and hands-on, above-the-waist, clothes-on petting, and its degree determines audience reactions. Critics who observe the practice may shout to a couple engaged in such an embrace, "Get a hotel room!" to express their disapproval of the practice. *Glamour* magazine sponsors a website, *Smitten*, which issued a post on August 15, 2011, by "Howaboutwe," offering several "common-sense guidelines" for public displays of affection: not in front of kids, not while people are eating, not when you're a couple accompanied by a friend, don't block a path, and avoid straddling. Writers have published a substantial number of books on the subject, some of them soft-core porn in e-book form (for instance, Renee, 2015; Knightly, 2015; Sestina, 2015), so the topic is on a sector of the public's mind.

As we can see from table 3.1, disapproval of a restrained version of the behavior is mild to nonexistent. Only 7 percent of my respondents expressed the feeling that a heterosexual couple "making out" on a park bench is wrong; 17 percent said the same for a gay couple. Two-thirds (63 percent) said the practice was not wrong for both straights and gays, while the remainder qualified the answer by responding that it depends on how passionate the embrace is, and the more passionate the embrace, obviously the more unacceptable it is in front of kids. The respondents made a sharp distinction between "making out" and sexual intercourse, the latter of which nearly nine in ten (88%) said that if it took place in the park, it would be wrongful. Again, respondents justified their answer by referring to a public act as something to which children should not be exposed.

Dog walkers are very unlikely to let their dogs off-leash. Out of a thousand observations of dogs and owners, I saw only eight owners let their canines off their leashes. (I exempt the hour between six and seven in the morning, when dog owners frequently and deliberately allow their dogs to run free through the park.) Multiple reasons drive this tendency toward civility, certainly, as I've pointed out, the possibility of knocking over a small child or a frail, elderly, or infirm person among them. I approached and asked ten people who were sitting, holding a dog on a leash, "What are some of the worst offenses that dog owners and dog walkers in Washington Square Park can commit?" Not picking up after a dog's poop was mentioned by seven respondents; other answers included letting a dog off-leash, not controlling a dog, and allowing one to become overly aggressive or rough with other dogs, or to bark, growl, jump, or lurch at people. Again, dog walkers and owners seemed to have the communal spirit in mind when thinking about offenses that they could but shouldn't commit. As we might expect, dog walking in the square follows neighborhood residential lines; dog walkers and owners are overwhelmingly white. Nine of the dog walker/owners I interviewed were white and one, judging from his name, was of Middle Eastern descent.

Following the theme of compliance as a continuum, of the 557 bicyclists I observed while I was tabulating these observations, 62 percent complied by wheeling their bike through the park; 38 percent violated the ordinance by riding their vehicle. In contrast, skateboarders *usually* violated the statute: Out of 196 skateboarders I witnessed during a particular stretch of time, 33 percent carried their board while 67 percent rode it. No doubt their youth drives their violation of the ordinance, but the contrast in noncompliance for the two categories is striking. The contrast between the largely negative attitudes my respondents expressed toward skateboarding—with only 27 percent saying it was "not wrong"—and the staunch defiance of the statute expressed by the actions of the skateboarders themselves, rebelliously zooming past vulnerable pedestrians, is striking and interesting. Perhaps, the observer might speculate, the very defiance of the act of skateboarding in the park tests the skill and demonstrates the bravado of the skateboarder.

Though a park is a human institution, it is also a physical environment in which a diversity of people make a place, settle into it, spend some time in it, and leave it more or less intact. Most visitors would say that they want the greatest good for the continued maintenance of the park, for the greatest number of park visitors. That being said, most park-goers recognize that Washington Square Park welcomes members of *multiple* constituencies, not all of whom have the same interests.

Violators of each activity are drawn from a specific social category of the population and hence, age and general predilection are relevant as to likelihood of violation. Constituencies may have a special *interest* in violating the statutes that restrict their freedoms. Hence, vaguely supporting "the greatest good for the greatest number of people" doesn't address the fact that park-goers tend to react most emphatically to the abridgement of the rights and freedoms of particular interest groups to which they belong.

Still, as we saw in the results of my survey, it is also in the interests of park-goers *as a whole* to have dog walkers pick up after their dogs; hence, it is in the interests of dog walkers specifically. It is in the interests of park-goers as a whole not to have to hear amplified music—but is it in the interests of musicians? Should it all boil down to a matter of which music group has the most powerful speaker? Obviously, music in the park would be unlistenable with a dozen *amplified* music groups simultaneously blasting away. Some park visitors come to Washington Square specifically to feed the pigeons; they too represent a constituency or interest group. Park-goers are torn down the middle, with roughly half who made a judgment saying it's wrong, half saying it's not wrong. The observer might feel that the occasional park bench encrusted with pigeon poop convinces some visitors that the practice should be banned. But it's not a major issue, and most park-goers agree. The PEP seem to agree as well; for the most part, they adopt a laissez-faire attitude toward the rule against it. Emily, our Joan of Arc of pigeons, aside, I've never seen a pigeon feeder—and I've seen hundreds—so much as receive a warning from a Park Enforcement Patrol officer, but I have seen PEP greet and walk by pigeon feeders.

In short, anyone interested in social control in public behavior has to consider whether enforcement of a given rule is overly stringent or contributes to the overall good. Most park visitors want certain bans enforced while others want a violation of the same ordinance ignored; permitting some practices may encourage a slovenly, neglectful modus operandi that, some feel, in turn encourages further anomie and decay, while enforcing others will seem nit-picking and senseless. Half of my respondents felt that sleeping on park benches is not wrong, but I did not ask about overnight sleeping; had I done so, their answers would undoubtedly have been different. What promotes the greatest good for

the greatest number of people? In all likelihood, it is discretionary enforcement of the rules and a balanced attitude on the part of the park's
constituencies. Park-goers do not want the park to become a trash-filled,
chaotic free-for-all, nor do they want it to turn into a concentration
camp in which every rule is enforced strictly, to the letter of the law.

Performative Deviance

For the most part, visitors have a casual, tolerant attitude toward the
unusual or eccentric behavior of the people they encounter there,
including those who are engaging in performances for the benefit of
others. In fact, some of these visitors *are* the performers, who would
attract dumbfounded stares and derision from Main Street America.
Some simply come for the show and would be accepted into conventional social circles more or less everywhere. Some are acting out a role
I refer to as *performative deviance*—they're behaving in a flamboyantly
off-beat, unconventional fashion to self-consciously display their eccentricity. Others are simply eccentric and off-kilter in their everyday lives.

No doubt psychiatrists have already diagnosed some of them as
schizophrenic and, as we saw, many of those are probably not taking
their meds. But some don't need meds and are in their "I'm in Washington Square and I'm allowed to do whatever I want" mode. Here, merely
eccentric behavior tends to be greeted with a blasé attitude. As we saw,
tolerance has its limits; not all park denizens find all nonnormative behavior acceptable. Mostly they restrain the impulse to suppress behavior
they find objectionable—unless it crosses some nebulous, shifting, and
arguable line.

A man who, to my ear, seems to have a slight Latino accent, wearing
a ponytail, black and purple silk-type cape, jeans, work boots, a black
leather vest, and a blue pullover, with a wooden Samurai-type sword
stuck in his belt and another at his feet, is standing on a stanchion on
the barrier surrounding the fountain, making a speech. A cloth bag with
three or four canes inside is resting against the stanchion.

"That's why I have to hook up with a ghost writer," the man intones.
"There's too much bottled up, I have to get it out. We all need a place to
sleep, uninterrupted. We've got to make this happen. If you feel as I do,
we can make it happen. I have not been happy for 12 years. I've been

donating various body parts. If it's a circle, it's continuous. If it's a square, it's discontinuous; it breaks off at right angles and goes off in a different direction. I started off 12 years ago a simple man. Now I've lost the use of one limb. I have no limbs to speak of. I can't fly, I can't walk without feeling it. I don't speak for myself, I speak for my broken limbs. I must go to the Japanese. They have been going for thousands of years. They are very high in their culture. We had warriors once—fifty years ago. I cannot go no further. I must replace my limbs. I must go to Japan. Knighthood is finished. We must awaken the Samurai. I have lost my fuckin' life. I must wake up. My life is not worth living. Because I stand alone. I can heal my body, I just need some help. I live today, I die tomorrow, and so will you. Our lives are not given to us for eternity. Learn to let go." He pulls the wooden sword out of his belt and holds it up in the air. He does not pass the hat, ask for money, or even demand the attention of his listeners.

"Believe in magic," he implores. "Believe in me. I died eight months ago. *I thank you for your attention!*" He's practically shouting. "You don't know how symbolic that is, people. Do you hear me?" the Cape Man asks rhetorically. "Do you touch me? Do you feel me?" Most people are ignoring him, walking by, sitting on the wall, talking to one another, looking away. By attending exclusively to the patterns of pedestrian deployment, a researcher of collective behavior would not be able to discern that he is making a speech. Finally, Cape Man steps down off the stanchion. After he climbs off his perch, an older, balding, middle-aged man sitting at his feet begins talking to him as he adjusts his silver necklace and pendant. Then a couple, perhaps in their twenties, walks up to him, shakes his hand, and begins talking to him. The couple seems sixties mod-British. I hear them praising Cape Man's performance.

We know Cape Man is putting on a show; he provides a dramatic example of "performative deviance." The sociologist, as well as the man and woman talking to him, might wonder what kind of person would put on such a show, and what kind of audience would consider such a show entertaining. Some visitors assume that such performances are likely to take place in Washington Square, and hence, the space attracts such deviant-seeming entertainers. And to the extent that such a show is deemed as weak, unworthy of an audience's attention, people would walk away from it. Is his performance a type of deviance? Again, the mental experiment comes into play here. Would passersby want to socialize with him in their everyday lives, invite him for dinner, have him as their friend? Perhaps one's answer to these questions reflects the kind of person Cape Man is and hence does, or does not, cast him into the status of *a* deviant.

Tic and Tac (Kareem and Tyheen Barnes), a twin tumbler act, has just completed its routine; they walk away from the dry fountain. The Cape Man decides to do an encore and climbs back up onto the center platform and announces his act. Tic and Tac's percussionist continues to drum. Kareem has put on a black baseball jacket and begins jogging around the center of the fountain, around Cape Man. Tyheen begins theatrically to banter with the Cape Man, saying—loudly, clearly addressing both him and the audience, "Cape Man, your act is lame, man, nobody want to see it. Lame, man, now get *down* off this stage. There are over fifty people here."

Cape Man decides to challenge their presence. "This is *my* stage, this is my act, I'm on now. You wait your turn." They continue in this back-and-forth vein for three or four minutes. Now seventy-five people are watching them.

"If you want to see these guys jump around, yell!" Cape Man commands.

The audience yells, "Yaaaaaay!"

"If you want to see me cut an orange with my sword, yell!"

The audience yells, "Nooooooo!" Tac grabs Cape Man's oranges and throws them off into the distance, toward a small copse of trees and some bushes.

"*You fuck!*" Cape Man screams, and steps down from the platform, grabs his rollie, and stalks off, north, to the right of the Arch, looking dejected. "Fuck this shit," he shouts as he storms off.

The tumblers take over and Tic stands on the stanchion while Tac makes an announcement about their performance. There are now about a hundred people watching. I go over to the Cape Man, standing about two dozen feet away from the fountain, and look at him. "They wouldn't let you perform, man?" I ask, trying to sound sympathetic.

"Nah, it's all politics," he grumbles.

"Yeah?" I ask, inviting him to elaborate. But he seems too upset to talk and turns away from me, so I wander off. Clearly, the audience defined his act as "lame," and hence, *deviant*. There are now about 130 people at the fountain, eager to see Tic and Tac perform. Were Cape Man and Tic and Tac colluding in a fake conflict to create a show—and a bigger crowd? I don't think so. Or were Tic and Tac manipulating Cape Man into a beef to drive him out and inherit the crowd exclusively for their own gain? I suspect the latter is true.

Facing north at the fountain circle, to the right of the Arch, there's a bearded, light-brown-haired man close to forty, short and lean, shirtless, wearing only a tiny leopard-skin-style bikini, who's making a speech. He's Matthew Silver and is self-described as "the crazy, fart-loving motivational NYC street performer who takes comedy to a level that many people don't have the bravery to venture to." Now is a "good time to get weird with life," he declares on his Internet site. About fifteen signs, painted in thick, red lettering on cardboard, rest at his feet; one by one, he holds up the signs, which read, "Everybody Fart," "We All Fart," "I Follow My Fart Heart," "Follow Your Fart," "There Is a Fart Support Group," and so on. Most of the time he's standing, his eyes focused on a point somewhere on the horizon, shifting his weight rapidly from one foot to the other. Then he gets down on his knees and implores those who are semicircled around him (about fifteen people), "Follow your heart. It's better to follow your fart-heart than to have a 9-to-5 job. Please, stop before it's too late." He stands up and makes farting noises with his mouth and goes back to the routine of shifting from one foot to the other. "Always love yourself. Sometimes you don't love yourself. Start loving yourself and follow your fart-heart. Don't go Christmas shopping because this present is *your* present. Please, I beg of you, fart and love yourself."

Fartman does not request donations and no receptacle of any kind is at his feet. Some of the people in his immediate vicinity stop and stare at him while wearing a supercilious smirk, while others look at him with a puzzled or astonished expression; the "deviance" of his performance is self-evident. This man is putting on a performance both portraying and exemplifying deviant behavior. Audiences may wonder about what such a man does in his everyday life and whether he walks or takes a subway from his apartment to Washington Square carrying his signs and dressed only in his bikini. He does not seem to perform comedy in a recognizable comedic venue, and he lives in the basement of his mother's house. While he was imploring and prancing and kneeling, *that was the real him.* That was *who he was* at that moment—or a side of him at any rate. But we also have to wonder what *kind* of a man came up with this routine and presents himself in that fashion to the mingling, swirling dozens, hundreds, of gawkers who walk by when he performs and how he came to behave in this particular way in this particular setting. With money out of the picture, *why* does he do what he does?

Following George Herbert Mead's conceptualization of the emergence of the *social self* (1913), we wonder about how Fartman developed the inspiration to present himself in the way he did, painting those signs, prancing around as he does, and uttering those words. Yes, Fartman engages in performative deviance, but the sociologist reflects on how successfully he is able to separate his public from his private persona. Washington Square is one among several venues where he feels comfortable acting out this ostentatious, flamboyant performance; this is one of his stages and this is how he defines himself. Since he wasn't asking for money, again, we have to wonder what his motive is for doing this. Still, his performance, however eccentric, is enabled by virtue of the fact that it takes place *in public*. On Facebook, in interviews, he remains in character, with his high, almost screechy voice and strange "fart" patter. Fartman—Matthew Silver—is indeed a street performer, a strange one, though in many ways, in the park, he is performing himself, that is, a quasi-comedic persona that he has assumed.

Fartman may be a psychiatric curiosity, but he is a sociological phenomenon as well. Following Erving Goffman's conceptualization of the "presentation of self in everyday life" (1959), we have to think about how the man fashions his performances to convey a certain impression about himself. Where's the dramaturgical "front" and where's the "backstage," what sort of role is Fartman playing, how does he relate to others in his everyday life, and what is he trying to achieve with his performance? How is he *taking heed of others* by adapting his behavior to his audience? He's clearly going off in his own direction. ("We are all the reincarnation of Jesus Christ, we're all aliens, there's something that connects us all," he declares on his website.) Mental disorder should be taken into account when considering self-presentations; quite obviously some interactants are less capable of staging themselves in a conventionally favorable light than others. And yet, Goffman situates many of his examples in the mental hospital. Even in Washington Square, the observer is likely to think, That man is mentally disordered and I wouldn't want to hang out with him. Still, here is Fartman, putting on his show—such as it is. To stress the point, the inevitable question that audiences are likely to ask about him is, Performance or not, what kind of a man would do such a thing?

Two guys arrive at Washington Square Park dragging a couple of boxes crammed full of some sort of folded plastic material and stop just south of the Arch next to a couple of people who sit behind a fold-up table on which rests a sign that reads, "Free Conversation." A thin, dark-haired white man in his twenties pulls out a deflated plastic couch and blows it up with a battery-operated device. The other guy, a young, chubby black man with curly, dyed-blonde hair, says, apparently to the people in the vicinity, "You have no idea how excited I am." He unfolds, then blows up, a naked, open-mouthed, plastic female doll. "People don't respect her," the curly-haired blonde man says. "She is thirty and she *will* be treated like a lady! She has three functioning holes—for conversation. You have to hold her under her arms." Numerous people take pictures of the man cuddling and "conversing" with the doll on the couch. I sus-pect the "free conversation" people had no idea that the doll guys would show up and settle in next to them, stealing everyone's attention. Then the chubby guy lifts up the doll and walks toward Fifth Avenue with the other one, accompanied by three men about their age. As he passes by me, he tells the other men, "We're taking *her* to Times Square," leaving the couch behind, indicating that they probably had an assistant in on this performance. It's undoubtedly a staged presentation of some kind, perhaps an assignment for a theater course, but it strikes me as very odd. To an astonished out-of-town tourist, the performers would probably say, "This is Washington Square—get used to it." The tourists learn what to expect; unlike mere schtick, with performative deviance, the line be-tween the act and one's true self is fuzzy.

Staring

There's a man sitting at one of the tables in the southwest corner of the park who's watching a chess match. I sit down at a right angle to him and turn around and notice that he's staring at me with an impassive look on his face. After thirty seconds, I smile. He keeps staring. After another thirty seconds, I shrug and give him an inquisitive look; he continues staring at me. So, I ask, "How are you doing?" No response, just the stare; thirty more seconds pass. Finally, I ask, "Why are you staring at me? What do you see?"

He says, "Why are you staring at *me*?"

I say, "I just glanced over at you and noticed that you keep looking at me." He appears to be in his forties, possibly of North African or Middle Eastern origin, but seems to have an American accent.

He says, "Why don't you go somewhere and bother someone else?"

I say, "I'm not bothering you, and this is a public park, I don't have to go anywhere."

He says, "Go argue with someone else!"

I say, "I'm not arguing—you are," but I finally realize the futility of arguing so walk away, sit near the entrance to this circle, and write all this out.

That was an odd encounter and it makes me wonder if what I'm doing makes people suspicious. It certainly challenges my assumption that I'm a fly on the wall, simply observing what takes place in the park. I'm concerned that simply *taking notes* is considered deviant here. But today, I notice at least a half-dozen people also taking notes—at least, writing in a notebook—and I doubt if any of them got into a beef. Following my definition of deviance—behavior that generates a negative reaction—I must have been engaging in a deviant act to inquire about his staring, but correspondingly, *his* staring should be regarded as an act of deviance as well. I decide to go back and apologize to him (not that I did anything wrong, but I am trying to enlist the cooperation of the people who hang out in the park), but when I get back, I don't see him at the chess table circle; he seems to have left.

Several weeks later, as I walk toward the chess table corner, I encounter the guy again. "What are you doing?" he asks, sternly. "I see you here every day. Stop what you're doing. Stop it! Get out of here! Get out!" he repeats, pawing at my notebook, which I pull away from his reach. He's yelling at me, and he seems very angry, and I can't figure out why, but I continue on my way. A couple of weeks after this hostile encounter, he confronts me again, though in a subtle but chilling fashion. As I step into the chess table area, I spot him. He's already staring at me; his head swivels as I walk, his eyes following me as I walk through the circle.

Passing him, I smile; he's contemplating me impassively, his head slowly turning toward me as I walk to the exit at the northwest corner. Each time I walk through the chess area and he is there, he stares—*glares*—at me, and I smile and say hello, but to no avail; he continues staring, with scowling intensity and total concentration. It's now fair to say that the man has a *thing* against me, but hardly anyone would be inclined to approach him and ask why.

When does a glance or a look at someone become a stare? Culturally established norms fix an approximate time limit on looking at strangers in public. One may look (or "stare") at a street performance, an animal, a small child, an unusual event (such as an accident or a fire), but ocular attention to a particular subject for more than a second or two becomes invasive, distressing, even threatening. When men do it, uninvited, to women, it is felt as especially nonnormative. And if the person being stared at is in motion and the starer's head swivels to follow the staree's movement, likewise, the act is deemed especially deviant.

It might seem oxymoronic for me to discuss staring as a form of deviance; after all, what is observation except a form of staring? Everybody in the park is *people watching*; in fact, they're watching people *watch people*. That's the point of being in the park. But the concept of staring is socially constructed—contested, to be sure, but culturally and contextually created and judged nonetheless. Open and unabashed, and unwanted, staring at strangers in a public space is *usually*, though not necessarily, a deviant act (Garland-Thomson, 2009). In *Behavior in Public Places* (1963, pp. 83–88), Goffman discusses the concept of *civil inattention*, the presumably benign mirror twin of staring; the person who stares violates the expectation of disinterested propriety. (Of course, the opposite of the coin is to ignore, or disattend to—as Goffman did—a violent crime, an event that I discuss in the appendix on ethics.) For a person to openly stare, the situation must, according to common consensus, *warrant* an intense, prolonged gaze—and how "prolonged" is *too* prolonged?—and usually such scrutiny is called for by a nonordinary event, and not simply because the party receiving the stare is visibly different from the run-of-the-mill individual.

So, here's a seemingly simple principle spelling out a rule that, when violated, constitutes a form of deviance that's not always easy to operationalize: *Don't stare* (unless staring is warranted!). Here's this rule as it applies to men staring at women: *Don't ogle or leer.*

In 2012, Lisa Wade, a professor of sociology at Occidental College, supervised a series of naturalistic experiments in which her undergraduate students engaged in three "mild" forms of deviance—holding a door open for people who are approaching a building but are very far away, walking too closely to people and getting in their way, and staring at people (Wade, 2012). In this experiment, staring at strangers in public made them uncomfortable, and their facial expressions and verbal responses indicated as much. "You're not gonna *say* anything?" "What's up, man?" "What? *What?*" were some of the reactions these accomplices elicited from the experimental subjects. In the Western world, virtually all parents admonish their children not to stare at strangers or at persons who are disfigured or physically impaired; nearly everyone regards it as rude, impolite, bad form—as Wade says, a "mild" form of deviance. Staring for a long time is considered hostile or at least condescending, and urban people tend to avoid doing it.

As Erving Goffman has pointed out, mutual glances, and even more so, a stare, should be avoided *unless* one wishes to engage in an encounter with the other party; "eye contact opens one up for face engagement" (1963, p. 95). On the other hand, the staring parties may be sexually interested in one another and may be *inviting* engagement. The "romantic gaze" indicates sexual interest and *in* the appropriate context, *from* the right party, is a much-sought-after gesture. When two parties are mutually interested, potential romantic and sex partners may stare at one another so that each may determine the potential desirability of the other. (If one of the two individuals is clearly and distinctly *un*interested in meeting the other, however, such staring *is* considered rude and invasive.) For the motivated person who is already sexually involved, or interested in sexual attention from and/or a sexual relationship with, an *inappropriate* partner, gazing may feel flirtatious and exciting. But for me, being stared at by this strange man in a public park was an unpleasant experience; one of the two of us in the above encounter was manifestly engaged in some form of interactional deviance. Moreover, there's often a sexual angle to staring: When a man directs an uninvited and unwanted stare at a woman, most of us regard it as a form of sexual harassment. Perhaps male-on-male staring is so offensive to the straight man because it seems to imply that he might be gay.

Garland-Thompson writes of people with unusual physical attributes (armless shoulders, missing or disabled legs) as possessing "stareable bodies." In fact, a stare can be "a social act that stigmatizes by designating people whose bodies . . . cannot be readily absorbed into the visual status quo" (2009, p. 44). But, she argues, the more that such people appear in public without attempting to hide themselves, in a natural and comfortable way, the more the rest of us are able to "expand the range of the bodies we expect to see and broaden the terrain where we expect to see such bodies," thereby creating a "new public landscape" and helping "create a richer and more diverse human community" (p. 9). I agree, but we're not there yet.

But as I say, staring is not always a form of deviance; whether and to what extent it is depends on the context in which it takes place. For one thing, open and unabashed staring is more normatively permitted in non-Western societies than in the cultural West. Such staring often denotes distance from or the strangeness of the party being stared at. It seems to say, "You are an outsider, an anomaly; you don't belong here." But staring is only situationally inappropriate; audiences are supposed to "stare" at public performers. This is usually one-way or *asymmetrical* staring and typically, there are many more observers than performers. In many parks and squares, buskers—jugglers, magicians, musicians, and tumblers—*want* people to stare at their act; the more starers there are, the greater the sum of cash that will cross palms. A particularly spectacular parade or procession or performance may result in the onlookers staring in admiration or astonished wonder at the parties in the cavalcade or act. At one time, customers were allowed and expected to stare at the "human oddities" who were presented "for amusement and profit" in a freak show (Bogdan, 1988). As I said, an accident, such as an airplane crash, a fire, or an explosion, will inevitably invite staring. But linguistically speaking, these forms of close, intense looking are not *called* "staring." Under ordinary, everyday circumstances, staring makes people feel uncomfortable; they will feel that their bubble of individual space has been invaded.

Cruising in the Park

For centuries, sex between people of the same gender constituted a crime and was considered morally indecent—yet, in many places, it often took place in public (Humphreys, 1970, 1975; Delph, 1978). In *Gay New York*, historian George Chauncey mentions that, late in the nineteenth century, men having sex in public parks was "a common practice" in a half-dozen New York parks—Central, Riverside, Mount Morris, City Hall, Tompkins Square, and Battery—which resulted in the park police arresting a number of men for the offense. (Most of these arrests did not take place out in the open, but in a more "private" public place, that is, in men's restrooms.) Early in the twentieth century, the police added Washington Square Park to the list (1994, p. 196). On October 7, 1964, according to a brief, anonymous notice in the *New York Times*, then–police commissioner Michael Murphy announced plans to "increase surveillance" of Greenwich Village in order to "curtail loitering and solicitation by homosexuals." In addition, he considered assigning female police officers in plainclothes to Washington Square "to halt annoyance of female patrons by drunks and hoodlums." Murphy made the move in coordination with a drive by Democratic leader of the Village, Ed Koch, "to rid the area of degenerates and other undesirables."

It is interesting that, even in the sixties, many politicians, as well as the police, considered homosexuals as belonging in the same category as "drunks and hoodlums" and "degenerates and undesirables." Moreover, most of the men who have sex in public restrooms are straight, not gay, in their identity and orientation (Humphreys, 1970, 1975), but sex with another man is nonetheless a homosexual or same-sex *act*, even when performed by a heterosexually inclined man. Locales that once attracted a substantial proportion of homosexuals—including Boystown in Chicago, the Castro district of San Francisco, and New York's West Village—have become more mixed as to sexual orientation. Gays who once preferred living in a community with a dense concentration of gays have become scattered and integrated into the community at large; there has been a "de-gaying" of former "gayborhoods" (Ghaziani, 2015)—a kind of gentrification of gays.

One major reason for the disappearance of gays as a distinctive category both in Greenwich Village and in Washington Square Park is the widespread acceptance and assimilation of homosexuality as the expression of a particular lifestyle—rather than the manifestation of immorality or pathology. Washington Square, once regarded as a traditional hangout for gay men, has lost the distinction. The transition of Washington Square away from being a gay sexual nodule is more than symbolic. The park has become a space where interest groups jostle for the right to express and represent themselves: a major player now active in this drama—families. With children. (A not-inconsiderable proportion of whom are themselves gay.) Behavior that was previously tolerated is less likely to be acted out today because mothers and caretakers don't want children to be exposed to it. Once a locale for outrageous gay escapades, Washington Square Park has become tamed—*domesticated*—and one of its villains is the family. But enter into the equation the fact that gay couples are increasingly likely to adopt children; hence, we may see both gay and straight families—but very little gay cruising.

In 1974, in *Male Homosexuals*, researchers Martin Weinberg and Colin Williams mention Greenwich Village as the most active locale in Manhattan—indeed, in New York City generally—for gay cruising, its "fulcrum" being Christopher Street, four blocks west of Washington Square, and to its west, the Hudson River waterfront, with its parked trucks, which had "become the scene of orgies that continue for hours with a stream of new participants" (1974, p. 45). At that time, reputedly, a particular discotheque in the Village, unnamed in the book, featured go-go boys with a back room for "impromptu orgies." The authors mention Washington Square Park specifically as a prime gay cruising locale (p. 45). That entire scene—from the "trucks" to the disco to Washington Square Park as major gay activity centers and pick-up spots—is gone, done in by gentrification, the "de-gaying" of formerly largely gay neighborhoods and their invasion by families with children, as well as the specter of HIV/AIDS, as well as the substantial takeover of real estate specifically around the square by NYU. Local experts say that the epicenter of New York gay life has shifted to Chelsea; more importantly, gay life has diffused throughout the society generally. The "gay ghetto" has become deghettoized.

Drug Selling in the Square

Nearly all African American visitors to Washington Square are law-abiding, but all of the small handful of men (and one woman) whom I have witnessed selling marijuana in the park are black. As park visitors walk along the pathway that leads to Holley Plaza, they notice several mostly middle-aged African American men trolling for customers. "Weed, smoke," they mutter to each passerby. Then, angling southwest, the observer may notice a few more sellers on the pathway that terminates at the chess circle, where mostly black players wait for mostly white customers willing to challenge them. Nearly all the customers of the marijuana sellers whom I've seen making purchases have been white, and the transactions are more or less entirely concentrated in the east-west walkway from the fountain to the Holley Plaza. The small number of marijuana sellers milling in and near the Holley Plaza pose a threat to no one, and they are chased from this spot as a result of a police crackdown, but they always return to resume their business.

Buying, selling, and using illicit substances have taken place in Washington Square for the better part of a century—though the sellers have been predominantly African American only comparatively recently—and the media have reported *news* about illegal drug sale and use for nearly as long. Even after police drug sweeps aimed at selling and using, and in spite of the installation of surveillance cameras, the drugs keep coming back. In an article published in the *New York Times* in November 1987, Peter Kerr reported that, months earlier, members of the community, outraged by the "drug bazaar" atmosphere of the park, "went underground to take on the dealers alone," found out about the who, where, and how of selling and buying, and enlisted the police, who issued summonses to cars illegally parked to make drug transactions, closed the park at midnight, and made fourteen hundred arrests. By November, Kerr stated, looking around the park, though one "can still find a handful of people"—generally crack-addicted marijuana sellers—who offer marijuana "in whispers of street jargon," for the most part, the police and the community "crushed the drug trade." The operation, everyone agreed, "has worked" (Kerr, 1987).

But drug use is persistent and hence, so is drug selling. Said Emily Kies Folpe a decade and a half later, "vestiges of drug dealing stubbornly remain despite all the enforcement efforts" (2002, p. 314). In 2004, Neal Hirschfeld reported in *Wired New York* (March 7) that the drug sellers of Washington Square "do business with impunity" in the park. "'Yo,'" shouts a seller, "'how many you need, my man!'" and transacts the sale "in plain sight of everyone walking by."

Though the Rudi Guiliani administration (1994–2001) installed video cameras all around the park in 1997 and, presumably, a narcotics team was working there "all the time," and though they scatter the sellers when their presence becomes known, the police remain stumped as to how to permanently clear Washington Square of drug dealing. Hirschfeld ruminates on the depth of the problem by raising fanciful solutions. Some of these dealers have been arrested sixty or seventy times, and yet they keep coming back. The average park-goer wishes they would go somewhere else, he says, and engage in a different activity to put cash into their pockets. "What, then, should be done to keep Washington Square free of drug traffickers? Have the police patrol it every 15 minutes? Turn it into a gated enclave, like Gramercy Park? Lease it to the Mafia?" He invokes the almost certainly apocryphal story—there is no historical evidence that the event ever took place—of George Washington showing General Marquis de Lafayette twenty hangings that were supposedly carried out in 1824 on the military grounds that became Washington Square Park. We can't *hang* drug sellers, Hirschfeld implies, so what on earth *can* we do? Very little, he seems to say.

Consider the following transaction, one of several I've observed. I'm sitting in a spot on the west side of the Holley Plaza. A tall, thin black man, about forty, is leaning against the lamppost adjacent to the Holley Plaza; to his left there are five other black men about the same age, some slightly older, milling around. (One of them told me he was fifty-seven.) He's wearing a dark-blue sweatshirt, fashionably ripped jeans, light blue-and-white running shoes, a black backpack, and a baseball cap that rests on top of a handkerchief. He's looking around—no doubt for customers. Right on cue, a short white man wearing a very stuffed black backpack, pulling a rollie, and leading a medium-sized, mixed-breed, black-and-white dog on a leash, is walking briskly south, away from the northeast corner of the park, toward the Holley Plaza. As he enters the plaza, the two men make eye contact, and the shorter man stops and hands a tightly folded sheaf of bills to the taller man, who takes it and sticks it into a link in the chain enclosure at the edge of the walkway, rights himself, reaches into his pocket, draws out a pack of marijuana cigarettes stuck into what looks like an empty Gauloise packet, then takes out two, and hands them to the other man, who turns around and walks back the way he came. The taller man then retrieves the bills and counts them—it looks like five singles—and puts them into his wallet.

So, yes, it is true, dealers *routinely* sell marijuana in the park. From time to time, the media or concerned citizens will attempt to generate a moral panic about drug activity in the park. These panics flare up and die down. The uneasy truce between the police and the drug dealers is likely to continue—punctuated by occasional mini-flaps from the media—for the foreseeable future. Given the volume of people who frequent Washington Square, the use and sale of hard drugs is extremely rare in the park; though the *sale* of marijuana is routine and ongoing, its overt use is fairly uncommon but far from nonexistent. The point is, short of a continual, massive, and oppressive police presence, "stamping out" the sale of marijuana is all but impossible, but the moderate surveillance and occasional arrests do keep a lid on the situation, preventing said sale from becoming rampant and blatant. It is worth noting that the sale of marijuana in state-licensed shops is legal in more than a dozen states of the United States.

Homelessness

What makes homelessness a form of deviance? On the surface, it might seem that conventional, respectable folk exclude the homeless from public spaces as a result not so much of what they *do* as of who they *are*. But most of us would hold that the homeless are *responsible* for their deviant status; they don't work, maintain a more or less well-tended household, dress in acceptable garb, or observe widely accepted standards of cleanliness or hygiene. They've failed to make their bed, and now they must lie in it—in the form of social rejection. Few respectables want to associate with or even get near the stereotypically undomiciled, who, for most of the mainstream, remain, in all likelihood, the stereotypical deviant. These images do not apply to many of the homeless, but they are, nonetheless, decisive in how that mainstream treats them.

If one looks in every direction around Washington Square, it is difficult to imagine how some people can be denied access or excluded there.

There are no gatekeepers; anyone may walk in. And these rules don't say that certain types of *people* can't enter—only that the people who do enter can't engage in certain types of *behavior*. In principle, rules apply to everyone, equally. "No smoking" excludes smokers only when they are smoking; "no drinking" excludes drinkers specifically when they drink; and so on. How can one say that "exclusionary tendencies" keep certain people out? This is, however, something of a rhetorical question. One of the most notable statements in Bartlett's *Familiar Quotations* was written by Anatole France at the end of the nineteenth century, in his novel *The Red Lily*: In its "majestic equality, the law forbids rich and poor alike to sleep under bridges, beg in the streets, and steal loaves of bread." In an unequal economy, even equal rules may exclude persons most in need of being included. Parks are not expected to eliminate unequal tendencies, but they should not exacerbate them. Still, social class and the economy always loom over accessibility to public spaces like a dark specter; they cannot be removed from the equation.

According to Beckett and Herbert, during the 1990s, many cities in the United States began passing "civility codes." Like their cousin, the vagrancy laws, they criminalized a range of behaviors that most citizens regard as nuisances rather than serious crimes. But these newer ordinances were both broader and more specific than vagrancy laws in that they criminalized not merely the *status* of homelessness and transience, but *behavior* that is commonly engaged in by persons who are undomiciled. "The most widely adopted civility laws made it a crime to sit or lie on sidewalks or in bush shelters, sleep in parks and other public spaces, place one's personal possessions on public property for more than a short period of time, drink alcohol in public, engage in public elimination, sell newspapers and other written materials in public spaces, and panhandle aggressively." The outcome of such statutes seems almost preordained: "Because these laws criminalized many common behaviors (such as sleeping, lying down, sitting, and urinating) when these behaviors occur outdoors, the homeless and unstably housed bore the brunt of the codes" (p. 14). And more broadly, Beckett and Herbert argue, these statutes "provide the police with an important set of order maintenance tools." They can now "make stops and conduct searches" that they would not have otherwise been able to accomplish. "Even if vagrancy laws remain unconstitutional, the new legal tools that entail banishment function as their twenty-first-century replacement" (p. 14).

One does not have to be particularly astute to notice the homeless in Washington Square Park. On a warm day in spring or summer, out of several thousand visitors, a handful will fit the classic stereotype. Some are pulling a cart or dragging a garbage bag full of possessions, or a collection of cans and bottles; some are sleeping, lying, stretched out, or sitting, befuddled-looking, on a bench, or on the grass; and a few are standing, and once in a while, mumbling to themselves, or even screaming to an audience that tries not to take note of them. Many will be unshaven, wearing grimy, tattered, shabby clothes, and some are drunk, and stagger as they walk; close up, the passerby's olfactory sense verifies their lack of access to hygienic facilities. Almost certainly, some undomiciled persons who visit the park don't fit the stereotype and do not *look* homeless, but the ones who *do* look the part stand out. What is interesting for us, as observers of deviance and social control, both formal and informal, is how the modal park-goer reacts to parties who are so clearly nonnormative and, as they presently subsist, are unassimilable into the societal and cultural mainstream.

Near the comfort station, on the bench to the right of me, the guy who was sitting there gets up and wanders away from the bench (he's making a call on a Smartphone) and leaves a blue folder bulging with materials inside. A white man with long, dark hair who's pushing a trash cart walks by, sees the folder, leaves his cart, walks over to it, picks it up, and begins thumbing through it. The owner, who is to my left, sees him and walks back and says, "Looks pretty good, eh?" The trash man hands it back to him and within his (and my) earshot, the phone caller says, "Some guy was about to walk off with my folder." Alongside the wall of the comfort station, a man is shaking out several blankets and stuffing them into plastic bags. The trash man continues rolling his bin along the walkway, sees the guy with the blankets, and says to him, "You can't keep your stuff here. The park isn't your apartment."

The guy says, "Yeah, but I gotta have some place to live."

The trash guy, obviously irritated by his previous encounter, says, "You gonna fight with me—like every other fuckin' person in the fuckin' park? I gotta do my fuckin' job. *You can't fuckin' sleep here!*" And so, the homeless guy, kicked out of a comfortable, grassy spot, protected by a wall on one side and a fence on the other, slings his bags over his shoulder and trundles off to find a new place to sleep; the trash man keeps an eye on him as he's walking away.

As permissive as the denizens of this space are, the park constitutes webs of power and influence, from top to bottom and from side to side, multiple hierarchies and circlets that enable particular parties to promulgate and exercise dominion over others. The homeless are at the bottom of everyone else's hierarchies. They make up the army of persons Holly Whyte (1980, pp. 60–65) calls the "undesirables." They are the socially marginal, the *banished* (Beckett and Herbert, 2009); virtually everyone else stigmatizes them, wants to get rid of them, force them out of *their* parks and neighborhoods. Still, the Washington Square community tolerates them—but barely.

Why investigate homelessness as a form of deviance? What makes the homeless *deviant*? And, in so doing, aren't we *blaming the victim*? (Ryan, 1976). To the extent that homelessness negates whatever values a society holds dear—family and marital life, occupational achievement, access to material possessions, affluence, comfort and security, assurance of a reasonable day-to-day existence, even the very food that sustains life— anyone who succumbs to it will be widely looked upon with disfavor. And surviving day to day as a homeless person demands activities that the mainstream considers unacceptable. Having no funds often entails begging, which can turn into aggressive importuning, or dumpster diving, which may involve tossing garbage onto the sidewalk, which in turn attracts vermin. Cleanliness requires access to water, which often means that the homeless must bathe either in a public restroom that others use or, in the case of Washington Square, a fountain; being able to urinate and defecate demands access to toilet facilities—or doing one's business in outdoor places where other humans gather. Sleeping may be accomplished in the open air, but in bad weather, and where urban sidewalks and parks are off-limits to outdoor slumber, shelters may be unacceptable from the point of view of one's own safety. Sprawling out on the sidewalk or on benches blocks access to the conventional pedestrian or park-goer. Many people find the very *sight* of people in ragged, filthy clothes—whether sleeping on sidewalks, begging, hanging out on the corner, or in parks, or just walking down the street—offensive, repulsive, and distinctly *deviant*. And the sociologist of deviance has a ready reply to the "blaming the victim" mythology: *We're* not labeling anyone as deviant—*mainstream society* has already done that! We're simply recognizing, and analyzing, a system that already exists.

The distaste for the homeless goes beyond the simple categorical rejection of persons who don't have a roof over their heads; sheer urban survival is not free, and in order to accomplish it, the unhoused have to have access to resources that make it possible. And as homelessness has increased in the United States during the 1980s and 1990s, municipalities from Boston and Philadelphia to Los Angeles and Seattle have passed "sit-and-lie" legislation restricting the rights of the unhoused. Though cities have enforced panhandling and loitering statutes for a century, the more recent laws strengthened and elaborated the older public space controls (Loukaitou-Sideris and Ehrenfeucht, 2009, pp. 160–77). Public spokespersons defend the more recent legislation by arguing that the activities of the homeless tend to crowd out the course of conventional family life, recreation, and commerce. "To the bewilderment of pedestrians in the 1980s," says Robert Ellickson in a law journal article, "panhandlers, aimless wanderers pushing shopping carts, and other down-and-out individuals appeared with increasing frequency in the downtown areas of the United States"—this, paradoxically, at a time when the skid row neighborhoods of the country, including New York City's Bowery, were emptying out. "By the early 1990s, the increased disorderliness of the urban street scene had triggered a political backlash" (1996, p. 1167). In 1994 alone, says Ellickson, three of the most liberal municipalities in the nation—Berkeley, Santa Monica, and Santa Cruz, California—"compelled their local officials to take steps to limit street disorder." Public spaces "are precious," he argues, "because they enable city residents to move about and engage in recreation and face-to-face communication" (p. 1169). The rules of proper street behavior, he adds, "are not an impediment to freedom, but a foundation of it" (p. 1174). But who interprets "proper street behavior"? A street person and a housed neighborhood resident are likely to have different interpretations.

Currently, even with a recent relatively low unemployment rate (under 4%), the United States has a homeless problem. Washington Square has an almost unique problem in that its reputation bends toward tolerance and diversity; the homeless come to the park specifically because they know that the locals and most visitors tend to be liberal, are more likely to put up with them, and will feel guilty if they don't. But tolerance has its limits; homelessness is a *problem* that's in the eye of the beholder. The homeless would *like* to have a roof over their heads; why *don't* they? Respectables in most neighborhoods don't want them around, considering them, as we saw, in William H. Whyte's terminology, "undesirables": the NIMBY problem—"not in my backyard"—in a nutshell. The comfortably housed would prefer the homeless to be "out of sight, out of mind," regarding them as a problem only when forced to cross paths with them. As we see, to live day to day, the homeless find it necessary to engage in troublesome behavior. A certain proportion are mentally disordered and can't or won't tolerate the effects of psychotropic substances, and today, safe, affordable residential mental health facilities virtually don't exist. Many affluent members of the society consider the unhoused unsightly, disgraceful—a stain or stigma on their community. An encampment of the homeless is not merely offensive; it is illegal, contrary to municipal ordinances. Screaming "bloody murder," says one observer, blocking cars in the street, using the sidewalk as "an al-fresco urinal," importuning passersby, frightening children—critics accuse the homeless of committing these and multiple other offenses (Peyser, 2015). Where do they go? They are most likely to go where residents tolerate deviance, but some don't know when they've worn out their welcome.

Cities offer a contradictory picture with respect to their exclusionary tendencies, that is, the likelihood that a community will exclude or banish *certain kinds* of people from its ambit. On the one hand, urbanism fosters a cosmopolitan outlook, an acceptance of strangers, and tolerance for diversity of all kinds. On the other, cities are so large that they can sustain neighborhoods that are relatively homogeneous with respect to race and ethnicity, income and socioeconomic status, even culture and lifestyle. And homogeneity often fosters the disposition to exclude persons who violate the template, who don't look and act like everyone else who lives in the neighborhood. Aside from race, the most formidable tendency to exclude certain kinds of people from certain kinds of neighborhoods is energized by indigence—people who are too impecunious and perhaps too personally disordered to put a roof over their heads, feed themselves, accomplish quotidian necessities, and abide by conventions. As we've seen, Whyte refers to the indigent as the "undesirables," those "derelicts who drink out of half-pint bottles in paper bags . . . , the bag women, people who act strangely" (1980, p. 60), the babblers, ranters, screamers, and gesticulators; those people who have no apparent means of support, persons on welfare; people who push shopping carts festooned with plastic bags into which are stuffed redeemable bottles and cans; the rarely or casually employed; people who sleep in shelters, on the sidewalk, on benches, or in some out-of-the-way nook or cranny; the vagrants, the beggars, the people who used to be called hobos and bums. These are the people most likely to be banished from the streets, parks, squares, neighborhoods, and communities of respectable people by the police or as a result of hostile or rude remarks, threats, even physical attacks from locals (Beckett and Herbert, 2009). Research indicates that the homeless are stigmatized as severely as the mentally disordered, indicating that there is a "robust tendency to blame the disadvantaged for their predicament" (Phelen et al., 1997, pp. 323, 337); of course, many people are both homeless and mentally disordered.

Virtually by definition, a ban on loitering is nugatory, null, void, and of no relevance in a park; loitering is what one *does* in a park. A park's primary function is to *encourage* loitering—that is, lingering, tarrying, resting, relaxing, contemplating, lounging, *occupying a space in public.* So how can the police exclude the homeless from Washington Square Park—a historical refuge of the unconventional, the offbeat, the wind-tossed, the stigmatized and vexed? The simple answer is, they can't; the more complicated answer is that it depends on exactly what they do and how they do it. *Certain kinds* of long-term occupations of space are legally and righteously banned, while others are tolerated, while still others represent what parks are *for.*

At approximately six in the morning, park staff shoves aside the temporary barriers blocking access to the park, signaling that all may enter there; and at midnight—again, approximately—after herding the laggards out, they put the barriers in place again. We've seen that, in today's stagnant global economy, the nation's, and New York City's, homeless population is at an all-time high, at least since the Great Depression. Do homeless people sleep in the park? Do large numbers hide from the PEP and NYPD at midnight and then bed down there for the night? New York City's Department of Parks' twelve o'clock curfew presumes that, at the chimes of midnight, everyone has a place to go. Almost by definition, anyone who sleeps in an urban public park is homeless—that is, other than a shelter, has no domicile in which to sleep. Until the summer of 2016, my informants say, a dozen or so homeless men slept in Washington Square Park overnight, but since then, the police have made a more concerted effort to roust midnight-to-six o'clock sleepers from the square. Here are a few observations, taken from my field notes.

Friday, October 14, 2016. This morning, I wake up early (about 5:30) & decide to use this opportunity to go to the Park at 6, when it opens, to determine if any homeless people sleep there overnight. So, I get dressed, gulp down some coffee, get a pen, a notebook, and a flashlight, and, at 6:05, walk toward WSP. Just as I get to the SE corner, a parks worker opens the temporary barrier. This is a good omen. I walk along the pathway that leads to the fountain, shining my light onto the grass to determine if I can see anyone sleeping; I don't. Then I notice an NYPD cruiser parked next to the fountain & I walk up to the driver's side. The driver has the window down & so I explain my situation, asking about homeless people sleeping in the Park. It seems that policing before this last August was unsystematic and sporadic. Cops'd roust someone at midnight, at 2, or at 4 in the morning, advise them to go to shelters, make sure they left, then the police would come back a couple hrs. later & find the same homeless men back in the Park, sleeping. Average number of people in the Park during the night? "About a dozen or so," one officer told me. In August, they explained to me, the NYPD decided to institute a crack-down on sleeping in the Park/s & they'd roust them more often, more systematically, more emphatically. Since then, they haven't encountered anyone in the Park. "For instance," one of them said, "there was nobody here tonight." I thank them for their time and leave. Of course, I have to do some more checking—asking more people, going out there a few more times at 6, but it's possible that that's the way it is.

Wednesday, October 19, 2016, 6:30 AM. I discover that at this time of the year, there's very little light at 6 but much more at 6:30. One NYPD cruiser is parked just north of the fountain, with its lights on. I walk west. A person wrapped up in a white blanket is sleeping *on* one of the non-chess tables. Apparently, the cops missed the sleeping, shrouded guy. A 2nd

NYPD cruiser drives into the Pk. from a SE walkway and pulls alongside the one near the fountain. As the car passes me, the officer on the passenger side says to me, "Good morning." I say the same to him then ask, "Any excitement?" He replies "Not yet." I laugh. Within fifteen minutes, the Park is bustling with activity. I count over 50 people there, including the Tai Chi guy who's doing his thing on the Garibaldi Plaza theater platform, multiple dog-walkers—one of whom, an attractive middle-aged woman who smiles at me, holding my gaze, making sure I smile back—several power-walkers, a maintenance man emptying trash cans into his bin, a half-dozen runners, two guys having an animated conversation in a language I can't even identify, a woman who's very fashionably and stylishly dressed, and one apparently homeless man who's stuffing some clothes into his rollie. In other words, by around 6:30–6:45, a *lot* of people have entered the Park, the majority of whom are conventional and far from homeless. Clearly, in pleasant weather, soon after the Park is opened, it comes *very* alive. Of course, when we go off Daylight Savings and push the clock back an hour, it will still be dark at this hour.

Wednesday, October 19, 2016, 4:30 PM. I have a conversation w. an elderly man whom I've seen a number of times in the Pk. "Hey, how ya doin'?" he asks. "I'm doing fine, and you? The Park gets up early, I notice. There are a lot of people here in the morning."

"Yeah. We got to move on out. It's time for us to git goin'. This is the *neighborhood's* park. I respect the people who live around here. They pay a lotta money to live here."

"It's everybody's park. But yeah, that's true, it is an expensive neighborhood. Listen, do people sleep here at night?"

"Oh, yeah, they sleep here."

"A cop told me they roust all the sleeping people out of here late at night."

"Naw, they keep comin' back. Me—I don't sleep here. I keep movin'. I walk around. See, if you lie down, they mess wit' you. You stay on your *feet*, don't nobody *mess* wit' you."

"Where do you sleep?" [Pause.]

"Wherever I can." [I hand him a $5 bill.] "Thank you very much." He gives me a fist bump. "Now I can eat," he says.

I'm glad I could help the guy out. For the homeless who don't want to live in shelters—which, some have told me, can be dangerous places to stay—Washington Square Park might seem an almost paradisiacal outdoor hotel in which to spend the night. But most nearby residents don't want men they think of as bums snoozing nightly in what's practically their back yard. Hence, the police crackdown of the overnight snoozers. But crackdowns come and go; poverty and homelessness are likely to be features of the American landscape for some time to come. I go back to the park several times in November, after the end of Daylight Savings. Several times, I ask the early morning cops about the sleepers, and I always get the same answer: Through the night, we roust the sleepers, and by 5:00 or 6:00 a.m., there are none. Of course, as common sense dictates, cold weather, especially if it is accompanied by rain or snow, minimizes the inducement to sleep outside.

I conducted a brief, separate interview with ten park-goers specifically on their attitudes toward the homeless. If I were to draw out a consistent theme the interviewees expressed, it would be *compassion with a major strain of ambivalence.* The factor of socioeconomic state lends a certain flavor to the space. The square is located, let's recall, in an overwhelmingly white, predominantly upper-middle-class neighborhood, and across the street from a major private university that enrolls sixty thousand students. Parents spend substantial sums of money to send their kids to NYU. Many Americans can empathize with the tendency in affluent neighborhoods to banish the indigent (Low, 2003; Beckett and Herbert, 2009), but my respondents reject this exclusionist bent, though most express reservations. Only one out of the ten says that there are "too many" homeless people in the square. Park ordinances specifically prohibit begging ("solicitation"), but park-goers are divided on the matter; two said that begging should not be allowed, four said it should, and the remaining four weren't sure or believed that it depended on how importunate and insistent the beggar was. When asked if begging should be allowed, Gerad, a sixty-year-old male, shrugged and said, "It's their civil rights. What can you do about it? Some go about it in a decent way. Some are more aggressive. If they're just begging, it's their right, they should be allowed, but if they become too aggressive and demanding, and won't leave someone alone, that shouldn't be allowed." When I asked the same question, Delbert, seventy, said, "Oh, boy! Well, if you live in that situation, if you're destitute, you're hungry, what can you do? It's a matter of survival." On the other hand, he added, "if you beg, then others come to beg, and pretty soon, the park has a major problem with the homeless begging."

When I asked what should be done about the homeless problem, nearly all said that it was a structural problem and so, it required a structural solution. Peter, in his early forties, said, "I think the social welfare system should be better. There should be more shelters. In the U.S., nobody should be homeless." Rick, retired, in his seventies, said, "Institutionally, more money should be allocated for homeless shelters, safer shelters, shelters that provide more services. But basically, it comes down to a bifurcated economy—the gap between the rich and poor is growing. We need a stronger economy, more money flowing into the lives of the poor, the fragile, the disadvantaged. More psychiatric and counseling services." All of my respondents were especially insistent that law enforcement should play no role in the condition or status of homelessness; the NYPD and the PEP have an obligation to help and protect the homeless when they are in need, but they have no right to harass, shoo away, or arrest them simply because they are shabby looking and undomiciled. "The cops shouldn't arrest homeless people," said Davon, a black man in his late twenties, "who aren't doing any harm or breaking any laws." Said Kelsey, a white woman in her late thirties, "It's not a law enforcement issue." The homeless "aren't doing anything illegal just by being homeless. The people should leave them alone, unless they need to be helped."

Crime in Washington Square and Elsewhere

In addition to behavior that seems bizarre, unconventional, annoying, unacceptable, or out of place to most of us, *common crime* is a major category of deviance. "Common crimes" are the seven FBI Index Crimes—larceny or simple theft; burglary; motor vehicle theft; robbery; rape; aggravated (or serious) assault; and murder. All crimes are the violation of *formal* rules or norms, called laws, and some are serious enough that formal agents of social control, mainly the police and the courts, are likely to arrest and prosecute violators. What is the *arc* of crime in the nation, in the City, in the Village, and in the square over the past half-century?

An article in the *New York Times* during the sixties (Sibley, 1964) painted a dismal picture of Washington Square. Derelicts, alcoholics, narcotics addicts, sexual perverts, and other "undesirables," claimed the author (Sibley, 1964), appeared to be taking over Washington Square. "You're not safe from the scum that infests the park," said William Passanante, the neighborhood's state assemblyman. "I spent my boyhood here," he stated. "The Village has always had its odd-balls and weird characters. That's what was so wonderful about it." There used to be, he added, "a live-and-let-live spirit." Times have changed, he told me. "Right over there," he said, pointing to a fenced-in playground near the Arch, "a couple of mothers came over to me shouting for help." It turns out a man was exposing himself to the children in the sandbox; after he was arrested and led away, a woman ran toward the police and screamed, "Where are you beasts taking this poor man?" A report, commissioned by James M. Hester, then-president of New York University, described the park as a haven for drunkenness, disorderly conduct, prostitution of both sexes, and the sale of narcotics. Hester convinced the then-NYPD commissioner, Michael Murphy, to beef up foot patrols in Washington Square Park; the change improved conditions, but not substantially. The derelicts, most of whom descended on the park from other neighborhoods, tended not to confine their activity to the park; they spread out, harassing patrons in nearby cafés and restaurants. "Sure, they have civil rights," a local resident told the reporter, "but so do we family people. And their rights end when they begin to trample on ours" (Sibley, 1964).

Fast-forward three decades, that is, into the 1990s; the passage of time seems to have brought virtually no improvement. Along Eighth Street, a block north of the square, thugs routinely robbed stores behind the business end of a shotgun, and harassed customers; vandals smashed shop windows and sprayed graffiti everywhere; and at the end of a business day, shopkeepers had to sweep up empty crack vials on the sidewalks in front of their stores. One by one, retail proprietors began abandoning their establishments in fear of becoming the next victim. By 1992, "8th Street looked like a gap-toothed smile capped with FOR RENT signs" (Gross, 1993, p. 32). Thieves openly sold stolen goods in the park; bums, he claims, urinated in the bushes, on the grass, against walls, even defecated in front of apartment or store doorways; drug dealers solicited and sold all manner of controlled substances. One resident counted one hundred "boom-box" cars passing by his apartment in a single hour; "the noise started at 9:30 p.m. and went on until 5 a.m." (p. 35). Alcoholics drank booze out of bottles sheathed in paper bags right in front of police officers, then got up and staggered along walkways, oblivious to their surroundings, as park visitors scurried to avoid a collision or being vomited on—and no one did anything about it. Arrests in Greenwich Village, and in Washington Square in particular, plummeted; seemingly, the neighborhood had reached the "anything goes" point on the permissiveness spectrum.

"These are political decisions," said Antonio Pagan, a city councilman. "They've deprioritized street crime" (Gross, 1993, p. 32). "The milieu of the Village has always accepted all kind of people and their artifacts, from dogs to nipple rings," said Mitchell Moss, a Village resident and director of New York University's Urban Research Center. But the culture of 'Anything goes' in Greenwich Village has stretched the boundary of civility" (p. 32). What made the Village an attractive and desirable place to live—its tolerance for diversity and unconventionality—has "made it nearly unlivable." But after tolerating an accelerating spiral of crime, disorder, and decay, Villagers and the police who patrol their neighborhood had finally recognized that they needed to crack down on the chaos around them; in order to save their community, they needed to launch a "battle for a civil Village" (p. 37).

Two years later, by 1994, the Village had changed, and dramatically. Crime in New York City, in Greenwich Village specifically, and in Washington Square, had fallen precipitously—and unexpectedly. Residents found themselves in a "suddenly safer city" (Krauss, 1995; Horowitz, 1995). The decline in crime had taken place for two years in a row, but in only one year's time—the first six months of 1994 versus the first half of 1995—in New York, robberies declined by 22 percent, burglary by 18 percent, motor vehicle theft by 25 percent, and murder by over half. The incidence of most street crime was at a quarter-century low.

How did this happen? Most criminologists were mystified, insisting on more evidence to answer the question. Jeffrey Fagan, director of Columbia University's Center for Violence Research and Prevention, said, "There's a miracle happening before our eyes and we don't know why it's happening" (Krauss, 1995). Journalists, criminologists, and sociologists proposed several theories to explain the crime drop—which seemed to be happening in most large cities in the United States—including a decline in crack cocaine addiction, a decline in the city's level of unemployment and an improvement in the economic picture, the middle-aging of the baby boomer generation, and the increase in the incarceration of the most crime-prone segment of the population.

William J. Bratton, commissioner of the NYPD, declared that he knew the answer to the criminologists' conundrum: *He* was responsible for the crime drop. Armed with detailed statistics on where criminal complaints and arrests were taking place, Bratton introduced community policing, turned precinct commanders loose in devising their own strategies, beefed up patrols in more crime-stricken neighborhoods, and increased arrests by 25 percent. Before Bratton assumed command, officers were told to adopt a hands-off policy toward minor offenses, including drug possession; after Bratton, all that changed. It is true that New York seemed to represent a success story—but so did many cities, including Houston, Boston, Phoenix. Still, New York experienced the most consistent and steepest decline, for all crime categories, and for violent crimes most especially. Yet criminologists remained skeptical, citing demographic factors as more influential. Said James Alan Fox, a criminologist at Northeastern University, "Most of the decline that has occurred would have occurred anyway" (Krauss, 1995). "Understanding takes time," added Jeremy Travis, director of the National Institute of Justice.

As we can see in table 3.2, according to all available measures, the crime rate in the United States declined *substantially* between 1990 and 2015. In fact, during the past quarter-century, the crime rate for the country as a whole dropped by more than half, for New York City, by almost 90 percent, and for the Sixth Precinct (more or less encompassing Greenwich Village, which surrounds Washington Square), by over 95 percent. No criminologist predicted a crime drop at all, let alone such a stupendous one. And yet, as New York's crime rate has sharply declined, Chicago's 2015–2016 rate increased. For instance, in 2015, Chicago's incidence of criminal homicide was 17.5; a year later, it rose to 26.8 per one hundred thousand in the population—seven times that of New York City's (3.9) and a rise of one-third. A few of America's largest cities, like Chicago, experienced an uptick in crime during the

TABLE 3.2. Crime in the United States, New York City, and Sixth Precinct, 1990 vs. 2015

Unit	1990	2015	% Decline 1990–2015
United States Population	249,464,440	321,418,820	
Number of Murders	23,440	15,696	33
Murder Rate	9.4	4.9	48
Number of Robberies	639,270	327,374	49
Robbery Rate	257.0	101.9	60
Vehicle Thefts	1,635,907	707,758	57
Rate of GLA	657.8	220.2	66

	1990	2015	% Decline 1990–2015
New York City Population	7,322,564	8,550,405	
Number of Murders	2,262	352	84
Murder Rate	26.9	4.1	85
Number of Robberies	100,280	16,931	83
Robbery Rate	1,198.7	198.0	83
Grand Larceny Auto	146,295	7,332	95
Rate of GLA	1,804.1	85.8	95

	1990	2015	% Decline 1990–2015
Sixth Precinct Population	65,132	66,880	
Number of Murders	7	0	100
Murder Rate	10.7	0	100
Number of Robberies	1,433	114	92
Robbery Rate	2,200.1	170.5	92
Grand Larceny Auto	1,092	32	97
Rate of GLA	1,814.8	47.8	97

Source: Adapted from Uniform Crime Reports, U.S. Census, and, for New York City, CompStat. Data for Sixth Precinct obtained from David Kraiker, New York Regional Office of the U.S. Bureau of the Census, based on the American Community Survey; rape not included due to controversy over definition.

last year or two, but the overall trend is decidedly downward. Though no criminologist has adequately explained this decline, it is welcomed by all concerned.

The FBI requests, compiles, and makes information publicly available on crimes reported to the police in parks and recreation areas (the "Park Crime Reports"). Four Manhattan parks are relevant here: Washington Square, Bryant Park (adjacent to the New York Public Library, between Fortieth and Forty-second streets, just east of Sixth Avenue), Tompkins Square Park (on the Lower East Side, between Avenues A and B, between Seventh and Tenth streets), and Union Square (between Fourteenth and Seventeenth streets, just east of the extension of Broadway). As table 3.3 shows, none of them is a dangerous or "unsafe" park; during 2015, a small though significant number of Index Crime felonies took place within their borders. More than half of these offenses entailed felony larceny—the simple stealing of money or an item worth more than fifty dollars. Nine violent felonies were committed in all of these parks during this period—none in Washington Square, two in Bryant Park, and two in Tompkins Square. Union Square seems to attract the most violent crime—four aggravated (serious) felonious assaults and one rape. Why there and not the other parks?

TABLE 3.3. Crime Reported to the Police in Four NYC Parks, 2015

Park	Size	Crimes
Washington Square	9.75	5 grand larcenies
Bryant Park	9.6	1 robbery, 1 felony assault, 3 grand larcenies
Tompkins Square	10.5	1 robbery, 3 grand larcenies, 1 felony assault
Union Square	6.5	5 grand larcenies, 4 felony assaults, 1 grand theft auto, 1 rape

Source: FBI, UCR, "Park Crime Reports." Size of park is in acres.

As we all know, the number of crimes reported to the police is not a perfectly reliable measure of the number of crimes that take place; for all crimes (except for motor vehicle theft and murder), a substantial proportion that occur are not reported to the police—they are the "dark number" or "dark figure" of crime. Still, most criminologists believe that the more serious the crime, the greater the chance of reporting, and that violent crimes (except rape) are vastly more likely to be reported than property crimes. Murder is a very *reliably* reported crime. As we've seen, Union Square is decidedly not a neighborhood park. Seven subway lines converge at its southern border, and many commuters walk to work from this Metro stop, often through the square. In other words, many of its visitors are transient. Many office workers eat lunch there. On the plus side, having a job means that they are probably more law-abiding than people who don't work, but the square also attracts transients for whom office workers are an attractive target. In addition, on select days, on the sidewalk adjoining the park, green markets set up booths and sell produce, and some of their customers relax in the park before and after purchasing farm-fresh foodstuffs—in other words, a domestic activity that would generate cohesion and sociality among visitors. Hence, two major factors (lunch visitations by office workers and food shopping) would seem to incline Union Square in a "safe" or law-abiding direction, though these factors are operative only at particular times or during particular days. In contrast, the transiency factor, engendered by the Metro station and by the park's location, is operative all the time.

Counting the number of people in Union Square's social units— singletons, dyads, triads, and triads-plus—I found that three-quarters of all the *person-units* who were inside Union Square (76%) were singletons; only one out of five was in a dyad (20%), and the rest, only 4 percent, were in triads or triads-plus. And of the total number of *people* in the square, roughly six in ten (59%) were alone, that is, in a singleton, and most were males. In contrast, in Washington Square, only 58 percent of all units are singletons, and only 37 percent of the total number of people there are alone. The *typical* or modal visitor to Union Square is solitary; the typical visitor to Washington Square is in a social group of two or more. This lends a certain anomic quality to the ambience of Union Square, and the coupled-up quality of Washington Square's relations, which means substantially more sociability, results in less anomie. Hence, the fact that no serious violent crimes have taken place recently in the latter and several, including one rape, have taken place in the former makes a certain amount of sense. However, none of these Manhattan parks is unsafe, and, as a whole, as we've seen, Manhattan and—even more broadly, compared with other cities (such as Chicago)—more generally, New York City, are comparatively safe environments.

New York City, through its Department of Parks and Recreation, operates 28,000 acres of parklands. The NYPD tabulates the incidence and rate of the seven felony crimes for time period and location; these tabulations are crimes "known to the police." In 2015, the department tallied more than 900 Index Crimes (as we saw, theft, burglary, robbery, motor vehicle theft, rape, aggravated assault, and murder) taking place in New York's parks, including nine murders and 20 rapes. In an editorial dated August 16, 2016, the *New York Times* stated that there was a 23 percent increase in the number of crimes in the City's largest parks for the previous nine months in 2016 versus 2015's same previous nine months—to 417, up from 340. "Should you be worried?" the *Times* asked. "Not really," it responded. The data add up, the editorial read, to less than a crime a day; that's a "tiny percentage" of the City's crime total, and lower than it has been for decades. Look around, the editorial suggested. "If you can see trees, benches and squirrels, you are safer than practically anywhere else in the city. The so-called 'surge' in crime is based more on fear and panic than on facts" (p. A20). As we saw, in Washington Square, during 2015, the police recorded only five of the felonious Index Crimes, all grand larceny: no murders, no rapes, no robberies, and no felonious assaults. Of course, many other types of crimes take place there, most of them drug transactions, but very few felonies take place in the park; most observers consider it, in comparison with other park locales, extremely safe.

Still, even aggravated assault in Washington Square is not completely unknown; in February 2011, a male tourist was punched in the face in the restroom facility during the day, by an assailant, a park "regular" who was described as being "emotionally disturbed." The victim was left on the floor, "bloodied and knocked out." As of eight months later, no arrest had been made. In response to the crime, unusual though it was, along with the rumored marijuana selling, the Parks Department began closing the toilet facility at five o'clock (Swalec, 2011). In June 2016, a man in his fifties removed a broken bottle from his sock and slashed two men in their twenties; he was identified as the same man who, two hours earlier, had assaulted a parks maintenance worker.

But here's an example from the opposite side of the crime coin. In August 2017, I visited the park, sat on a bench, talked with a friend for two hours, then walked to my apartment. Patting my fanny, I realized my wallet was missing. At home, my wife canceled the relevant cards. An hour later, a representative from NYU's Department of Public Safety knocked on our door and told us that someone had found the wallet, which I could pick up in the department's office; the next day, I did, and everything that had been in the wallet was intact.

One afternoon, I came upon two NYPD officers writing citations, which they handed to two young men, wearing t-shirts and shorts, sitting on the fountain wall. A man (who appeared to be homeless) rushed up to them and asked what offense they received the "tickets" for. "We were fighting," one of them said. (They seemed slightly drunk.) "Yeah, we were really going at it. He couldn't defend himself," one of them says, somewhat pridefully, with reference to the other. "I was getting the better of him, and they [the cops] said, 'Hey, go easy on him.' We were in the pool, fighting, and they gave us a $20 ticket." In short, Washington Square is not a crime-free environment—nor could it be, given the volume and extreme diversity of its clientele and the precariousness of the existence and mental condition of some of them. It seems self-evident that the police are likely to restrict themselves to the most serious felony offenses.

Larry the birdman was feeding his birds. He reached down and held up one of them and reached for its leg. Another man approached Larry and shoved him. Both assumed a pugilistic stance, and Larry hit the other man in the jaw, not a powerful blow but a "back off" jab, and the other man swung at Larry a couple of times, never landing a solid blow. They swung at one another several times but each time, missed. Larry yelled, "Back off, get outta here!" The other man wore a stunned, almost deranged look on his face, but refused to move away. This stand-off took place over the course of several minutes, but there was no real fight, just swinging, missing, and yelling. Within about five minutes three PEP came and grabbed the other guy—who was very quiet compared with Larry, who was yelling the whole time—by the arms and took him away. Meanwhile, two NYPD approached, saw the guy in PEP custody, realized they were redundant, turned the corner, and walked down another pathway in the direction from which they had come. Larry sat and fumed and talked to himself for a while.

I was with a friend who urged me to talk to Larry, but the birdman quickly hopped on a bike and rode off. "You missed your opportunity," my friend said. The next day, I went back to the spot and Larry was there, so I walked up to him, put a couple of dollars into his bucket, and we chit-chatted. Finally, I asked him, "Hey, man, what was that beef about yesterday with the guy you swung at?" And Larry told me, "That guy was upset about me trying to cut the string off a pigeon's legs. He thought I was trying to cut the bird's leg off. That's why he swung at me." I talked to him a bit more. We parted on what passes for amiable terms, but I still wasn't satisfied. I was intrigued by the fact that the police trundled the other guy away but did not even question Larry; perhaps it's because he's a park regular, a known quantity, and, according to his statement, he didn't start the fight.

Comparing the major New York City parks with respect to the Index Crimes (defined above) that have taken place there suggests that it is possible that there's something about the parks that conduces visitors toward or away from crime. During 2015, the NYPD reported all the crimes that had taken place in New York City's parks. As we saw in table 3.3, which presents figures for Washington Square and three other, comparable New York parks, no violent crimes were reported in Washington Square in 2015—only five nonviolent thefts or larcenies— whereas there was at least one in all the others. More crime, and more violent crime, has taken place in Union Square than in the others, and Washington has been the safest park, crime-wise. I suggest that the denser sociability that prevails in Washington Square versus the higher proportion of singletons in some of the other parks, especially Union Square, as well as the surrounding residential neighborliness of the former versus the more commercial quality of the latter, significantly contributes to this contrast.

* * *

Interview with Buddy, a Formerly Homeless Man

Buddy is a sixty-year-old man, until recently homeless; he lives in a shelter and, last week, received a key to his own room. The homeless maintain a noticeable presence in the square.

ERICH: How did you get to the park? And where did you sleep last night?

BUDDY: Actually, I didn't get to sleep last night. I got up, left the shelter I'm staying in, walked around, over to First Avenue, Second Avenue, around Tenth Street, Fourteenth Street, went over to Ninth Avenue, Twenty-third Street where the clubs are, I walked around a lot, then I came down here to check out the park.

ERICH: Where do you live—not the address, just the neighborhood or the town.

BUDDY: I go to different locations. I'm homeless, actually, but right now I've been staying at [names the shelter]. I have my own room now. I have an outreach team that works with me. Being homeless is rough. It's really *rough*. But I have my own place to live now. Homeless people need a place to live. I was contacted by an outreach person about a month and a half ago, and I'm now where I want to be. I wasn't before.

ERICH: How did you get here?

BUDDY: I walked here. I like to check out the scene. I like to move around, do different things.

ERICH: What do you do when you come here? What do you like most about the park and what do you most like doing here?

BUDDY: Once in a while, you meet nice people. I like to check out the women who come here. There's all the pigeon people—the people who feed flocks of pigeons. You meet the tourists with their maps, I like to help 'em out, talk to them about where they're from. Things like that.

ERICH: Do you think most people accept and follow the rules of the park?

BUDDY: Not really. You're supposed to take your dog to the dog run, but a lot of dog walkers walk their dogs on the grass.

ERICH: Have you ever witnessed anyone in the park engaged in behavior you believe is a violation of parks ordinance?

BUDDY: Some people go into the park at night. It's okay if they're respectable, middle-class people. But if they're homeless, the parks police will lock them up.

ERICH: Do you see any special problems here? What do you think would improve the park?

BUDDY: I think they fixed up the park *real* good. I feel good here. There aren't any social problems because there are too many eyewitnesses. Plus, a lot of people carry phone cameras. You can see everything. It's like being on *Candid Camera*. Things are too out there in the open. Plus, the park has its own cameras. There's nothing anyone can do and get away with it.

ERICH: Have you ever felt menaced or threatened or fearful of someone harming you? Are there people in the park who make you nervous, anxious, or uneasy?

BUDDY: I'm a good judge of character. If I meet someone, he lets me know he's no good. I can tell. Their energies, their demeanor aren't right. So, I avoid them. I have my own way of telling.

ERICH: Are there any questions I've asked but didn't—which I *should* ask people?

BUDDY: I'm concerned about the future of the park. You know, NYU has been buying up all the property around here, kicking people out and taking over. Now they want to privatize this park, put a fence around it, only allow NYU students in. It should remain a public park. [My face must have registered skepticism.] Is or isn't NYU buying up property all around here?

ERICH: It is.

BUDDY: Well, that's what I'm talking about.

ERICH: Do you really think that NYU will try to make Washington Square Park private, only for NYU students, with all the powerful interests that oppose it? All the wealthy residents in One and Two Fifth Avenue? All the rich people who would be shut out?

BUDDY: Definitely. Definitely. I believe it. They can do it. They've been doing it with everything else.

ERICH: OK, well, thank you very much. This has been very helpful to me.

BUDDY: OK, now, I've done something for you, now maybe you can do something for me.

ERICH: I was about to come to that. What would you like? I was thinking maybe I could pay for your breakfast.

4

Social Control

Walking south on Sixth Avenue past a mini-mart located around the corner from Waverly Place, about a block from Washington Square, I observe a couple crumbling up slices of white bread and letting them drop among a circle of pigeons, who greedily gobble up the pieces. Suddenly, a woman runs out of a Starbuck's and admonishes them. "Stop doing that!" she commands. "Don't feed the pigeons, the rats'll come around and eat it! It's *terrible* food for pigeons!" Looking chagrined, the man closes up the bag and both of them walk north, toward Eighth Street. Some observers would say that this woman is being a "meddling busybody" (Becker, 1963, p. 148). But others are likely to believe that this woman is exercising her civic duty—that is, to intervene when someone engages in clearly wrongful behavior. The episode reminds us to pay close attention to the interface between deviance and social control. Who exercises social control, and when do audiences regard *intervention* against nonnormative behavior to be meddlesome and unjustified? Where is this interventionist line drawn and which *audiences* draw it?

To be plain about it, social control is an act or a set of coordinated acts and one or more institutionalized practices that are intended to reduce or eradicate what some actors consider wrongdoing. Revenge, retaliation, and vindictiveness cannot be eliminated as motives, but scratch revenge and you'll find social control.

The intersection of deviance and control articulates a *dynamic system* within which the lines of right and wrong are drawn and redrawn by the very enactment of social control. The reason why public behavior in Washington Square and its environs is not "out of control" is that, when parties in the park exercise social control, persons inclined to engage in similar kinds of behavior contemplate the wisdom of doing so. This is true everywhere, but, I argue, contrary to its laissez-faire reputation, such control does take place there, and it may very well be exercised in a more flexible—and effective—manner than elsewhere. Unpunished behavior surely encourages similar infractions; putatively wrongful behavior, when visibly sanctioned, produces fewer violations. (Of course, social control is far less effective on the mentally disordered.) These observations are hardly surprising; we need to move beyond these widely accepted platitudes.

Over time, the boundaries of all social systems are pushed, tested, drawn, and redrawn, and hence, the ante to challenging their norms is likely to be upped when parties activate effective social control. To be crude about it, one pile of unscooped-up dog poop may encourage another; intervening against the first pile is likely to discourage the second. (But no, following up on my critical view of the "broken windows" theory, ignoring nonscooped-up dog poop does *not* encourage robbery, rape, or murder!) But the thing about dog walkers in Washington Square is that they form a kind of loose community with like-minded interests; why on earth would they befoul their own nest? Moreover, *flexible* as well as appropriate social control may more effectively keep a lid on more serious violations; in an environment such as Washington Square, the *unrealistic* clamping down of the rules is more likely to foster rebellion than conformity. Enacting and enforcing rules against embracing and kissing would be folly there (though doing so for sexual intercourse is not only realistic but reasonable). Still, as we saw, even affection between partners may "go too far," attracting, as it does, the censorious stares of onlookers or audiences. Washington Square does *not* become a "broken windows" setting because, for the most part, the social control exercised by both official agents of social control and the ordinary parkgoer manifests the flexible, realistic, and reasonable reactions to what audiences there consider wrongdoing. After all, an *intentionally* broken broken window (say, in the comfort station) constitutes a serious offense in the park that the majority of park denizens would *not* tolerate or ignore. The dog owner cannot simply walk away from a pile of dog poop deposited in a dog run; he or she would be immediately called on it. There is the sense, among a substantial proportion of park-goers, that this is our place, we're all in it together, you must *not* befoul our nest.

Some sociologists regard the concept of social control as residing entirely in the realm of *formal* social control—that is, it is embodied only by the reactions of the police, the courts, the criminal justice system, and the many bureaucratic agencies that attempt to control wrongdoing (Cohen,

1985; Horwitz, 1990). Here, I don't focus exclusively on the forces of the state and their agnate institutional embodiments and representatives. Though the attempts of such agencies do indeed constitute a *form* of social control, most attempts to exercise control over what audiences regard as unacceptable actions or beliefs manifest themselves *informally*; observers *do* react when they encounter unacceptable or deviant behavior. Interpersonal forces are foundational; they are the lynchpin holding the society together—they determine how society operates. The jostle, the give and take of informal reactions are what drive the enterprise of reining in the supposed sins of parties who stray. Neither species of control, formal or informal, should be neglected; both are essential.

During between one and two thousand hours of observation of behavior in Washington Square Park—an unusually laissez-faire environment—I have witnessed multiple infractions of social conventions and park ordinances, not to mention violations of the criminal code. I have also seen reactions *to* these violations and infractions by both informal "audiences" or interpersonal observers as well as formal agents of social control (mainly the PEP and the NYPD), which forced me to think about the dynamics of reactions to such infractions. Most of the efforts at social control flow from ordinary citizens, while others, the minority, emanate from official agents; hence, the details are different but the principle is the same. Putative wrongdoing may be admonished, or not, punished, or not; hence, social control is a variable, not a constant, modulated according to the audience's view of the action in question and the specific agent in question, that is, formal or informal. And when it is applied, social control may restrain, deescalate, or prevent said unacceptable behavior—or it may not. Hence, the question, "What do people *do* when they witness what they consider wrongdoing?" is far from trivial. Likewise, agents of formal control may or may not act when *they* witness infractions of the criminal code—and, along similar lines, some agents may act one way, while others act in another fashion. Some spring into action and confront the violator; others condone the behavior and pass by the violators without comment or reaction. And some violators respond to a putative violation by growling, "Why the hell don't you mind your own damn business?" Exactly *how* social control is exerted, and with what consequences, remains a major issue for criminologists and sociologists of crime and deviance.

Let's contextualize our central issue: deviance *and social control* in Washington Square Park. How is putative wrongdoing in this public space *tamed*? What are the factors that make for so much deviance and so little *serious* crime? What is it about this place that makes the Kelling and Wilson "Broken Windows" hypothesis, as it applies to Washington Square, such a hopeless failure?

Washington Square is the kind of place where actors are likely to go against the grain, and audiences likewise tolerate a broad range of unconventional behavior. But even here, they deem *certain* kinds of behavior to be wrongful. Park-goers draw a sociological *line* that, when crossed, triggers off a negative reaction. What goes on here that is different from most other places? The seeming paradoxes that run through human interaction in the square, as compared with elsewhere, intrigue me—as they should every interested observer of social processes.

Does it need saying? No matter; I'll say it anyway: Social control is neither benign nor malevolent. How it operates depends on what unit or system we look at. It works relativistically: Social control for the hegemon—the dominant entities in society—may represent deviance for a revolutionary group, and vice versa. In Washington Square, it makes sense to examine the social control of the majority, as well as that of agents of formal social control, the latter mainly the mandated exercise of law wielded by the NYPD and the PEP, as they interpret it. But it is entirely possible that the park-going majority may disagree with the patrol officers; the PEP or the NYPD may be too strict in their interpretation of the norms, rules, or laws. What about minority audiences? Social control entails intentionality, that is, an action oriented toward the goal of preventing behavior that violates a norm that a social collectivity believes is right: I spank my son for stealing cookies, an act I consider bad, and I believe my act will reduce the likelihood that he will do it again. But, to use an often-wielded argument, what if a boy steals a loaf of bread to feed his family, which is starving? From the loaf's owner's perspective, the boy violated a norm and should be punished; from the humanist's perspective, he did a good thing and should not be punished. Various groups or subcollectivities may attempt to control their members'—variously defined—wrongful behaviors, which may be at cross-purposes with one another. Such is the nature of social control;

it takes us into multigroup realms. Keep that in mind and we can move on to more or less firm sociological ground.

Informal Social Control

There's a man on a wooden bench at the south side of the walkway that runs between the fountain and the Garibaldi Plaza. He's wearing khaki shorts and has an artificial leg, he would appear to be about forty, he wears a blonde beard and dark shades, and a handkerchief in the pattern of an American flag is wrapped around his head as a cap. There's a shopping cart close by which contains several odds and ends, including a tiny folding table, a small folding chair, and a golf club, a 3-iron. He has propped a cardboard sign up against the cart which reads, "My name is Jim. HA!!!! Disabled homeless veteran trying to get home. *Anything* would help. Thank you! Semper fi!" An older man with a dark beard, wearing a red and black flannel jacket, walks up to the cart, draws out the 3-iron, and places a purple rubber ball on the ground. The man with the flag kerchief yells, "Fore!" and the older man swings at the ball, sending it toward the fountain. He hits a woman in the leg who's standing and talking with a man near the fountain; she seems startled and turns around. The bearded man retrieves the ball without acknowledging that he hit her, and returns to where he hit the ball. The woman and her companion say nothing but walk away. The man who hit the ball tells the guy with one leg that he knows how to play golf. "I'm a real Tiger Woods," he boasts. He hits the ball again and it bounces against the fountain wall and rolls to the feet of a woman sitting on the stone bench. She hands it to the man who hit it, and he walks back and sticks the 3-iron back in the shopping cart and walks off. Nobody admonishes our would-be Tiger Woods, though the bystanders I observed scrutinized the hapless pair of pseudo-golfers as if they were insects. Everyone who observed the transaction is likely to draw the conclusion that this is a very laissez-faire locale; the act in which he engaged clearly violates the norms of everyday civility, and mere incivility can become experienced as serious and offensive personal disrespect.

In the small circle east of the Garibaldi Plaza, Colin Huggins is playing a piece by Philip Glass. To my left, there's a tall woman in a blue-and-white dress, lying down, with a blue scarf covering her face, and, since her legs arch over the metal armrest in the middle, she's occupying virtually all of a full, four-person bench. Her outfit communicates to me that she is affluent—tastefully upper-middle-class. When Huggins finishes the piece, he walks over to the woman and shakes her arm. "Hey, Miss! Princess! You're taking up four seats!" She doesn't stir. I say to the pianist, "She's out," but Huggins is persistent; the woman begins to show some signs of life and sits up, but she leaves the scarf on her face for fifteen or twenty seconds then finally pulls it off. She's of Asian descent, in her early forties, and wears glasses. Huggins goes back to his piano. A shirtless man with a t-shirt sticking out of his back pocket ostentatiously sticks a can of Budweiser America into a plastic bag, sits down on the walkway to the right of and behind Huggins, and begins swigging the beer. Huggins says he's thinking of playing either another Glass or Chopin. The man sitting on the ground yells, "Don't play Rachmaninoff, you'll fuck it up! Play Chopin! Chopin!" Huggins begins playing the Beethoven *Appassionata* Sonata, but sloppily and with choppily inconsistent tempi. Then the formerly sleeping woman puts on her sneaks, which were resting on the ground, makes a subtle hand gesture to a young woman—shorter, and to my eye, biracial—across the walkway that she should leave, and after about a minute or two, stands up and walks off to my left, followed by the younger woman, then by a white man, next to her, clearly her companion, all walking toward the Washington Place exit. When Huggins finishes, the man drinking the Bud yells loudly, "The man's great! He just did what none of you could do in fifty years of practice! They don't teach that at Juilliard!"

In this episode, parties present exercised three instances of informal social control. First, Huggins did not want the woman to sleep during his performance; he woke her up and forced her to listen to him play. Second, undoubtedly annoyed at the pianist, she retaliated against him by walking out on his performance, and by encouraging two others to do so as well. And third, Huggins retaliated against the loud Bud drinker by not playing what he requested and playing badly—though the man clearly didn't have the ear (and was probably too drunk) to realize that he was being chastised. Of course, the rest of us suffered as well.

Agents of informal social control in Washington Square Park are people who exercise influence, whether directly or indirectly, on others in a face-to-face or interactional context. Generally speaking, agents of social control include one another; we are audiences to the behavior of others, and they to ours. People may overtly verbally admonish wrong-doers, in the fashion of the chastiser of the pigeon feeders, or they may simply withdraw from the presence of persons who do something they don't like, or they may ignore an invitation to interact with them, or they may wear a facial expression of disgust, outright disapproval, or annoyance, or roll their eyes. At the same time, some have more influence to effectively admonish normative violators than others.

Interpersonally, in the case of a genuine threat, parties are likely to withdraw sociability and indeed, their very person, from the presence of the offending individual; in the most offensive cases, this process is inevitable and usually fairly swift. Two people walk into the park, separately, one behind the other; I'm walking behind the second party. Suddenly, the lead person, a tall black man in his thirties, rips off his leather jacket, begins screaming incoherently and flailing at a bench with the jacket. The second party, a petite Asian woman in her twenties, walking directly behind the man, is busily pressing the keys of her cell phone. She looks up from her device, notices the man's furious activity, stops in her tracks, whirls around, and begins expeditiously walking in the opposite direction, hurrying past me with a dazed, resolute look on her face. By rushing away, the woman was rightly and understandably protecting life and limb. Withdrawing from the man's vicinity was commonsensical; for her to continue walking past him would have been potentially harmful to her person. In doing so, she reacted rationally to a particular form of deviant behavior, behavior that seemed deranged and seemed to threaten to become more violent. (Being somewhat foolhardy myself, I simply walked past him.) We can designate such a reaction as *protective social control*—which results in avoidance of the offender—but, to emphasize the point, most responses to nonnormative behavior are not straightforwardly protective.

Formal Social Control

In Washington Square, the NYPD and the New York City Parks Department itself—specifically, the PEP, which constitutes an agency whose representatives (at the micro level)—exert social control by approaching park visitors and informing them that amplifiers violate park rules, warning skateboarders and bicyclists that they're not allowed to zoom through the park, telling smokers to put out their cigarettes, asking hawkers to show their permits to engage in commercial activity. Social control also includes multiple layers and instances of *organizational* control, "social control agencies"—on-the-job supervisors, managers of all kinds, the entire educational system, our religious leaders, everyone who works for mental hospitals, unemployment offices, politicians, social welfare workers, social workers, psychiatrists, the people at the IRS, INS, DMV, FBI, CIA, NSA, DoJ, DEA—the entire alphabet-soup panoply of agencies enforcing notions of what we *ought* to do and ought *not* to do—and what happens when we *do* what we ought not to do. For thousands of years, commentators on social rules have recognized society's functional need for some form of social control—a structure of rules that must be promulgated and enforced to protect the generic collective from anarchy, chaos, and disintegration. To be effective, rules and their enforcement should seem to the ordinary member of society to be legitimate, inevitable, necessary, and reasonable. The Hebrew Bible describes a "covenant" between God and Abraham, the first Jew; it is explicit about the sanctions the ancient Israelites should visit upon the person who curses his father and mother, has sex with an inappropriate partner, and ignores the distinction between "clean" and "unclean" beasts. The Nordic supremacist sociologist Edward Alsworth Ross wrote a book entitled *Social Control: A Survey of the Foundations of Order* (1902), stressing the importance of "controlling the delinquent class" (p. 52), but he seems to have believed that social control included preventing Asian immigration to the United States to avoid white America's "race suicide." (In the speech that led to his resignation from Stanford University in 1900, Ross stated that it would be better for "us," meaning the United States, "if we were to turn our guns upon every vessel bringing Japanese to our shores than to permit them to land.") In *The Social System* (1951), Talcott Parsons regarded deviance as a tendency on the part of one or more actors "to behave in such a way as to disturb the equilibrium of the interactive . . . system" (p. 250), and social control, an effort to restore that equilibrium. (Parsons was clearly not overly fond of deviance nor of putative threats to society's equilibrium.) The student of deviance is likely to argue that most nonnormative behavior does not threaten the social system's "equilibrium" and yet, much of it nonetheless does attract negative sanctioning. Just as important, multiple social systems may function within a given society without interfering with the others' functioning. The matter of social control has always been a major theoretical issue in the field of sociology, and has been a major concern of multiple philosophers, social theorists, and political thinkers for thousands of years, as well as religious and political systems in societies everywhere throughout human history.

The Park Enforcement Patrol are employees of the New York City Department of Parks and Recreation, whose mission is to ensure that the City's parks serve the public, a mission that banned activities may undermine or disrupt. Social control, the efforts to enforce a norm, including a rule, a law, and an ordinance, includes both formal and informal types. In principle, social control's mission is to ensure a workable version of the social order. A pair of PEP officers and, less frequently, members of the NYPD, patrol Washington Square, and surveillance cameras watch park-goers on an hour-by-hour, day-to-day basis, but for the sociologist, the paradigmatic deviance dynamic is measured by the informal action-reaction-interaction sequence, that is, what ordinary individuals say and do to and with one another. In fact, in Washington Square, formal rules, regulations, and ordinances are often ignored; the enforcement of norms there is probably more informal than determined by formal law enforcement.

But the obverse of this is that some ordinances are specific to New York City parks; certain behaviors that are regarded as acceptable elsewhere are formally banned in them—smoking cigarettes, riding bikes, skateboarding, feeding pigeons. Moreover, the person sitting next to you may not consider them wrongful, and the PEP officers citing you for committing the offense may not even consider the offense they are citing you for as *personally* offensive. Indeed, many strange or offensive behaviors are specifically *not* citable—to draw from the example of Fartman. For a century, battles have exploded about, around, and in Washington Square Park that reflect incommensurable, even conflicting, interpretations of what defines the soul, the heart, the essence of the place. They entail foundational issues such as who is welcome there and who isn't; what visitors may do and what they must be prohibited from doing; and who exercises *dominion* over the spirit and the appropriate protocol of Washington Square.

A brawl—more like a tussle—breaks out near the Washington Square fountain among four thirty-something white males who, judging by the way they are dressed, are indigents, and judging by the way they move and yell, are probably intoxicated as well. The altercation begins with some shoving, then finger pointing, finger wagging, grappling, shouting, and groaning; two of them hold out their fists like boxers and one takes off his shirt as if to say, I'm getting down to some serious fighting. I don't see a single punch landed, just a lot of flailing, though one of them—who, a few hours earlier, I was foolish enough to hand my pen to when he asked to look at it, then walked off with it in his possession—ends up sprawled on the ground. After about five minutes, two PEP officers approach them and they force the would-be pugilists to separate; sitting on the steps inside the fountain, the bumbling brawlers explain to the PEP what happened, with much gesticulating and vigorous body language. None of them are cited; indeed, it seems, no one involved was sober enough to have committed a violent offense.

As the PEP are walking away, one of the guys stands and shouts, presumably as an apology, "I feel like an idiot. I'm sorry. Everything's cool." The PEP stop about ten feet away from the men, turn around, and scrutinize them. An NYPD squad car appears and the two PEP talk to the driver. Then four NYPD approach on foot and the PEP officers talk with the NYPD, and then they all leave, the squad car circling the fountain. It stops on the other side, but soon drives off. It's clear that the appearance of the PEP and the NYPD was prophylactic—to keep a mini-fracas from becoming an all-out melee involving injurious fisticuffs—but if it *had* escalated, officers would have been there to break it up and, if necessary, deal with its consequences, namely, injury and hospitalization. The scuffle didn't even get close to that. I'm *impressed* by how quickly law enforcement showed up—in substantial and, as it turns out, disproportionate numbers. Three PEP and five NYPD represent the exercise of a great deal of social control, and the observer might be likely to wonder about such excess.

Thirty-two in-line skaters pour into the park from the pathway that enters at LaGuardia Place and roll past three PEP, two men and a woman, who are standing in front of me, watching them. "What are we going to do about the skaters?" one of the PEP asks. The woman walks toward and approaches one of the skaters, who has paused near a stone bench. "You know," she informs him, "skating isn't allowed in Washington Square Park." The skater blows a whistle and instantly, all of his companions make a hairpin turn and skate out of the park through the Schwartz Plaza exit. It is probably the swiftest, most direct, and most graceful cause-and-effect instance of the exercise of social control in response to a normative breach I've ever seen. (For a detailed listing of the "Rules and Regulations of the New York City Department of Parks & Recreation," go to www.nycgovparks.org/rules.)

Behind the Garibaldi statue, a middle-aged man who bears a strong resemblance to the late Philip Seymour Hoffman is sitting two benches away from me, drinking what appears to be orange juice out of a large Tropicana bottle. He appears drunk; his eyelids are half-closed and he has the slack, loose face of someone who is besotted. Two PEP, one a sergeant, the other substantially younger, who seems to be a rookie, spot and approach him. "Don't you know that consuming alcoholic beverages is illegal in the park?" the sergeant asks him. From where I sit, the drinker's response is incoherent, guttural, and slurred. "We're going to have to issue you a citation." The younger PEP takes a summons tablet out of his back pocket, fills out the form, rips it off the pad, and hands it to the seated man as his partner glares at the pickled park-goer, whose gaze is focused somewhere off in the distance. I scurry a few feet away so I can write down what I've just observed, unnoticed. Their task completed, the PEP pair walk toward the fountain as the seated man stares at the ticket in his hand, uncertain as to what to do next. While I'm scribbling these notes, the PEP pass by, and both glance at me suspiciously. Wondering how they *knew* the man was drinking alcohol, I rush over to the bench where the imbiber had been sitting, but he is gone. I walk toward the fountain circle in the direction the PEP had trooped off, but the officers are swallowed up in the crowd.

Tight and Loose Control Systems

Erving Goffman (1963) characterizes the situational involvement that is normatively and proprietarily demanded or expected of participants of specific settings or gatherings. In "loose" settings, such as "a park on a summer Saturday afternoon," he tells us, "a man does not have to closely attend to his surroundings and can exhibit his minimal situational presence by visibly loosening his tie and taking off his shoes, by dozing off, by wearing torn or rumpled clothing, by showing lessened concern about concealing belches" (p. 198). In the park, he may also interact with others latitudinally and casually by "quarreling, love-making (to a degree), or shouting to a friend coming up the path." No one would object if he were to "immerse himself in auto-involvement as he cleans out the wax from his ears, eats chicken from a basket, or massages the muscle of his leg" (p. 199).

In "tight" or "tighter" contexts, such as the ordination of a priest or a bishop, a wedding, a presidential inauguration, the performance of chamber music, a board meeting in which the CEO is summarizing the firm's previous quarter's profit and loss, "each person may be obliged to show constant orientation to the gathering as a whole and constant spirit of the occasion" (Goffman, 1963, p. 199). Even in the same sort of setting in different societies or communities, audiences are bound by varying degrees of "tightness" or "looseness." On the street, Parisians are expected *not* to express surprise at the appearance of unconventionally, unusually, or "oddly costumed" persons (p. 200). In a like manner, to repeat my request for a thought experiment, picture the shabbily dressed, grimy-faced homeless men who frequently inhabit and shuffle through Washington Square Park entering the shops of Oscar de la Renta, Giorgio Armani, or Tom Ford on Madison Avenue; chances are that the guards in these shops would politely but firmly escort the men back out onto the street. Clearly, in comparison with Washington Square, these exclusive men's clothing stores enforce a "tighter," more vigilant interpretation of a clearly defined norm regarding, in this case, appearance—as well as hygiene—not to mention impecuniousness.

Again, we are forced to confront the issue of how much control in a public space is too much and how little is too little. Erving Goffman provides illustrations of whether and to what extent an extreme freedom from the social and normative constraints usually imposed by bystanders produces a dangerous, chaotic environment for the modal visitor or denizen. "One individual's right to be lax in his orientation to the gathering," Goffman writes in his study of a male mental ward, "implies a duty on the part of others present to accept this laxity without taking corrective action" (1963, p. 207). In some of the wards, he explains, "patients had an understanding with attendants that it was permissible to sleep on the floor, drool, hallucinate, and spit into cups." Goffman observed that when "a patient urinated against a hot steam radiator to save himself the trouble of going to the toilet, fellow patients sitting in the cloud of evaporating urine seemed to appreciate that they had agreed to forego the right to respond with anything but a slight frown or ironic smile to what was happening around them" (p. 207). We may recall that "a man urinating in the bushes" attracted an 87 percent disapproval rating in Washington Square Park; as in the park, so it was in Goffman's mental ward—perhaps some inmates *disapproved* of such behavior, yet pretended to disattend to it.

Many sociologists and anthropologists—myself included—have observed criminal behavior without intervening; research on deviance and crime cannot be conducted in any other way. But many argue that this practice is not ethical. Of course, criminologists set aside their noninterventionist pretenses if the behavior in question includes rape or murder. My guess is, had they the capacity to prevent such actions, nearly all sociologists and criminologists would do so—but as we'll see, at least one sociologist did not stop or report the crime when he observed a sexual assault. To remind the reader, if criminal behavior veers beyond a certain point with respect to harm, it threatens the society with disorder; social control attempts to restore the social order. But not all societies exercise the same measure of control, nor do all collectivities within a given society. *Tight* systems of control incline us in one direction, *loose* systems in another. We began our exploration through the permissive habitat of Washington Square by raising these questions, and yet we don't have a definitive answer—nor, in my estimation, could we. According to Nachman Ben-Yehuda, it depends in large part on how much the illicit behavior challenges the status quo.

A Dialogue with a Sociologist of Deviance on Social Control

It's the summer of 2016 and I'm sitting with Nachman Ben-Yehuda, a friend and a sociologist of deviance (1985, 1990, 2013) on a bench in Washington Square that's adjacent to a pathway just west of the fountain. Dozens of people stream by in singletons and multiples. I ask him to appreciate the diversity of humanity passing by this spot—possibly more diversity than obtains in any other place on earth. One by one, I take note of the variety of the human species parading before us. "You talk of diversity here," he responds, "but consider this: In this park, most people are very well-behaved. Hardly anyone commits serious deviance in Washington Square. No revolution is being plotted here, no murders are committed, no robberies or rapes—no serious crime of any kind. This place is not a breeding ground of deviance. Everybody gives room to others to do their thing. Nothing earth-shaking is happening in this place."

"I'm not sure if I follow you, Nachman. There's very little crime here, but that's the point. People are civil to one another as long as their behavior doesn't infringe on the rights of others. They exercise informal social control on one another for the preservation of a common good. Unless you want to say that crime is the only form of serious deviance and any other type of deviance is trivial."

"Well, one of the issues you have to address is change over time. There were bigger rifts and challenges in the past than is true now. Race and civil rights used to be a more important source of conflict in the fifties and sixties. Now, no race riots, no civil rights movement, no civil rights demonstrations in the park, and a black man was elected and reelected president of the United States. Race isn't as much of an issue as it was in the past. And there's no major conflict that's comparable to Vietnam, just smaller ones, so there are no antiwar protests in Washington Square. Women have rights they didn't have and have won lots of political victories. Change over time means that there are no serious schisms tearing the country apart, so diversity has been tamped down or swallowed up, both here in the park and throughout the society. And you also have to look at differences among parks. You see more crazies in Washington Square than in Tompkins Square Park and Union Square. Craziness and other extreme eccentricities are more accepted here and not there, and that's why the mentally ill come here—they know they'll be tolerated."

"But that's what I'm talking about. You're making my point exactly. But if they go beyond a certain point, we, or the authorities, will come down on them."

"Craziness doesn't challenge the system. What we see here is the successful exercise of social control," my friend responds. "People here are being controlled."

"*By whom?*" I ask. "And to whose end? And how? In what way? What's the *nature* of this control? There's a lot of angry people in this country. White, uneducated males who worked for industries that left for China, left for Mexico—they *had* a good job, made a good wage, they had medical care, hospitalization, retirement—now they don't. That's all gone. They got nothing now. Flipping burgers at McDonald's for chump change. They're pissed. They think the blacks and the effete snobs in New York and San Francisco are making monkeys of them. These are the guys who are going to vote for Donald Trump—angry white males. This is a big, big rift. Who's controlling them? They're not being controlled—or at least, not by the people in Washington. Frankly, I think the controlologists missed them. The angry white males want to control everybody else—or at least they don't want others to control them. Plus, they want the jobs, the money, the respect, and the power they lost. They want it all back. They're regionalists or nationalists in an increasingly global, internationalist world—and they aren't getting on board with the program. Where's the social control here? This is a big rift and they're not falling into line."

"The question still boils down to a matter of control—this an environment in which a shifting crowd of extremely varied and diverse people are being controlled by invisible and taken-for-granted forces."

"Nachman, this all sounds very mystical. I don't see actual people engaged in identifiable control. I return to the question: Who's doing what? Anyway, *these* people are not the ones in West Virginia, Idaho, or Mississippi. Those people want what they used to have."

"Think about Stan Cohen's notion of the *deviancy control system*. Picture this place, Washington Square Park, as a mini-society that's a lot like a sea, and the control system is like a fishing net. There are people with authority casting the net, fishing for deviants, who are caught, punished, corrected, tossed back into the sea. Then the cycle starts all over again. The agents of the social control system make decisions or assumptions about the net, as do the fish: where the net is located, how large the holes are, when it is pulled up, these sorts of considerations. And how the fish react to these matters. When socially and culturally varied people enter Washington Square, they have a good idea what to expect in advance. They eventually realize that certain kinds of behavior are acceptable in the park here while other kinds of behavior are not. Socialization is taken for granted. It's in the background, it's the foundation; it has already taken place. And the sorts of deviance that were allowed in 1959 are very different from those that are tolerated now. There are shared understandings about what's acceptable and what's not, which reveals the power and influence of the cultural socialization processes at work. It's like a black hole; you do not see it but then you see its consequences. You see *that* it works—the results of its existence."

"But I don't see any control here," I reply. "There are no fish. Nobody's being caught or processed. The Parks Enforcement Patrol walks by, sure, but we just saw a park ranger do nothing to a skateboarder who whizzed by; all he did was take out his cell phone and call his superior. Nothing happened to the kid. I've seen PEP smile and say hello to people who are feeding the pigeons and the squirrels and just walk by them, but their feeding is a violation of the statutes."

"These are not important. They don't shake up the system. If skateboarding kid had hit somebody, that would be a different story," Nachman responds.

"Yes, of course, and that's the point. The social control here is mainly informal. The PEP and the NYPD almost never *apprehend* anyone; they hardly ever take a suspect into custody; they mostly just warn offenders. Notice that the skateboarder left the park and didn't come back. Nachman, look at that guy" [pointing to a clearly homeless man, barefoot and dressed in tattered clothing]. I've heard other homeless guys call him 'Floyd.'"

"He probably lives in a shelter. Imagine him walking into the lobby of One or Two Fifth Avenue, demanding to go up to an apartment to visit somebody. They would kick him out onto the street."

"Of course they would. But those buildings are private. Out here, he's tolerated. People look the other way."

"Take a good look at him. He's a social isolate. People ignore him. He's shirtless, and shoeless and he's begging people for money. Look! He's begging the hot dog guy—a guy who earns a living by *selling* hot dogs—he's begging him to give him a couple of hot dogs! Look, the hot dog guy ignored him, now he's babbling to himself. Now he's asking that guy over there for a cigarette."

Floyd is lying, face up, on the stone bench and says to no one in particular, "Y'all live in Houston?" in a southern accent. He walks over to the guy who plays guitar at the walkway that exits south to Thompson Street. Floyd asks him for a dollar but the singer ignores him and Floyd walks away. "I'd say Floyd is a pretty serious deviant, wouldn't you? He gets rejected everywhere, by everybody. He can't establish interpersonal contact because he's too needy and too weird."

"It depends on what you mean about the guy," Nachman says. "It depends on whether we're talking about the interpersonal or the structural level. And interpersonally, we are *already* shaped by the structural level." We get up and stretch our legs, walk around the fountain several times, and stop at the northeast quadrant, continuing our discussion of deviance and social control. "All these guys," Nachman says, "Foucault, Stan Cohen, the contrologists, they would all say that, by its very nature, deviance is controlled."

"*Of course* it is, by definition—I mean, it's *deviance*, deviance is that which society *attempts* to curtail or control—but controlled *by whom*? *Who* does the controlling? Again, this seems like some mysterious force. It sounds like a tautology—true by definition. The question is, how successful is the control? Naturally society, or some social unit, attempts to control deviance, that's in the nature of the beast, but what *kind* of control are we talking about? Who's doing what? It *seems* trivial, but it involves people and behavior that most of us don't want to have anything to do with, and that seems pretty serious to me. We're *all* socialized to behave a certain way, but the socialization doesn't always take. Sometimes it works, sometimes it doesn't. The consensus is high for some things but not for others. Nachman, I did this little survey of sixty people in the park. I asked them about what they considered wrongful, behavior like feeding the pigeons, women appearing topless, amplified music, drinking alcohol, skateboarding, that sort of thing. I got some consensus from them about certain behaviors, but for others, very little. Nobody likes seeing littering or a man peeing in public, or a naked man walking around. But for some issues, the consensus was nil."

"But again, that's not *seriously* wrongful behavior," Nachman responds. He sniffs the air. "What's that smell? I smell urine." We turn around. Standing in front of one of the stone benches behind us there's a barefoot guy whose shabby garb tells us he's homeless, there's a pool of liquid at his feet, and his face wears a contorted mask of guilt.

"Let's move away from here," I suggest. We walk to the southwest side of the fountain circle. "See, we avoided that guy," I say, "and our reaction to him was strictly interpersonal. We moved away and withdrew any possibility of sociability with him. Nachman, *he* is seriously deviant. What sort of social control just got exercised? We're just two guys, and yet other people, one by one, are going to do the same thing."

"We've already been socialized to reject that guy. All of this happened decades ago, but it stays with us, it still exerts control over us. A consensus about what's wrongful behavior has been built up. It gets exercised when people react the way we did. The work has already been done and, yes, we do exert social control. But this is a result of structural and cultural forces. It's part of power arrangements in the society. The controlologists would say it starts at the top and it's relentlessly exercised. It serves its purpose. There's little room for serious diversity. Think of Socrates. He got put to death because he corrupted ancient Greek youth. That's not going to happen anymore because in America, and in all the Western societies, they've already achieved widespread agreement about *seriously* wrongful and rightful behavior. By the way, everyone remembers the name of Socrates but no one recalls the judges who condemned him. Who were they?" Nachman has a sly smile on his face.

"I have no idea who they were," I respond. "That's very interesting."

"Nobody knows. Asking that question is not original to me. Stan Cohen told me that."

"Let me tell you something. In 1961, there was a demonstration right here at the fountain about the right to perform in the park. About ten folk singers were arrested and taken to a police station. The next day there was a headline in the *New York Mirror*—a newspaper that doesn't exist anymore—that read, '3000 Beatniks Riot in Village.' The news story was hugely overblown—in fact, there were only five hundred people in the whole demonstration, there was no riot, and they weren't even *beatniks*, they were folk singers, and only ten were taken into custody."

"It sounds like Stan Cohen's so-called riot in Clacton. It started a moral panic about delinquent youth. That sort of thing'll never happen here again. There's too much agreement about what's permitted and what shouldn't happen. It's all been settled, and Stan would say it's the successful exercise of social control."

"I still don't get it, Nachman. These are basic issues and lots of these deviancies are also considered wrongful elsewhere. So, where's the co-ordinated control?"

"This is a pretty tame place. Nothing earth-shakingly wrongful takes place here. We've been successfully socialized to act in a certain way."

"Well, I still don't get it."

So, who is right? Who's wrong? The answer may be somewhat elusive—in fact, there may be no straightforward right or wrong here—but what is clear is that social control is the foundation stone of the sociological conception of deviance. I tend to emphasize informal control and keep trying to bring it into the micro situation, while Nachman is operating on a larger canvas—the macro, institutional structure of an entire society.

Either way, sociologists of deviance and social organization regard control as a bulwark against societal disorganization, disorder, and disintegration: If there were no audiences monitoring and sanctioning the actor's behavior, no negative consequences to violating norms that others accept as valid and binding, actors would be free to do whatever they wanted, much of it wrongful, harmful to others, destructive to the social fabric. But a multiple number of micro orders may challenge or attempt to undermine the larger dominant structure. The formulation of Thomas Hobbes leads to the inevitable question: "How is social order possible?" And the answer is virtually always: the establishment and exercise of social control—efforts to ensure conformity to a norm, to acceptable behavior. *But according to whose definition?*

Foucault, Cohen, et al.: The Controlologists

In Discipline and Punish: The Birth of the Prison (1979), Michel Foucault devotes three pages to a description of his most famous—and notorious—example of the barbarism of the traditional exercise of social control: the torture and execution of Robert François Damiens, a domestic servant, who, in 1757, feebly attempted to assassinate King Louis XV of France by stabbing him with a small penknife. Damiens's torture was gruesome; his tendons were slashed and his body was ripped apart, limb by limb, by harnessed horses. The attending crowd cheered as his presumably still-alive torso was burned at the stake (1979, pp. 3–6). Then Foucault shifts forward in time eighty years and describes a timetable drawn up by one Leon Faucher, a journalist and politician, who proposed, in meticulous detail, a systematic program of a proposed prisoner's schedule, item by item, activity by activity. During these eight decades, Foucault argued, the prison system in the West had become transformed from a barbaric crowd spectacle that entailed the infliction of severe physical punishment on the body of the prisoner (the "iron fist") to a modern regimen of enlightened, rational resocialization of his mind, through observation, instruction, scientific knowledge, psychological expertise, and the sophisticated, judicious application of influence (the "velvet glove"). The penal system is no longer geared to revenge or even retribution, nor to the physical punishment of the prisoner's body, in large part because such sanctions are ineffective—they do not touch his soul or transform his thinking or feeling or, in long run, his behavior. In contrast, a humane and enlightened exercise of the state's, and the institution's, power transforms the way the miscreant, the behaviorally errant human being, functions. Today, most social scientists and criminologists recognize that the late-eighteenth-century execution of Robert Damiens and Leon Faucher's nineteenth-century convict timetable were not paradigmatic or characteristic of the state-sponsored social control of their day. Most penologists would say that Foucault selected extreme examples to demonstrate his point; he aspired to literary rather than empirical truth. The penal system was not characteristically as barbaric in Damiens's day as his execution implies nor as enlightened as Faucher's timetable then seemed to indicate; certainly today, punishing the prisoner's body remains in effect, at least in the United States. *Public* executions have not existed here since 1936, but most states (thirty-one) can impose the death penalty, fourteen hundred prisoners have been executed since 1976, twenty-eight in 2015 and twenty in 2016, and the mass media—which, as Foucault argued, have replaced public spectacle—report on some of those executions, pleasing much of the public, a majority of whom favor the death penalty (63%, according to the latest Gallup poll).

But Foucault was saying something broader and more sweeping than addressing the dynamics of state-sponsored execution. His conception of the prison extended vastly beyond treatment and rehabilitation of the prisoner. Yes, of course, society has transformed—and reformed—the prison and the prisoner. But much more than that, argues Foucault, *the prison has transformed the society*. The enlightened prison has come to be built along the lines proposed by English utilitarian philosopher Jeremy Bentham (1748–1832), which are those of a *panopticon*, where a small staff can monitor and control the behavior of a large number of inmates. Foucault proposed that society has become one vast, gigantic panopticon, where agents of social control can observe and sanction the behavior of miscreants as well as the society at large—far more today, in the twenty-first century, than in Foucault's day (he died in 1984); consider surveillance cameras, space satellites, drones, spy networks, snitches, informants, and the like. In fact, suggests Foucault, the distinction between judicial confinement and punishment on the one hand and civilian "institutions of discipline" on the other has disappeared to the point where all social control constitutes "a great carceral continuum that diffused penitentiary techniques into the most innocent disciplines," sanctioning "even the slightest illegality, the smallest irregularity, deviation or anomaly, the threat of delinquency" (1979, p. 297). The authority that sentences and incarcerates "infiltrates all those other authorities that supervise, transform, correct, improve." Nothing distinguishes them except by degree; in its functioning, the state's power to punish "is not essentially different from that of curing or educating" (p. 303). The fundamental question here is how members of the society came to tolerate and accept a centralized authority that wielded the authority to punish miscreants. Legal carceral power has become generalized to normative power. The *mechanism of discipline*, Foucault declares, is to *suffuse the power of the carceral apparatuses into omnipresent mechanisms of discipline*. "Judges of normality are present everywhere," Foucault declares. "We are in the society of the teacher-judge, the doctor-judge, the education-judge, the social worker–judge." It is "on them that the universal reign of the normative is based" so that everyone in the modern society subjects each individual "to his body, his gestures, his behavior, his aptitudes, his achievements" (p. 304). In the Western world, the prison network is the paradigm and indeed the wellspring of *generalizing and normalizing power*. And more to Ben-Yehuda's point, by the time in their lives when park-goers encounter one another in a locale such as Washington Square, they have already been subject to society's normative power, and are unlikely to engage in the sorts of behavior that substantially threaten the social order.

In his book on social control, Stanley Cohen complained that the sociological study of social control had "lost its political thrust" and had become "less structural and more social-psychological"; it had, in fact, become something of a "Mickey Mouse" concept, "a neutral term to cover all social processes to induce conformity," ranging from infant socialization to public execution. "Oppression, repression and suppression now become the normal properties of the society." Consensus has become either nonexistent or else "precariously maintained by awesome and cunningly disguised systems of social control" (1985, p. 5). "Social control has become Kafka-land, a paranoid landscape in which things are done to us, without knowing when, why or by whom, or even that they are being done" (pp. 6–7). But the professional literature, Cohen declares, "reveals little of such nightmares and science fiction projections. Textbooks . . . still use an older and blander language of social control: how norms are internalized, how consensus is achieved, how social control evolves from pre-industrial to industrial societies" (p. 7). But the fact is, Cohen's notion is extremely narrow; the more widely accepted conceptualization of control, the one I adopt here, which realistically takes into account all parties who influence us to act in certain ways, is indeed much broader.

Cohen's notion of social control centered on *organized responses* to criminal, deviant, and problematic behavior. He was interested in how the system of repression works and how the recipient of social control experiences being processed by the system. Cohen believed that organized responses to deviance, problematic behavior, and supposed wrongdoing are elements or features of an interlocking system of agencies that address and deal with delinquency, drug abuse, mental disorder, crime, sexual irregularities, family instability, and pathology. The state is increasingly involved "in the business of deviancy control—the eventual development of a centralized, rationalized and bureaucratic apparatus for the control and punishment of crime and delinquency and the care or cure of other types of deviants." Supposed experts divide up the universe of deviance into types according to a vocabulary and body of knowledge legitimated and wielded by themselves and deal monopolistically with each according to this diagnosis, resulting in the increased segregation of deviants into *asylums*: "penitentiaries, prisons, mental hospitals, reformatories and other closed, purpose-built institutions. The prison emerges as the dominant instrument for changing undesirable behavior and as the favoured form of punishment" (p. 13). As Foucault argued, the physical punishment of the body has declined as an instrument for punishment and rehabilitation, to be replaced by more mind- and psychology-centered methodologies dedicated to transforming the miscreant though segregation, isolation, and rehabilitation.

Where one stands influences what one sees. Much of the relevance and validity—the resonance—of what Michel Foucault, Stanley Cohen, and their allies, the controlologists (Scull, 1988; Lowman, Menzies, and Palys, 1987), argue depends on matters of definition and emphasis. I define social control as the effort of the society—or the units within society—to sanction counternormativity, ensure the social order, and regulate itself by discouraging that which is wrongful and supposedly harmful, and encouraging what its members, or the powers that be, consider beneficial. In my scheme of things, social control is predicated on constructionism. By that I mean that what's *regarded* as disruptive or harmful, and what is seen as beneficent, is socially and culturally institutionalized in the first place. Even more basic, a given specific, concrete act has to be conceptualized as a member of a larger category of things that are supposedly good or bad. Laws concretize these categories and establish state-sponsored penalties for enacting what's defined as wrongful. Let's be clear about this: Social control is not entirely or always benign; it has a strong political and ideological component (Ben-Yehuda, 1990), and in authoritarian regimes, its minions routinely trample on human rights. In the old South, lynching was a form of exercising social control—*for* the hegemonic racist white power structure—by "keeping Negroes in their place." Even in contemporary democracies, some types of control repress the freedoms of their citizens. Social control is an instrument, a process, a social and political mechanism, not an outcome.

Deviance and Control in Washington Square

Social life is a continual back-and-forth, action-reaction-interaction sequence and, in a busy public place, *someone* is usually around to observe and object to someone else's supposed wrongdoing. One party, the "actor," engages in a particular form of conduct; another party, an "audience," reacts to the behavior of the other, defines wrongfulness in a certain manner, and reacts accordingly; the first party, presumably chastised, may or may not continue the interaction. What is wrongful to one party may be acceptable to the other. Formal social control—as we saw, here, the PEP and the NYPD—claims dominion over the entire enterprise, a claim that may be contested by one or the other of the contending parties, but, relative to the universe of the entire public, formal agents of social control are in the distinct minority. There's always a chance that a member of the public at large will report a hypothetical malfeasance to the authorities, but for minor offenses, such reports are atypical. Informal social control—unofficial, interpersonal reactions to putative wrongdoing by audiences—is far more common and, in all likelihood, more influential. The wonder of it all is that most of these interchanges are resolved more or less peacefully, and the social order remains pretty much intact.

Deviance is context bound and time bound; what's considered wrongful depends in part on *where* and *when* the actor performs it. Contemporary Washington Square is a kind of community, a tiny one, and what a few parties do may negatively impact on the rest of them. At the foot of the Garibaldi statue, a PEP officer tells a young guy with a small, triangular-shaped electric guitar to disconnect it. The guitarist refuses, saying he won't do it. They have an argument. The PEP says he'll give him a summons and it's going to cost him a $250 fine. It goes back and forth. "Listen, pal, I'm just trying to work with you here, I don't want to give you the fine, but you gotta disconnect the guitar." The guitarist slowly, reluctantly, expressing visible annoyance, unplugs the guitar and puts it back in its case. The PEP officer says "Have a nice day," and walks away. The guy with the guitar clenches his fist and says to his companion, with a certain amount of anger, "You know, this gets me so mad, I wanna . . ." and he brandishes his fist. Of course, the young man does not punch the park officer; he restrains the impulse. Judging by the expression on his face, however, he stays angry for another fifteen minutes, when I walk away.

But the fact is, the rules are unevenly—though usually judiciously— enforced. Two men in their twenties are performing just south of the fountain—an electronic guitar and a boom-box percussion. They have a smallish audience, including four young women taking their pictures on their cell phones. A New York City Parks Department cruiser stops near them and a PEP officer gets out and talks to the guitarist. He nods and she gets back into the vehicle and drives off; within a few seconds, they resume playing. I assumed she told him that no amps are allowed, so I wait for their break to talk to them. After a five-minute riff, the young women alternately applaud and take their picture, and I walk up to the guitarist, who's now smoking a vape cigarillo. He's just told the older guy that they are not buskers and are not collecting money. "Did that PEP tell you to stop playing because of amps?" I ask the guitarist. "No," he says, "she said fifteen minutes till quiet time."

"I'm surprised," I say.

He says, "So was I."

I exit the park under the Arch and turn right; affixed to the fence next to the sidewalk I notice three signs, one after the other, the third of which reads, "Musical Instruments may not be played in the Park between 10 pm and 8 am. Please respect others." In this case, the "others" are the neighbors of the park. I check the time; it's 10:30. Plenty of flexibility all around. This is the genteel way of doing things; discretion and communality seem to be the twin lodestones around which Washington Square authority exercises social control. The PEP told the musicians to stop, and they did, at their flexible schedule; the officers did not issue a citation.

Two PEP, a man and a woman, walk by me. As they're walking west, a boy perhaps twelve years old carrying a skateboard is walking east, just inside the fountain area. The man says to the boy, "You know, there's no skateboarding in the park." A broad, gleeful grin breaks out on the boy's face, and he slams the skateboard to the ground, pushes it forward, and hops on, zooming off on it. The PEP stop and watch but do not pursue him. "I can't believe it," the man says to the woman. "He skated away right in front of us." They watch him until he disappears, then they turn right and walk south, in the opposite direction. A minute later, an older boy, in his late teens, possibly twenty years old, zooms by them on a skateboard, going west. They do not chase him.

As we saw, by glancing at the signs posted at the park entrances, everyone who walks into Washington Square knows that using amplification without a permit violates a New York City Park ordinance, as does skateboarding. It makes sense because amplification is contrary to the rules of civility: It forces everyone in every corner of the park to listen to the loudest music, and this would drown out the music of nonamplified players. Multiple musical groups do perform simultaneously in the park—during one afternoon, I counted seven clusters of musicians playing—but if all the instruments were amplified, their simultaneous sounds would become a cacophony. However, from a distance of a few dozen feet away, most nonamplified music (our clamorous-sounding drummer excepted) is not loud and can be ignored. Rather than restricting the rights of park-goers, in a sense, the "no amplification" rule expands them, allowing more speech makers and music makers to be heard; it is, in fact, a lesson in civility. And skateboarding? Its violation of public civility inheres in the fact that a reckless skateboarder can do serious harm to children and the frail and elderly. The dissonance of competing amplified musicians assaults all listeners; the din is inescapable. A collision with a speeding skateboarder offends only one person— but potentially, all of us; in some cases, only the nimble and the alert can avoid it. Yet the skateboarders I've talked to are confident of their skills and assure me that they'd never bump into, let alone hurt, anyone. It is in the thicket of such dilemmas that the PEP must fashion a reasonable and sensible-seeming path.

In important respects, Washington Square is the opposite of Foucault's panopticon. Official agents of social control ignore most violations of the park's ordinances, and exercise social control *mostly* by their presence. Moreover, for the most part, park visitors factor one another's rights into their equation of right and wrong, and the line-of-sight from the central fountain area allows, as I said earlier, *the many to view the many*—quite a different proposition from Bentham's hypothetical prison and Foucault's reformulation of it. Still, acts that the majority would consider unacceptable behavior—our loud Heineken guzzlers, for instance—are committed not by the majority but by the few. Everyone in the fountain area, including the PEP and the NYPD, can *see* the dealers at work, but as long as they stick to marijuana, don't sell to minors, and stay in their space, not much is done about their illegal deeds. Social control is exercised in the square, but Foucault's vision fails to illuminate its dynamics.

The most outstanding feature of serious or felonious crime in Washington Square Park today is that there is very little of it. (Technically, a felony is a crime that can draw a penalty of more than a year in prison.) This does not mean that we should therefore ignore it; indeed, it's my job to venture an explanation of *why* felonies are so rare here. A great deal of criminological research centers on victimology—that is, the relationship among locale, time, and circumstance, as well as social category of criminal victimization versus perpetration. Suffice it to say that the park's location, its historical tradition, the tendency of its visitors to practice sociability, and the clientele it attracts, its design (a sight-line from the fountain to much of the rest of the park), as well as the effectiveness of its mechanisms of formal and informal social control, have a great deal to do with how little predatory crime takes place within its borders.

Washington Square Park is not a typical park. As I've said multiple times, serious crime is relatively rare there, partly because the park is usually relatively well populated, partly because of its multiple surveillance cameras, and partly because, in spite of its substantial size, the line-of-sight view that the observer has from the fountain or center to the park's peripheries is fairly good. (The park closes at midnight and opens at six in the morning.) Surveillance by the PEP and/or the NYPD *somewhere* in the park is more or less continuous, but in any given locale, it is fitful. The media report on crime in Washington Square in part because it is news when it happens, and serious assaults have taken place in years other than, but not during, recent years. But less serious crime, the infraction of Parks Department ordinances, as well as much "deviant" behavior, does take place, and fairly frequently.

These are some of the factors, I suggest, that constitute the keys that help us unlock the mysteries of Washington Square's deviance and social control conundrum. Would Thomas Hobbes have agreed with me? I'd love to hop into a time machine and put the question to him.

* * *

Interview with Communications Officer, NYPD Sixth Precinct

This interview was conducted in the Sixth Precinct station house in Greenwich Village, with James Alberici, communications officer, NYPD, who indicates that laws, rules, and regulations are mitigated and interpreted by individual officer discretion—a point made by Jerome Skolnick over half a century ago in his classic *Justice without Trial*. Still, there seems to be a common core of agreement with regard to how to handle the more serious infractions.

ERICH: What do you think is the most important mission that the NYPD has in patrolling Washington Square Park?

OFFICER ALBERICI: Keeping the peace. Maintaining order. Seeing that the people involved get along.

ERICH: In your estimation, in what ways is Washington Square different from other New York City parks, for instance, Bryant Park, Union Square, or Thompkins Square?

OFFICER ALBERICI: They're all different. The NYU students come here, and the neighborhood is different from the others. Tompkins Square, Bryant Park, they used to have a serious drug problem, now they've been abated. Washington Square isn't as problematic as the other places.

ERICH: What do patrol officers do when they witness a violation—smoking, drinking, off-leash dogs, riding a bike or a skateboard, that sort of thing?

OFFICER ALBERICI: We prefer to issue a warning. It makes more sense than issuing citations. You get to know who the offenders are. If they repeat the offense, you can get more serious with them, maybe issue a summons the second or third time. A first-time offender, a warning is intended to discourage them from repeating the violation.

ERICH: There's a theory called the "broken windows" theory, Kelling and Wilson [1982], it's that if law enforcement ignores petty offenses, the offender will be emboldened to engage in more serious violations, even crimes. Yet, in the square, there are many minor violations and very few serious crimes. So, is that a refutation of the broken windows theory?

OFFICER ALBERICI: I believe in the broken windows theory—to a degree. But when you issue a warning, the people know what the law is, they're aware that they've violated it and that we know it, and they're discouraged from engaging in more serious offenses. It works for most people. Once warned, most people abide by the law. On the other hand, if the warning results in belligerence, then we can take sterner steps—if they get irate as a result of just the warning, then we have to act. But each person is different, each situation is different, each interaction is different. We operate on a case-by-case basis.

ERICH: What are the most common violations that take place in the park?

OFFICER ALBERICI: Alcohol, smoking, marijuana use.

ERICH: What about the most serious offense?

OFFICER ALBERICI: Maybe drums at night. Making loud noises. Amplified sound. Bothering the neighborhood, keeping them up at night.

ERICH: What's the secret to Washington Square's success? Why is it so safe and peaceful?

OFFICER ALBERICI: People come to the park to have a good time. Nobody's looking for trouble. Yet, years ago, the park was not as nice.

ERICH: Within a week's time, how often does a patrol officer in the park witness a violation so serious that they would take a suspect into custody?

OFFICER ALBERICI: I don't think, even in a week's time, the average officer takes a suspect into custody.

ERICH: If you were to give a rookie officer advice on patrolling Washington Square, what would it be?

OFFICER ALBERICI: Be willing to listen. Approach every individual *as* an individual. Sure, there's a potential that something really bad can happen—that's true everywhere. Especially at night. But an informed flexibility makes the most sense.

ERICH: If you were to characterize the difference between Washington Square at night and during the day, what would you say?

OFFICER ALBERICI: It's Mayberry during the day, Bangkok at night. It's amazing that there isn't more crime at night. It's chaotic, a madhouse. But it's safe then, too.

ERICH: Thank you very much for your time and your views, Detective Alberici. I appreciate it.

OFFICER ALBERICI: You're quite welcome.

5

Race

On the performance stage at the Garibaldi Plaza, a brass/woodwind ensemble, all white teenagers, are playing "On Broadway." They've attracted a crowd of thirty or forty listeners, and when they complete a tune, about half the audience wanders off, to be replaced by a more or less equal number, who stop to listen to the next selection. They then play some New Orleans jazz, but when they finish, two Park Enforcement Patrol officers show up, and several of the band's reps walk over to them. Wearing an officious look on his face, one of the PEP announces, "We need a permit." The music director hands him several stapled-together sheets of paper. A permit it is, and they seem satisfied, so they back off. After two more musical numbers, the band begins breaking down the chairs and the music stands.

As the band packs up, across the walkway from the stage, in front of the Garibaldi statue, a middle-aged black guy begins playing a number on the tenor sax. The PEP, one male, one female, approach him, interrupt his performance, and begin discussing its legality. They say that they "don't want to risk a lawsuit." They're standing next to a woman who seems to be affiliated with the band, probably an official of some kind, but clearly unaffiliated with the saxophone player. The sax player responds, with more than a hint of annoyance, "Oh, a black man demanding respect. When the kids were leaving, you could see it on their faces—the disrespect. You're running a number on me. And it's because I'm a black man. I'm going to demand my rights. I'm going to educate you. You hear me play!" he insists. "That wasn't enough? I don't play like any musician you ever heard. I'm coming at you with that black shit in your face! All day long!"

As the dispute continues, a glee club chorus mounts the stage. The nub of the issue began about permits and documentation, but it seems to have morphed into a matter of race. "You can look me up on the Internet," he pridefully tells the PEP officers. "I'm there." Clearly, the—

organized, officially sanctioned, white—chorus, like the musical ensemble, exemplifies a conventional, and authorized, musical organization that is not requesting donations, while the saxophone player, who is black, is a busker who's soliciting contributions, and whose performance falls outside the NYC Parks "Regulated Uses" and within its scope of "Prohibited Uses." In short, the Parks Department defines the saxophone player as a *deviant* performer. However, within five minutes, the beef seems to have exhausted itself, and the PEP leave. Now the representative of the music group and the sax player seem to be having an amiable conversation; whatever source of disagreement they had before seems to have dissipated.

My guess is that a conflict-resolution observer would say that the female band-rep managed to defuse a potentially antagonistic situation. She asks about the fact that the sax is silver colored. The chorus sings "The River Is Wide." There's a violinist and a cellist on stage playing with them. The sax player is talking to an Asian man who is standing next to both of them. The woman comments, "They are *so* cute!" meaning the teenagers in the chorus. The sax player laughs. They express rapport with one another. He's talking at length with the Asian man, showing him pictures on his cell phone. The Asian man is laughing. The woman says to the sax player, "I gotta walk away now. I gotta walk away." They hug and laugh. The saxophone player continues talking with the Asian guy, then asks him to watch his instrument, which he has placed in its case, then he exits toward University Place. About a half-hour later, the sax player returns, picks up his instrument, and begins playing "For All We Know." He ends to polite applause. A young woman drops a bill into his case and begins conversing with him. The Asian guy joins in. The sax player leans down, picks up and collects his money and stuffs it in his pocket, packs up his instrument, shakes the Asian guy's hand, thanks him, and leaves by the same exit, this time carrying his saxophone. Weeks later, I talk to the saxophone player. He tells me that, several years ago, he sued the Department of Parks for harassment and won a substantial settlement. His name is Dusty Rhodes, and he frequently plays in Garibaldi Plaza.

The institutional and societal mechanisms are such that race inadvertently yet *perforce* plays a role in the square, while, in this case, the social/interactional attempt by the officials only *mitigated*, for a time, the larger forces at work. As Hakim Hasan—former proofreader, bookseller, and contributor to Mitchell Duneier's volume, *Sidewalk* (1999)—explained to me, in his account at the end of this chapter, blacks and whites may be treated in an equal fashion in the park, yet race is an *elongated* issue; it plays itself out obliquely but with certainty. The U.S. economy has not yet fully assimilated African Americans into the economic mainstream—in the music industry as well as elsewhere—in the same proportions as it has whites. Hence, more likely to be outside that mainstream, some blacks must innovate in order to achieve what most of us want—a chance to ply our craft, express ourselves, earn enough to live comfortably, and make our way through life with a measure of self-respect, security, and well-being. *Some* of us who haven't yet achieved the middle-class ideal seek unconventional means to achieve that end (Merton, 1938). These alternate paths may be somewhat different for persons of color than for whites.

I cross the fountain circle and settle into a bench along the double pathway leading to Washington Place, near the Holley Plaza. To my left about twenty feet away, there's a man, perhaps in his midthirties, sitting on a bench, screaming; I move closer to hear what he is saying. He seems to be addressing a young Asian woman, probably an NYU student, sitting on the grass, who's reading, studiously ignoring his incoherent oration. "During World War Two, the Nazis made the Japanese honorary Aryans. That's what you are—an honorary Aryan!" the man shouts—on and on and on, along politico-racial themes. Judging by his referents, he has had some higher education, but at some point along the way, he seems to have fallen off the middle-class escalator, probably because of his mental disorder, and now he's unsupervised and unmedicated.

The man is both in and out of place here. Everyone ignores him, but neither the PEP nor the NYPD descend upon him and trundle him away. In many places, a screaming black man would raise alarm bells—would cause a visitor to feel threatened and complain to the police, who would activate law enforcement; here, he's simply a clanging, discordant presence. He has wisely chosen the setting in which to rant. The majority of the people streaming by him are white, but they seem not to feel menaced by his presence. Would visitors to a less cosmopolitan park be more likely to feel that he could become violent? Possibly. Still, the man is engaged in deviant behavior—his screaming violates the informal norms of public behavior to an extreme degree—and yet, he is simply ignored. How does his behavior intersect with the fact that he is black? I didn't see any evidence of his race making a difference; the man could have been white as far as anyone could tell from the reactions of bystanders— they would have ignored him either way. Judging from the fact that only 2 percent of the population of Greenwich Village is black (and this man is very unlikely to be among that tiny minority), it is clear that the man does not live in this neighborhood; he chose to come *here* rather than to the community parks near his residence. And thinking about *that* seems interesting.

As Hakim Hasan explains, Washington Square is not a utopia—all of us have an elongated life that stretches before and after our appearance in the park—but, for the most part, it is a place that welcomes diversity. But diversity stretches only so far, and when a contradictory voice falls too far outside the park's reach, the violator becomes an outcast—a deviant.

Randy, who's white and with whom I've conversed, told me that, for years, he was homeless; he has experienced serious psychiatric and impulse-control difficulties, but now lives in his own apartment. One day, I hear him explode in an outburst, loud enough for dozens of park visitors to hear. "Fuckin' Arabs! Fuckin' Muslims! We ought to ship 'em all back home! Hell, those countries wouldn't take 'em, they'd send 'em back *here*! Fuckin' niggers come here to the park," Randy screams, "and fuck everything up!" Within two minutes, the entire area in his vicinity, halfway to Washington Place, empties out as a result of his screaming; one by one, his neighbors abandon their spot and scamper away from his vicinity. "Hey, you! Yeah, you! Fuck you!" He stands and looks around, with an angry expression on his face. "Yeah, yeah, I'm talkin' to you!" The content of his out-of-control diatribe is not random; psychopathological (or drunken) rants tend to travel along social-psychological, cultural, and subcultural grooves, and in this case, Randy, the ranter, a middle-aged white man apparently with a preexisting animus toward Arabs, Muslims, and African Americans, has drawn on his background in supplying the content of his verbal spasm, spewing his racially charged feelings into an otherwise amicable park atmosphere. Though Randy's park neighbors no doubt disapprove of the content of his rant, they likely also fled for their safety. The observer cannot help but wonder about how the local and situational context holds multiple prejudices in check.

Racial Ambivalences

In Washington Square, as elsewhere, the stereotypes, biases, and hierarchies of race, class, and gender prevail and are acted out. What occurs in public places is filtered through a racial screen; the same behaviors are likely to convey somewhat different meanings according to who the actors and observers are. In that respect, the square shares much in common with heartland America. On the other hand, many of the behaviors that take place in the park between and among visitors of different races, social class levels, and sexes, are inconceivable in most other places in the United States. And actions that would touch off alarm bells elsewhere are absorbed into the behavioral landscape here. Washington Square is accessible to all; no gates stop anyone from entering. Social interaction is common and fluid across categories, and for the most part, people tend to be civil to one another. And outsiders—marginals, William H. Whyte's "undesirables"—are not at all excluded. Yet, today's stereotype of African Americans, according to sociologist Elijah Anderson, holds that "black people start from the inner-city ghetto and are therefore stigmatized by their association with its putative amorality, danger, crime, and poverty" (2013, p. 32). This is a stereotype with which the African American is burdened and that he "must disprove before he can establish mutually trusting relationships with others" (p. 32). In an affluent, predominantly white locale, such as a "fancy hotel lobby, on a golf course, or, say, in an upscale community, he can be treated with suspicion, avoided, pulled over, frisked—or worse" (p. 33). In a more cosmopolitan locale, whites may ignore him or handle him with kid gloves. It is a public space where all who would be civil are welcome, but where alarm bells are more readily sounded for some visitors than for others. An alignment of incidents may activate an unspoken racial coding and release responses that may affront and wound parties who are present. In Anderson's terminology, Washington Square Park is most decidedly a "cosmopolitan canopy" (2011)—but with a twist or two.

Urban sociologists Mitchell Duneier and Harvey Molotch (1999; Duneier, 1999, pp. 188–216) discuss the fraught social interaction that takes place in Greenwich Village, on Sixth Avenue, three or four blocks north of the square, between upper-middle-class white women and African American men who are begging for money. When the panhandlers ask for a contribution from men, the entreaties are fairly straightforward. "Can you help me out?" would represent a typical request. But with women, the entreaties work in such a way as to make the black man feel entitled—as a man—to ensnare the white woman in "a series of compliments and assertions of intimacy which are difficult to ignore without feeling rude" (Duneier, 1999, p. 211). The researchers' informants attempt to manipulate women, knowing that "even privileged women occupy vulnerable positions in public space" (p. 210); hence, the interaction centers on the mind-and-power games that men with little power use to assert themselves as more than equals ("Hello, doll baby," "I love you baby," "Marry me," "I'm watching you. You look nice, you know," "You married?" "Where your rings at?"). What these men are doing is attempting to subvert the hegemony of the power of whites over them, delegitimating it by overturning interactional conventions in small street encounters with vulnerable parties who feel coerced to go along with their one-upsmanship strategies. In Duneieir's and Molotch's words, these men are in fact engaging in "interactional vandalism" (1999).

Like most males, both black and white, these men have been taught that to be a male is to possess power over women on the street and so, they feel entitled to control them (Duneier, 1999, p. 210). Duneier and Molotch draw parallels with construction workers who make lewd remarks to women passing by. In the case of the residents of Greenwich Village in the 1950s and early '60s, to which Jacobs referred, "eyes upon the street" often made public spaces seem welcoming or comfortable to the nonconformist and not merely the potential criminal. But sometimes, they say, "eyes have the opposite effect" (Duneier, 1999, p. 213)—they may be toxic to comfortable, egalitarian social relations. In some neighborhoods, outsiders are not welcome; people who are different will be viewed suspiciously, perhaps taunted, cruelly remarked upon, even stopped. Social class may enter in as well; the visitor who is dressed too shabbily, or too elegantly, may be made aware that it's time to move on. But even in the 1990s, and no doubt into the 2000s, Duneier and Molotch's informants have "troubled encounters" with the upper-middle-class white women on the street because they feel severely disadvantaged by the society and so, disrupt social interaction with women in such a way that they take advantage of their gender prerogatives. In their turn, the women attempt to avoid being rude to these men because they are operating on the basis of liberal guilt—the "morality of wanting to be nice to those at the bottom of the racial and class structure" (1999, p. 212).

The only man in Washington Square whom I observed engaging in the sort of outrageously flirtatious and male-*entitled* behavior that Duneier and Molotch describe was Justin, a recently released ex-convict whom I accompany on a stroll through the park. "Hey, pretty girl," he says to a young, attractive, smartly dressed woman; she ignores him and continues walking by us at the same pace. A twice-incarcerated felon—he has received convictions for armed robbery and the sale of a controlled substance—Justin is determined to go straight; he managed to land a fairly decent job driving a van, and begins work the next day. He looks a bit like a shy, soft-spoken, and more attractive Richard Pryor, if that combination can be imagined. Along the sidewalk bordering the square's north side, we spy a well-appointed, professional-looking woman approaching us. "Hi, sweetheart, how are you doing?" I pause a bit. We discuss the appropriateness of coming on to women. He says he doesn't see anything wrong with it. I say, "They take offense to it. You came on to ten or twelve women, and they all walked by, basically, they all ignored you, snubbed you. Yet you feel OK about all this."

"I'm not coming on to these women," Justin tells me. "I'm just saying nice things to them."

"Well, saying, 'You look beautiful tonight' is flirtatious. It means, 'I want to go home with you, I want to fuck you.' It's not so innocent. It asks for a response. If they don't respond, that *means* something; it means that they didn't take your comment too kindly. They wish you hadn't said that."

"I don't agree," he says. "They hear the comment, they feel good about it, they realize there are guys out there who like them, it boosts their spirits."

"Justin," I say to him, trying not to sound like a scold, "I don't think that addressing women out of the blue who are complete strangers is a good idea. Frankly, I don't think they like it," I add.

"Some of them do," he replies. We enter under the Arch, walk through the fountain circle, and angle left, toward Bobst Library. A tall, attractively dressed woman with a kind-looking face walks toward us. "Hello. You look very nice today," Justin says to her, making strong eye contact.

She stops before we pass her, turns her face toward him, and says, "Why, thank you very much," and continues on her way.

"I told you," he declares, giving me a sly smile. I decide to keep my mouth shut about Justin's street flirtations.

As I noted earlier, Jacobs barely mentioned race as a factor in public metropolitan life (1961); her comments were confined to the subject of segregation. Without reading too much into her interpretation, it's important to note that in the period during which she observed and wrote about behavior in urban neighborhoods, the population of Greenwich Village was roughly 1 percent African American. Today, as I've pointed out, it is barely higher (2%), but there's an important difference: If my tally is correct, almost one Washington Square visitor in ten is black; clearly, nearly all have made an effort to *come here* from somewhere else. But rather than being an "out of place" intruder, African Americans are regarded by most whites in the square as a component of the rainbow mix of the park's habitués. As we saw, in my survey of park-goers, only one black respondent out of eleven said he did not feel welcome in the park, and *not one* respondent I interviewed out of sixty of any race said that interracial romantic socializing ("an interracial couple") is wrongful; indeed, several thought the very question I asked was foolish and stupid, but I'm glad I asked it.

Racial Segregation, Racial Diversity

Residential segregation tends to be the rule in urban America, but the picture is changing. Since 1980, for both blacks and whites, the trend has been for a growing number and proportion of Hispanics and Asians to be in the mix of the population, but black-white segregation remains very high and has been declining very slowly; it is highest in Detroit, and third-highest in the New York metropolitan area. According to a slightly different measure, racial isolation, which measures the percent of members of each racial category in the neighborhood where the average minority group lives, New York ranks seventeenth most "racially isolated" in the nation: the average black person in its metro area lives in tracts that are 54 percent black. In addition, though segregation has been declining in the United States over the past three or four decades, New York ranks second among metro areas in both Hispanic-white and Asian-white segregation (Logan and Stults, 2011; Baird-Remba and Lubin, 2013; Silver, 2015).

Sociologist Reuben Buford May describes a system of "integrated segregation" in the night bar life of Athens, Georgia, home of the University of Georgia. Blacks and whites are "unlikely to have substantial interactions across racial boundaries," May says. Instead, he found, most nightlife participants "prefer to spend time interacting with people with whom they share common sensibilities and background" (2014, p. 8), that is, those who share the same racial characteristics. The "caravanning group" or bar-hopping "social capsules" that socialize together tend to be all black or all white, as well as all male or all female. An "ongoing social tension . . . runs along and across lines of gender, race, class, and culture" (p. 11). Blacks and whites share the same physical space—that is, many of the bars, and the streets connecting the bars—but they rarely socialize on an intimate basis with one another. Of course, on the street, bar patrons *pass* "individuals who occupy statuses unlike their own," giving the appearance of an integrated public space "where individuals share social relationships" (p. 18), but they are like ships passing in the night; they do not connect. Of course, the basis of clusters extends beyond race alone. Members of a given capsule who caravan with one another assume that the others share "tastes and sensibilities" based on the notion that "people like me will know how to have fun like me" (p. 18)—but race seems to be a basic entry requirement for clustering.

In *The Cosmopolitan Canopy* (2011), Elijah Anderson paints a substantially different portrait of public social life. He argues that the public spaces of America's cities may be "conceptualized essentially as a mosaic of white spaces, black spaces, and cosmopolitan spaces," the last of which are "racial islands of civility" (Anderson, 2015, pp. 10, 11). May (2014, p. 8) disagrees, stating that he does not believe such spaces are "widespread" and argues that they are unlikely to play a role in "improving race relations when they do exist." *White spaces* are areas where many of the whites who inhabit and visit them feel that African Americans don't belong; black people, they believe, are "out of place" in white spaces. As a result, many black people sense that they must enter such a place with caution; they must be vigilant and ensure that they never let their guard down, never act in a rowdy or ebullient fashion. Instead, they must try to be invisible among whites in such spaces. Most of America, Anderson argues, is made up of white spaces.

Anderson's research indicates that the territory constituted by the string of Philadelphia institutions along the route from Penn's Landing on the Delaware River, west along Market Street, past Liberty Place, to the Schuylkill, comprises a "cosmopolitan canopy" and is distinctly *not* a "white space" (2011). But twenty-first-century America, he argues, represents a "historic period of racial integration and incorporation" and a "growth of the black middle class, which is the largest in American history." Nonetheless, the society as a whole "is still replete" with white spaces that are currently being entered by a growing number of socially and economically mobile African Americans (2015, p. 11). My position is closer to Anderson's than to May's. When it comes to race, Washington Square is distinctively *not* a "white space," and is almost uniquely a *cosmopolitan canopy*, but it has not always been so.

A Brief History of Race in and around the Square

Washington Square is as multiracial a space as we can find in the United States, but for the better part of a century, its embrace of African Americans has been more prickly than hospitable. The chronology of the arrival of African residents to New Amsterdam—a document that is still in progress ("New Amsterdam," 2018)–begins its narrative in 1612; it mentions free Africans, mainly from Angola, with Portuguese names. As we've seen, later in the 1600s, a Dutch administrator deeded parcels of land that covered most of the geography of the spot that became Washington Square Park to a half-dozen former slaves to serve as a buffer against the Lenape, who often marauded against the settlements there and hence, represented a serious threat to New Amsterdam, located at the southern tip of Manhattan Island. (In 1655, one Henry Van Dyck shot and killed a Lenape woman who tried to steal a peach from his orchard, understandably causing the Lenape to attack several Dutch settlements.) Toward the end of that century, African Americans farmed about three hundred acres of lower Manhattan, plots that included much of what is now Washington Square (Folpe, 2002, pp. 51–55). But in 1674, the Dutch West India Company signed the Treaty of Westminster with the English, who seized control of the colony, passing this acreage into white hands (p. 54). And, as we saw earlier, in 1820, Rose Butler, a slave, was hanged in a spot that is occupied by the present-day square; it seems she tried to burn her mistress's house down.

By the mid-1800s, the landlords of the buildings along Thompson Street, adjacent to and just south of the square, and just north of Houston Street, had rented to so many black families that wags referred to the mini-community as "little Africa." Jacob Riis—among the reformers that journalists called the "muckrakers"—described these apartments as "vile rookeries," most notable for their squalor and crime, and the nearby black-and-tan saloons their residents patronized, as attracting the "utterly depraved of both sexes, white and black" (1890, pp. 161–62). Presumably a progressive, Riis shared the "widespread prejudice of the time, which held that racial mixing always had a deleterious effect on both races and was a sign as well as a source of social decay" (McFarland, 2001, p. 13). By 1900, this stretch of Thompson, along Minetta Street, and Minetta Lane, was declared "one of the worst slums in the city"; it included, commentators said, prostitutes, as well as some two thousand blacks, and it was time to clear out the "unsavory crowd," declared Riis (L.S. Harris, 2003, p. 226).

The most ruinous blow that white New York residents struck against African Americans took place during the Civil War Draft Riots of 1863. With the outbreak of the war, the names of all male citizens between the ages of twenty and thirty-five were placed into a lottery to be drafted into the Union Army; men of African descent, not being citizens, were exempt from the draft. In retaliation, within two days of the announcement of the lottery, resentful white mobs, many of them Irish immigrants, attacked black men on the street, lynching eleven. The riots lasted for five days. One horde burned down the Colored Orphan Asylum, located at Fifth Avenue between Forty-third and Forty-fourth streets; the asylum's staff, along with Union soldiers, had to protect the fleeing children from the angry rabble (L.M. Harris, 2003, pp. 279–88).

The white elite of Greenwich Village did not confine their racist views and behavior to persons of African descent. The New York University Archives house twenty-seven boxes of papers collected by the Washington Square Association; the racial history these files document is, from today's perspective, damning. In December 1906, says the introduction to this collection, a dozen householders of the Washington Square area between Fourteenth Street and Washington Square Park were invited to the West Tenth Street home of one Cornelius Berrien Mitchell, where he proposed the formation of an association in order "to maintain the present desirable character of the neighborhood." The "character" of Washington Square had been established in the 1830s as the "American Ward," that is, as a "model of cleanliness, good citizenship, and self-respect," in other words, upper- and upper-middle-class, white Anglo-Saxon Protestants. In the 1870s, in response to the influx of a large population of Irish to the east and west of the square, as well as a sizable African American settlement nearby, the old-line patricians politically allied themselves with the Tammany machine (most notably run by the infamous William Marcy "Boss" Tweed, in office 1868 to 1873, later imprisoned for political corruption), which intended to maintain the neighborhood as exclusively white Anglo-Saxon Protestant. However, during the next decade, both the Irish and the African Americans had indeed been pushed out of Greenwich Village, not by right-wing efforts but by a wave of Italian immigrants, hundreds of thousands of whom settled in Greenwich Village and its environs.

Two or three blocks south of Washington Square, in an unused space just south of Houston Street, poverty-stricken migrants set up a tent-and-shack encampment, the type of settlement that observers later referred to as a "Hooverville" (L.S. Harris, 2003, p. 226). Into the twentieth century, their children and grandchildren, born in the United States, felt a growing parochial and proprietary interest in their community vis-à-vis outsiders, and Italian American males often defended their neighborhood with physical threats or their fists. This proclivity continued for more than a half-century.

From the perspective of today, it is difficult to imagine the squalor, disorder, and decay into which Greenwich Village, and Washington Square Park, had fallen by the late 1950s. The subhead of a *New York Times* article during the era seems decades ahead of its time: "Beatings, Broken Windows in Café and Marauding Put Area on Guard" (Alden, 1959). Deputy Police Commissioner Walter Arm told the *New York Times* that more than the usual number of police officers had been dispatched to the neighborhood to quell the violence. "The situation is very explosive," Arm explained to the *Times*. "The police are trying to control the situation before there is an outburst of major violence."

The cause of the unrest? The *Times* suggested multiple factors, including organized crime, the encroachment of the honky-tonk bar and café nightlife, and the destruction of small neighborhood buildings for the purpose of constructing several skyscraper dwellings. But the lynchpin of the violence, "the principal factor causing the unrest," argued the *Times* in 1959, was the "racial antagonism between Negroes and old-time Italian residents" (Alden, 1959, p. 1); "here and there . . . are bands of young neighborhood toughs," both black and white, "spoiling for trouble." In the evening, the article continued, "the area about the fountain in Washington Square Park, once alive with the music of bearded guitarists and bongo players, has the aspect of a deserted battlefield. Only the police walk about the fountain." After multiple outbreaks of fighting, the NYPD put a curfew on walking through the fountain area after 6:00 p.m. One African American habitué explained that he had never seen the community as dangerous as it was then. There are some blocks in Greenwich Village, he said, "where it isn't safe to walk at all. They have what they call neighborhood recreation halls. I would call them torture chambers. God help you if they ever drag you inside one of them" (p. 42).

Local hooligans smashed coffee-house windows, threatened mixed couples, threw eggs at black men, and attacked homosexuals, bringing "the police in great numbers to the area." The *Times* offered a pessimistic assessment of the "deeply troubled" Village situation and the "sinister threat" it posed to a "peaceful way of life in one of the city's best-known neighborhoods" (Alden, 1959, p. 42). During this era, folk singers invaded the park, generating the ire of many locals, and in the sixties, motorcycle gangs roared through the park and developed a ritual of circling the Arch. This tendency of local Village hostility toward outsiders—or simply anyone who was unconventional looking—lasted well into the sixties. In 1966, at the corner of Bleecker and MacDougal, just two blocks south of the square, I myself was physically attacked by a local teenager who taunted me as a "dirty beatnik" and a "nigger-lover" because of my appearance (shoulder-length hair, granny glasses, sandals). During this period, once, the proprietor of a deli on Sixth Avenue announced to me, "We don't want your kind here." According to the *New York Times*, menace lay "just underneath the carnival atmosphere created by blinking neon signs, jazz music, writers reading their poems, and crowds of young people" (Alden, 1959, p. 42).

In 1970, then-congressman Ed Koch (later, mayor, 1977–1989) denounced the administration of Mayor John V. Lindsay (1966–1973) for "dumping" the city's unfortunates in the Village neighborhood's SROs (single-room-occupancy hotels). The Lindsay administration, claimed Congressman Koch, decided "to make Greenwich Village wide open for every circus program imaginable." This included an estimated fifteen hundred to two thousand "homeless men on welfare, 90 percent of them black, many of them recently released convicts," living in the SROs, who, Koch said, were a "major cause of the area's crime" (*New York Times*, September 28, 1970; quoted in L.S. Harris, 2003, p. 272). During July and August 1970, the NYPD made seven hundred arrests in Washington Square Park; 75 percent of those arrested were living in a single SRO—the Greenwich Hotel—and virtually all of them were black.

In September 1976, a throng of more than twenty white youths "swarmed through" Washington Square, "yelling racial epithets and attacking blacks with baseball bats and sticks." Witnesses said that they believed that the youngsters were "part of a group of youths of Italian descent" who hung out on the street at a particular spot several blocks away. A young woman who was present stated that the boys were chasing everyone in the park, including herself, "but the only people they hit were black. It was completely racist." Another onlooker stated that the boys were screaming, "Get the niggers out of the park." One black man was injured seriously enough to be hospitalized. No police were present at the incident (Treaster, 1976), and the badly injured man, Marcus Mota, a dark-skinned Dominican, died four days after the attack. Three of the attackers were charged with assault and three with manslaughter; their weapons of choice had been bats, chains, and pipes, and their motive had indeed been "to clear the park of blacks and Hispanics" (Jaynes, 1978). In short, the history of race in, and on the streets adjacent to, Washington Square has not been a smooth or easy one; encounters between whites and African Americans have been marked by conflict, hostility, and struggle. The observer might have predicted the era of the twenty-first century to be more of the same—but it was not.

The Demographics of Race in New York City

Greenwich Village has experienced a demographic pattern or arc that is worth investigating. Let's go back to 1943, during World War II. Table 5.1 tells the story we're interested in—the racial composition for that year of Manhattan's Greenwich Village. One warning: In this table, the lineaments of the Village were drawn at Fourteenth Street to the north, Canal Street to the south, Centre and Bowery streets and Third Avenue to the east, and the Hudson River to the west—five blocks south of its present lines and three blocks east. Of the foreign-born whites, a bit more than twenty thousand (60%) were from Italy, and, some said at the time, lived in "overflowing tenements." The percentage of African Americans (or "Negroes," the term typically used at the time) was very small, less than 1 percent, and the percentage of "other races," including Asians, was even smaller—only 0.2 percent. In short, in 1943, 99 percent of the residents of Greenwich Village were white.

TABLE 5.1. Racial Composition, Greenwich Village, 1943

Race	Number	Percentage
Native White	55,494	71.3
Foreign-Born White	21,595	27.8
Negro	602	0.8
Other Races	121	0.2
Total	77,812	100.1

Source: New York City Market Analysis, compiled by the *New York Times*, the *News*, the *Daily Mirror*, and the *Journal-American* (copyright 1943). Note borders of Greenwich Village, discussed in text.

Now examine table 5.2. Although in the 2000s, the population of the Village was and still is predominantly white, its proportion of nonwhites increased substantially, though they are mainly Asian, not black. The percentage of African Americans remains low—higher than it was in 1943 but lower than in 2000, though the proportion who are members of "other races," namely, persons of Asian descent, as I said, has increased substantially. Latinos were not counted as a separate category in 1943; they are today. Table 5.2 conveys the most recent statistics on the racial/ethnic composition of Greenwich Village.

In short, although this demographic exercise no doubt incorporates a measure of "apples-and-oranges" calculating, *for the most part,* it shows that the resident population of Greenwich Village remains overwhelmingly white, almost not at all black, and increasingly Asian. The most noteworthy demographic facts of the 2015 data on race and residence in Greenwich Village are these: Today, Greenwich Village is 33 percent more likely to be white than New York City as a whole (78% versus 45%), less than a tenth as likely to be black (2% versus 25%), only a fifth as like to be Hispanic (5% versus 26%), and about equally as likely to be Asian (11% versus 13%). And a majority of the adult residents of the two Village neighborhoods (the West Village and Greenwich Village) have a college degree.

Thanks to the Metro system, Washington Square is a subway ride, or several subway rides, away from every neighborhood in the City. Eight subway lines converge on stations that are just a few blocks from Washington Square Park. In addition, numerous bus routes run to stops within easy walking distance of the square. Hence, not only are the neighborhoods of the Village, the East Village, Chinatown, and Lower Fifth Avenue convenient to the park—a ten- or fifteen-minute walk—but all others are as well, by virtue of New York City's excellent MTA system. The Project for Public Spaces conducted a "user analysis and place performance evaluation" of Washington Square Park. Among other observations, it counted which entrances/exits pedestrians entered into or exited from. Of the more than twenty-six hundred entries, the Fifth Avenue opening was the most popular; of all visitors who entered the park, 21 percent came in through that entrance. It also drew the most exits, 23 percent of the total. Nearly a fifth (18%) entered through the University Place entrance a block east, but only a tenth (9%) exited through there. About one-twelfth (8.5%) entered through the Thompson Street entrance, almost directly south of Fifth Avenue, but more than twice as many (19%) exited that way. About an eighth (12%) both entered and exited through the southwest or MacDougal corner. The rest were scattered throughout the park. These entries and exits indicate possible neighborhood origin and, to a degree, racial composition.

Here, the designation "Greenwich Village" includes the entire Sixth Precinct: Greenwich Village and the West Village. Note that the area circumscribed by the 2015 data overlaps imperfectly with that designated

TABLE 5.2. Percent Non-Hispanic White, Black, Asian, and Hispanic in Greenwich Village, 2000–2015

Race/Ethnicity	2000	2010	2015
Non-Hispanic White	82.0	80.9	78.4
Black	2.7	2.0	2.2
Asian	6.6	8.2	10.6
Hispanic	5.4	6.1	5.1
Mixed and Other	2.3	2.9	3.7
Total	65,000	66,880	55,000

Source: Center for Urban Research, *New York City Demographic Shifts, 2000 to 2010*, www.urbanresearchmaps. org; for 2015, "Population of Greenwich Village, New York, New York," statisticalaltlas.com.

by the 2000 and 2010 censuses. Greenwich Village did not lose population between 2010 and 2015; the neighborhood lines drawn by the different agencies collecting these data varied somewhat.

On twelve separate occasions between fall 2015 and spring 2016, I did a little census of my own, making thirty-five hundred observations of park visitors and inferring the racial category of each person I saw in the fountain area; table 5.3 summarizes these observations. (This informal "census" is admittedly flawed and potentially somewhat inaccurate.) The most noteworthy feature of my tally is the substantially higher percentage of African Americans who *visit* Washington Square as opposed to the percentage who *live* in Greenwich Village. Since real estate is expensive in the Village and incomes of African Americans tend to be lower than those of whites and persons of Asian background, only 2 percent of the neighborhood's population was black in 2010, as tallied by the U.S. Census, and 2.2 percent, in 2015 (as tallied by the Center for Urban Research). Hence, my figure of 9.2 percent indicates that, of the City park choices that African Americans might make to visit, Washington Square is a desirable one. The figures that appear in table 5.5 are slightly different. Note that I did not include in this tally of members of racial or ethnic categories parties whose membership I could not immediately and unambiguously recognize—mainly, people whose ancestry hailed from the Middle East or from indigenous Latin America. My reluctance to do so was based on modesty, that is, an awareness of my fallibility with respect to such distinctions.

TABLE 5.3. Racial Composition, Washington Square, 2015–2016

Category	Percent	N
White	70.0	2506
East Asian	13.3	477
African American	9.2	330
South Asian	7.4	263
Total	99.9	3576

Source: Personal observations of persons entering and walking around the fountain area on twelve occasions, late 2015 to early 2016. These are the author's deduction of the racial identity of the observed parties. Note that the U.S. census counts self-identity. In this table, Middle Eastern, Hispanic, "mixed," and "don't know" are not included or tabulated, due to my inability to accurately make such distinctions by sight. These figures are rough and approximate. These observations are separate and independent of those that appear in tables 5.5 and 6.1.

There's an interesting confirmation of the fact that most African Americans who visit Washington Square Park do not live in the immediate Greenwich Village neighborhood but have, in all likelihood, taken public transportation to get there: dog walking. I have counted the gender and racial category of 662 dog walkers (whose categories I could readily determine). Some are professional dog walkers, of course, who may live elsewhere, but I only saw three persons walking more than three dogs at the same time; one of them was a woman walking seven dogs, including a mastiff mix and a chihuahua mix. In fact, over 90 percent of my observations were of walker/owners with a single dog on a leash. Another factor must be considered: *The KC Dog Blog* puts dog ownership in the United States as a whole at 50 percent of families; for African Americans, this figure is half of that, 25 percent. My speculation is that the reason for the lower dog ownership among black families is that they are more likely to live in a densely populated area, making the ownership of a dog inconvenient. (Roughly 600,000 New York City households own a dog.) Fifty-nine percent of the people I counted in Washington Square Park with dogs on a leash were females (392), the rest (271, or 41%) were males; nearly three-quarters (73%) of Asian dog walkers were female. Just under nine in ten (88%) were white, 2 percent were black, and one in ten were Asian (10%)—a ball-park near-approximation of the community's residential composition. Clearly, most dog owners live in the neighborhood, and the vast majority are white; dog walkers who did not own the dogs they walked, my guess is, were in a small minority of the people I observed. I also interviewed a small number of people who had a dog on a leash (ten), and all owned their dogs.

The current racial composition of New York City may shed light on its residents' park use, with respect to both who is likely to use a park and what its residents have to *do* to use it—that is, how far they have to travel to get there. More specifically, Manhattan's population size and density, as well as its racial composition, do not entirely explain or account for the composition of the visitors to Washington Square Park. A comparison between the 2000 and the 2010 censuses offers some interesting insights into recent changes in the City's demography. Unlike other eastern (Boston and Baltimore) and several midwestern cities—such as Cleveland, Detroit, and Chicago—New York's population actually grew between 2000 and 2010—by 167,000, or about 2.1 percent. Changes in its composition are particularly interesting. Unlike the City as a whole, substantially fewer whites lived in New York City in 2010 than in 2000—a decline of 78,000, or 2.8 percent—and the African American population decreased even more, by 5.1 percent. In contrast, the Latino presence increased by 7.5 percent, and Asians, by 31.8 percent, or 175,000 people. About 76,000 more New Yorkers declared themselves of mixed race (a 34% increase), the latter increase unquestionably a result of the census allowing respondents and members of the relevant categories willing to *identify* as biracial to do so, as opposed to an actual demographic change itself.

But more interestingly, for our purposes, and in spite of these shifts, slightly *more* whites lived in Manhattan in 2010 (48% of its population) than in 2000 (45.8%), and slightly *fewer* African Americans (15.3% vs. 12.9%) did so. In fact, Manhattan's Asian and white populations increased during the 2000–2010 decade, while its Latino and African American populations declined. The tendency of ethnic/racial polarization may reflect a larger and much more substantial trend taking place not only throughout the United States but around the globe: the increasing polarization of incomes, with the most affluent quintile (20%) of the population of the country as a whole earning an increasingly larger slice of the total economic pie and the least affluent quintile earning a smaller slice. Manhattan is increasingly becoming more gentrified and hence, increasingly out of the reach of growing sectors of the least affluent minority groups—hence the polarization of *races,* as well as *economic strata.* By 2020, whites will be the racial *majority* in Manhattan, yet a decided *minority* of whites will live in the City as a whole. As opposed to Manhattan's increasing racial polarization, New York City as a whole is becoming more racially diverse. The only statistical majorities currently in New York City's boroughs are those in Staten Island (64% white) and in the Bronx (53.5% Latino). Of course, *neighborhoods* tend to be more racially and ethnically segregated—and homogeneous—than entire boroughs: The population of Greenwich Village is predominantly Caucasian, Chinatown is largely Asian, Jackson Heights and Corona are majority Latino, and so on, but these figures, now more than a half-decade old, are changing over time and, of course, *all* neighborhoods in New York are racially and ethnically mixed to *some* degree. Between 2000 and 2010, the white population in Bedford-Stuyvesant grew by 633 percent, and in Harlem, by 400 percent.

Table 5.4 summarizes the U.S. census statistics in 2010 on the racial/ethnic make-up of New York City and its boroughs. A third of the population of New York City (33.3%) is classified as non-Hispanic white, just under a quarter (22.8%) is black or African American, just over a quarter (28.6%) is Hispanic or Latino, and just under an eighth (12.8%) is Asian. Except for Staten Island, Manhattan's population is whiter than that of the other boroughs, and less African American. Demographers project that the white and Asian populations of Manhattan will increase in the future and hence, chances are, African Americans and Latinos will have to travel further from where they live to get to Washington Square Park. The two reasons for this demographic shift are fairly straightforward but complex in their consequences: first, over time, the same polarization of incomes that is taking place in the country as a whole is likewise happening in New York City, that is, the rich are getting richer and the poor are getting poorer—at least, the incomes of the lower economic strata are stagnating; and second, housing costs are rising in Manhattan and hence, lower-income renters are forced to move further away, and that is more likely to affect African Americans and Hispanics than whites and Asians.

TABLE 5.4. Size, Density, and Racial Composition of New York City, by Borough, 2010

Borough	Number (million)	Area Sq/Mi	Density	White	Black	Hispanic	Asian
Manhattan	1.6	23	70,000	48.0	12.9	25.4	11.2
Brooklyn	2.6	71	26,300	35.7	31.9	19.8	10.4
Queens	2.3	109	23,000	27.6	17.7	27.5	22.8
Bronx	1.4	42	33,000	10.9	30.1	53.5	3.4
Staten Island	0.5	58	8,000	64.0	9.5	17.3	7.4
City Total	8.4	303	27,100	33.0	22.8	28.6	12.8

Does Race Matter in Washington Square?

I put one question in my survey as a kind of "anchor" to insure that respondents were not answering in a mindless, mechanical fashion—whether they thought that an interracial couple was engaging in wrongful behavior by being together. As I explained above, all sixty respondents (100%) said that being part of an interracial couple was not wrong. In fact, the question itself elicited some startled replies, which caused me to apologize for having asked the question in the first place. A seventy-five-year-old white woman stared at me, dumbfounded, and asked, "Now, why did you ask me *that* question?" I explained to her, "Well, I'm sorry, I have to establish a range of attitudes toward behaviors some respondents feel are innocuous and inoffensive, some of which are considered more seriously wrong. This question is at one end of the spectrum." She replied, with some indignation, "Well, there's absolutely nothing wrong with that!" Brother John, a lay monk, replied, "I think it's wonderful." Rick, a retired teacher, echoed the same view: "It's great. I love it. The more the merrier," "It's not even worth talking about," "These days, all of New York is interracial," and "Are you kidding?" represent some of the responses I received to this question. I'm almost embarrassed for having asked it—except for the fact that it elicited such colorful and emphatic responses. *And* they provide a contrast with the responses I received to the behaviors my interviewees considered truly wrongful. With respect to socializing, my respondents seemed to feel that race doesn't matter. It's my job to find out whether and to what extent that is true. Surely I can determine this through empirical observation, recognizing that my conclusions will be fraught with ambiguity and contradictions.

Of *course* race matters, but as a sociologist, I have to understand the *ways* in which it matters. And if, as a sociologist, I am conducting a study that relies, in part, on observation, I need to identify the racial categories to which the people I observe belong. All societies construct and promulgate racial categories and, as a member of one of them, I too am familiar with the racial categories that prevail in the society. Many people give stereotypical responses to questions about race—and these responses do matter, on some level—though they may act in a different fashion. In the U.S. Census, respondents are asked to which racial category they belong. In all likelihood, the respondents' answers to that question would correspond, more or less, to the perception that other members of this society have about what category they belong to. Again, race is a genetic semi-fiction, but knowing what the society's cultural rules are that determine who belongs to which category, most observers can approximately place the parties one observes in the categories they themselves no doubt would choose; the mistakes are likely to be, statistically speaking, minimal. In parts of the discussion that follow, I rely on my observations regarding who belongs to what categories. It's possible that some parties, including the person so identified, would say I'm wrong. However absurd and pernicious race is as a material-world phenomenon, it is *socially constructed* and these social constructions have social (and economic, and political) consequences, and I intend to look at some of them. Many people believe that race is a real-world constituent of our lives and so, it is real in its consequences.

Here's one partial exception: Hispanic or Latino is an ethnic, not a racial, category; hence, some Latinos who are of European ancestry are genetically white, while others have some African ancestry and may be perceived by others, both black and white, as black. And many Latinos possess a measure of indigenous or Native American ancestry—some of their genetic forbearers were American Indians. To repeat: ethnicity is not the same as genetic inheritance; the first is a matter of culture and identity; the second is a matter of testable DNA. And sociological categories are yet another system of classification. It is by this tangle of imperfectly overlapping systems that humans sort one another and, to a measurable degree, relate to one another.

Eleven of my sixty respondents were visibly African American (one was African), three self-identified as Hispanic or Latino, and four were of Asian descent; the rest were white. I asked each black respondent, "As a black man/woman, do you feel welcome in the park?" (I did not ask the Asian or visibly white Latino respondents the analogous question.) All except one said that they felt welcome. Samuel, a fifty-year-old resident of Brooklyn, the father of three, said, "Sometimes I feel unwelcome. There are still some people who feel you don't belong." I did not ask for an elaboration. Fernando, in his late fifties, a Latino of color, said, "Anybody can come to the park as long as they behave themselves. I see all nationalities here. Everybody is welcome here." When I asked Vincent, a resident of Harlem and multiply arrested marijuana seller, about whether, as a black man, he felt welcome in Washington Square, his reply was, "What I do have nothing to do with the fact that I'm black. I'm not welcome 'cuz I sell marijuana." John, a thirty-year-old unemployed, homeless man, answered, "No, I don't feel unwelcome here in the Park." Felicia, a Queens resident in her twenties, told me, "I don't think there's any difference, black or white, here." The results were substantially consistent and indicated that, with respect to their overall perception, persons of color *do* feel welcome in, and do *not* feel excluded from, Washington Square Park as a result of their race.

Nonetheless, race plays itself out in Washington Square, but in ways that even the experts may not have recognized. To emphasize the point, practically every well-informed person knows that race is a biological fiction; so-called or putative races blend into one another and there is no such thing as a "pure" race. But over the centuries, putative racial categories became "racialized" (Murji and Solomos, 2005). Race—the fiction now embodying the reality—may or may not be directly relevant to deviance and social control, but it could exert a subtle yet *determinate* effect on how parties react to putative wrongdoing. Race is *perceived* and unwittingly *acted upon* by the ordinary denizen of the park, by officers of the three agencies that police the park—that is, the NYPD, the NYU Safety Patrol, and, most particularly, the Parks Enforcement Patrol (PEP)—in an *indirect* rather than a direct fashion. (Most of the PEP, both male and female, are black.) For example, proportional to their numbers, the homeless are more likely to be black than white, and virtually all the drug sellers are black; these facts may very well work their way into the nervous systems of the PEP (black or white) and the NYPD, not to mention the ordinary park-goer, again, black or white. I'm also interested in how the relevant racial categories get along with one another. Putative racial membership may or may not be meaningful *to these actors*, and may, or may not, have an impact on how they socialize and interact with one another. Addressing such issues begins with taking a census or tally of persons whom most observers would classify as belonging to one or another racial category.

Interracial Socializing in the Park

We can see in table 5.5 the results of my observations for the purpose of determining interracial socializing—which were separate and independent of my racial count, whose results appear in table 5.3. Once again, my racial categorization is no doubt fallible; short of approaching all parties in the park and questioning every one about their racial/ethnic identity, perhaps it is best to remain with these distinctions. The fact that these counts, which were made on different occasions and specifically for the purpose of determining how members of different racial categories appear in public *with one another* (I focused on dyads), are almost identical to those that appear in table 5.3 indicates a measure of reliability. The likelihood of interracial socializing is obviously strongly related to the size of the category or categories in question—that is, the larger the group, the smaller the likelihood that its members will socialize with members of other categories, and the smaller the group, the greater that likelihood is. There are simply more in the larger categories available to socialize *with*, and fewer in the smaller categories. For instance, according to data supplied by the Pew Research Center, of the 6.3 million newlyweds in the United States in 2013, 12 percent married someone of a different race; among whites, the largest category, this figure was 7 percent, among African Americans, it was 19 percent, and among Asians, 28 percent. For American Indians, the smallest racial category, fully 58 percent married someone belonging to a different racial category.

Thus, returning to the park, if sociability were random with respect to numbers and the tallies that appear in table 5.3 are accurate, about 70 percent of whites would socialize with other whites (I tallied only dyad pairing), only 9 percent of African Americans would socialize with black persons, 13 percent of East Asians would socialize with East Asians, and 7 percent of South Asians, with one another. In other words, the number of people *in* a given social category is one factor that influences inter-group contact, and by that factor alone, whites would socialize mainly with whites, and minorities would also socialize mainly with whites. But sociability doesn't work randomly.

I conducted the racial census late in 2015 and early in 2016; at that time, I did not count racial pairing. Hence the total racial tallies in table 5.3 are slightly different from those in table 5.5, taken late in 2016 and early in 2017. These are two separate counts, taken during two separate time periods. Their percentage figures are almost identical: 70% versus 70% for the total proportion of whites; 9% versus 12% for blacks; 13% and 13% for East Asians; and 8% versus 5% for the category I referred to as "other" (Hispanics, South Asians, North Africans and Middle Eastern-ers, and possibly mixed). The fact is, when I conducted the first "census," I did not think about racial and ethnic pairing; that came in the second tally. Note that the results of the racial census that appear in table 5.5 *only* count parties in dyads. Still, the similarities between the counts in table 5.3 and those in table 5.5 are remarkable.

As we can see in table 5.5, *in dyads*, whites socialize mainly but far from exclusively with other whites (80%); their tendency to ra-cially out-socialize (20%) is substantially lower than for members of the other categories, which the statistician would predict from their larger numbers. Persons of African descent in dyads are somewhat less likely to socialize with members of other races (44%) than with other blacks (56%), though, given their smaller numbers, their out-socializing may be surprising, considering what some other research-ers have concluded with respect to the strong tendency of the races to exclusively interact within their own category (May, 2014). The tendency to racially out-socialize among East Asians is even stron-ger; over half of the dyads in which they appear (55%) entailed pair-ing up with non–East Asians. East Asians out-socialize, in pairs, far more than is true of any other major racial category, both considering and ignoring their absolute numbers in the square population. South Asians are somewhat more racially homophilous—and about as much as African Americans—than whites and East Asians, with 56 percent

TABLE 5.5. Racial Homophily/Heterophily of Dyads in Washington Square Park, 2016–2017

Composition of Dyads	Number of Units	Percent of Units	Racial/Ethnic Categories	Number of People	Percent of People
W-W	1165	55	Whites	2910	68
W-EA	254	12	East Asian	568	13
W-B	175	8	Black	505	12
W-SA	151	7	South Asian	279	7
B-B	141	7	Total Number of People	4262	100
EA-EA	129	6			
SA-SA	39	2			
EA-SA	29	1			
EA-B	27	1			
B-SA	21	1			
Total	2131	100			

Whites in Dyads: 2910
    Whites racially in-socializing: 2330 (80%)
    Whites racially out-socializing: 580 (20%)
East Asians in Dyads: 568
    East Asians racially in-socializing, 258 (45%)
    East Asians racially out-socializing, 310 (55%)
Blacks in Dyads: 505
    Blacks racially in-socializing, 282 (56%)
    Blacks racially out-socializing, 223 (44%)
South Asians in Dyads: 279
    South Asians racially in-socializing, 156 (56%)
    South Asians racially out-socializing, 123 (44%)

Source: Observations of dyads on six occasions in fountain area, 2016–2017. I did not tally instances in which members of these categories socialized with parties whose racial/ethnic origin I could not readily identify, that is, in all probability, Latino, Middle Eastern, and "other." I did not tally members of putative triads and triads-plus.

interacting with their racial peers. What we see is considerable intergroup contact; the optimist would hope that the racial mingling and mixing in the square would influence substantial intergroup harmony, although here, it is as likely to be caused more by preexisting fellowship than it is to cause it. Dyad socializing with persons belonging to a racial category other than one's own is not the last word on racial harmony, but it is a step in a positive direction.

* * *

Interview with Hakim, a Proofreader

Hakim Hasan is a former proofreader for a legal firm and a former street bookseller. I got in touch with him as a result of being struck by the insightfulness of his "Afterword" in Mitchell Duneier's book, *Sidewalk* (1999, pp. 319–30). We arranged to meet in Washington Square Park. Hakim proofread this chapter.

ERICH: I got in touch with you because you might have some insights on the role of race in Washington Square. You've come here lots of times, you wrote the "Afterword" to Mitch's book, *Sidewalk*, for years you sold books with the fellas on Sixth Avenue, and I can tell that you're a knowledgeable, insightful, and serious man. What's your take on race in the park?

HAKIM: Washington Square Park is one of the great public spaces— you might say, the *preeminent* spaces—in the City. Anywhere. It's a cosmopolitan place. I feel more comfortable here than in any other place in the City. It welcomes folks on the margins.

ERICH: One of the questions I raise in the book is whether and to what extent race matters here. I ask my respondents, "Are black people welcome in the park?" I selected sixty people, pretty much at random, and eleven of them turned out to be black. I asked the African American respondents, "As a black person, do you feel welcome in the park?" All but one said that they feel welcome here. What I was worried about was whether I was getting polite, stereotypical responses, that I wasn't getting their true feelings.

HAKIM: People come here from all over. All kinds of people come here. You go out on Sixth Avenue, race makes a difference. It matters there. You go to the lobbies of the fancy buildings up there [points toward One and Two Fifth Avenue], race matters. It doesn't much matter here [in Washington Square Park].

ERICH: You mean the square is kind of like a utopia?

HAKIM: It's not a utopia. It is a space of *cosmopolitan marginalization*; that is, all sorts of people come here. The Village is one of society's places of self-invention. Yes, this place is different from more conventional places in society, but I want to explain that. The race issue is an *elongated* question. If you talk about the matter of black folks, how does race play a role in general, in the larger structural picture, the answer is, it does. You can't understand the issue without looking at the broader context. Race in a public space like Washington Square is a narrow issue. There are larger structural forces that cause you to come to Washington Square in the first place. You need to understand the back story, the way that race plays itself out. In the general society, as you move up the food chain, up the socioeconomic ladder, there are fewer and fewer black people the higher up you go. They're held back by structural forces. I was exiled before I even got here. The question you ask, about whether race plays a role in Washington Square, is a different sort of question, it's a question of *navigation*. It's about whether you can move with comfort and ease through this space. That didn't begin in the park. That's the end point in an elongated process. If I can't walk comfortably through the park, that makes social assumptions about where I'm supposed to be and what I'm supposed to do. A black man can walk through the park with a white girlfriend and nobody would care. But that doesn't change anything; that doesn't change the barriers that I have to overcome to rise in the economic structure. Let me tell you something. I worked at a museum that was run by white women. I felt like I was in Tupelo, Mississippi, in the 1940s. I realized that they didn't want me there in the first place. When I was let go, I felt I had been released from a maximum-security prison. Everything I did was questioned, my decisions were questioned. In my job, they had no sense of what I was doing and where I was coming from. This one woman seemed to feel that I had disdain for white people. She asked me if I got along with white people. I was the only black person that was ever hired in that capacity; all the other black people there were working in custodial jobs, jobs of that manner. This is what I had to deal with all my life. In many ways, you don't ever stop having to deal with it. The women I worked with, when we went out on the street, they didn't want to acknowledge me. They'd look away. They didn't want to have to deal with black people. It was a very difficult place to work. I'd walk into meetings and people would look at me as if they were asking, who are you, what are you doing here? Washington Square, there's an inherent eccentricity to this place. So, what I'm saying is that the elongated view is when you look at spaces like Washington Square, you have to juxtapose how you're treated here with your everyday lives. This is one of the places where marginalized people can be accepted and feel comfortable, where they are welcome. The world is not a perfect place, right? So, where are those places where the marginalized can go and exist—in short, *to be*? This is why a lot of people from places like Kansas who might not fit in where they live come to places like Washington Square. It is a place of negotiated marginality. But I do not assign that same feeling to the community at large. This is still a largely white, upper-middle-class neighborhood. You pay a lot to live here. So, yes, black people are welcome here, as are a diversity of people, and no, race doesn't much matter here, in the park. But that's only part of the picture. It matters in the neighborhood, and it matters in the society as a whole. We all come from someplace, we all started out someplace else. To truly see what you see in the park, you have to look at the *genealogy* of the structure of the society. You don't realize how insane the idea of race is until you think seriously about it. Washington Square is a kind of *end point*, it's a cosmopolitan place where race doesn't matter, but you also have to consider what our everyday lives are like, what the structure of the society as a whole is like, what our lives are immersed in. We all have to walk out of here and return to the lives we lead and the roles we play in the society at large. And do you know why the mingling and mixing, what I call the "social miscegenation" of Washington Square Park, prevails here but not in the surrounding community? It's because the people in the community know that this miscegenation does not filter out into their day-to-day lives. They know that these marginal people, these so-called undesirables, will be gone by nightfall. The park is not open all night. This human ebb and flow is limited, it is circumscribed.

6

Sex and Gender in Public

A slender woman, perhaps thirty-five, with disheveled blonde hair, her face contorted into a smirk because a cigarette is dangling at an angle from the corner of her mouth, is standing in her socks—one of them missing a toe and a heel—next to a stone bench in the fountain circle. She's wearing jeans, a colorful cloth belt, and a sleeveless black pullover, the right side of which is yanked halfway down, so that substantial swathes of her back and chest are exposed; she does not appear to be wearing a bra. There's a small, bulging, violet-colored cloth sack at her feet, and a rollie leans at an angle against the bench, out of which she's busily yanking items of her wardrobe, including a jacket, which she stuffs back in and then takes out again.

The woman reaches into a pouch in the rollie and pulls out her shoes, places them onto the stone bench, then reaches in, scoops out, and scatters various small odds and ends, such as pens, books of matches, and makeup compacts, onto the bench, then grabs a fat, blue-and-white-barreled ballpoint pen out of the pouch and pitches it underhanded toward two conventional-looking men in suits and ties, one white, one Asian, who are sitting and talking about six or eight feet from her. It lands on the bench about a foot away from where the nearest one is seated and skids toward him, resting against his jacket. He looks at the pen, the pair look at one another, and, in concert, without saying a word, they stand up and briskly walk away.

As she's busily rearranging her items, a stocky, middle-aged white man sporting yellow-tinted sunglasses—who, though wearing a sports jacket, looks slightly disreputable—approaches her. He invites her to lunch at a nearby diner, and she shakes her head, visibly refusing his proposition. After talking with her for a minute or two, the man leaves. The woman then takes out a small plastic bottle, which a guest might have received as a complimentary grooming product in a hotel, flips off the top, which flies away and sharply clatters onto the ground, turns the bottle upside down and squirts its contents in circles on the bench area next to her, then tosses the empty away; it lands in the small, flat, circular planting area at the base of a tree nearly ten feet to her right. She takes an orange scarf out of the backpack, stuffs it into her back pocket, letting it hang down along her right leg, then wraps the arms of a gray sweater around her waist and ties the arms in front of her, takes out several other articles of clothing, including a jacket, and places them on the bench.

Another middle-aged man, also white and also wearing a jacket but appearing substantially more respectable than the first, approaches her, talks to her for a minute or two, takes out his wallet, hands her three bills, and smiles at her. She doesn't smile but accepts the money, nodding almost imperceptibly; he leaves, giving the viewer no hint of having made a proposition. The woman has created a space about ten to twelve feet on the stone bench to her right, where she has squirted the liquid, on which no one sits. Then, leaving her articles scattered on the bench, she jerkily, in a robot-like fashion, follows a pigeon for about thirty feet to a spot just south of the fountain, where it flies away, then she walks back to her stuff, puts the purple sack under her arm, takes two jackets out of the rollie, tucks them under her other arm, jams the rest of her items, including her shoes and the small objects she had tossed onto the bench, back into the rollie, zips all of it up, and trundles it away by its handle toward the south side of the park.

Curious about the contents of the small container she tossed away, I walk over to the planter, pick up the empty bottle, and read the label. It's Frescent Shampoo and Body Wash. And I think: Typically, the craziness of deranged men acts as a deterrent to women; they don't want to associate with such a man—unless they're crazy themselves. During the short period of time I observed her, the woman attracted two men into her interactional orbit. According to any and all psychiatric definitions of the term, this woman would be defined as mentally disordered— sociologically, a *deviant*. And yet, in the park, men did not shun her, at least not completely. One wonders what the first man had in mind by inviting her to lunch, but perhaps one does not have to wonder very much.

Our disheveled, mentally disordered Washington Square female drew stares from many park-goers who passed her or sat nearby, no doubt as a result of the flamboyant eccentricity of her behavior. This woman seems vulnerable on her own. Her encounters with the two apparently normal men bring together representatives of different sectors of the society—and yet, no genuine mingling took place. She fended off the advances of one would-be suitor and accepted the gift of another without obligation, thus playing her conventional feminine role competently, but her attractiveness and her vulnerability as an anomalous, disordered female on her own in a public place who attracts the attention of males interested in contact with her introduces the speculation that she has probably engaged in such fending-off maneuvers in the past—possibly some of them unsuccessful—and will have to do so in the future. She combines notions of conventional femininity with a distinct "otherness": transforming the shampoo and body wash product from material that fosters daintiness and conventional femininity to something that supplies her with the means by which she engaged in her strange act of defiance—making the bench unusable for ordinary park-goers as a place to sit—and littering the park by hurling the empty bottle onto a landscaped space designed to reflect orderliness and attractiveness. I had observed her earlier in the day, wildly, jerkily daubing her face with make-up, an act that both affirmed her feminine role yet contradicted it with her frenzied, spasmodic movements. Her apparent vulnerability dramatizes to us that women in public spaces may find it necessary to develop *strategies of defiance and resistance* (Casey, Goudie, and Reeve, 2008). At the same time, this woman's presence and activities in the park also jarringly remind us that the park is not a pleasure garden made up of mere conceptual heterotopic qualities but an all-too-real material one that occasions contradictions, dilemmas, and potentially unpalatable encounters. Men are no less subject to criminal victimization than women—in fact, statistically, they are substantially more so—but many men consider themselves invulnerable, and they tend to act in a more cavalier fashion when it comes to the possibility of threats to their person in public places.

As we've seen, civilization's creation of the public square is one of the most significant innovations in the history of humanity; further, the acceptable comingling of men and women in public who are strangers to one another—a much later development—is not far behind in its import, I'd speculate. But even in more gender-restricted societies, not all public locales are off-limits for women in equal measure, nor are they off-limits for all women. For instance, in Cairo, upper-middle-class women may engage in mixed-gender sociability in upscale, Western-style coffee shops—not to be confused with the traditional male-dominated sidewalk cafés—and nonetheless remain within the bounds of respectability (de Konig, 2009, chapter 4). But given the nature of gender roles in societies around the world, and given the vulnerability of most women in relation to men, any kind of public stranger heterosociability generates issues that the interested observer must address. Among other things, such behavior pressures the social order to define and redefine the nature of gender-related normativity and deviance in public.

Societies must address the issue of intergender socializing: who may talk to whom, who may do what with whom, what is permitted and what's prohibited, and *who says* what's permitted or prohibited. How does the society protect women from contact with men unknown to them, and what should an acceptable response by a woman to such a man's attempt to establish sociability be if he does approach her? Among other things, she must protect herself against possible harm from such strangers. To reiterate the point: Men are significantly more likely to be victimized by violent crime (murder, robbery, assault—but obviously not rape) than women, but society does not take the same protective measures toward them, and men themselves unrealistically feel they can take care of themselves.

The role of women in public spaces is one of the more consequential issues societies have had to address; as a general rule, historically, paternalistic societies have tended to restrict women's public appearances mainly to functional locales (drawing water, shopping at markets, accompanying children), whereas more gender-equalitarian societies place far fewer limitations on women's comings and goings. Oddly enough, in many of the major, classic statements describing and analyzing behavior in public, some of them written by women, the role of sex or gender barely makes an appearance (Jacobs, 1961; Harrison-Pepper, 1990; Low, Taplin, and Scheld, 2005; Lennard and Lennard, 2008). And, as we'll shortly see, at least one observer of public behavior (Gardner, 1989) has critiqued the premier sociological analyst of the public realm, Erving Goffman (1959, 1963, 1971), for his inattentiveness to the difficulties women face on the street. Women are particularly vulnerable to being victimized by men in public places by way of multiple offenses, including verbal harassment and illegal, unlawful, unwanted, or non-consensual sexual groping, fondling, or touching. Surely the subject of women in public merits our attention.

Gendered Public Spaces

For centuries, societies have typically defined public spaces as masculine. As we saw, prior to the emergence of the urban square and park, women were chiefly confined to the marketplace and fountains and wells. Females who violated the rules of such confinement—barmaids, prostitutes, night-workers, or, centuries later, feminists who demanded the same ecological and temporal rights as men (Findlay, 1999)—were branded as deviants. Gottdiener and Budd (2005, pp. 27–29, 81–83), refer to "feminine space" ("A woman's place is the home") and "masculine space" (most bars, especially sports bars, "monster" truck stadiums, audiences of "extreme" sports, and locales that host the playing of "extreme" video games), which define where women and men, respectively, are normatively appropriately emplaced. In spite of the retreat, in the Western world, of exclusively male-dominated spaces, the claim that "existing environments are increasingly bi-sexually controlled may be an exaggeration. Societies still invest men with the power to dominate. That fact alone implies that, in most spaces, it is male-biased activities that will prevail" (p. 82). It is not that women never visit "masculine" spaces; it is that the sex ratio among visitors is lopsided, though no doubt in varying degrees, not to mention hegemonically masculine. Such characterizations apply even more strongly when the scene shifts to nighttime activities in such spaces. Of course, traditional societies, including the American past, harbored such spaces *outside* the household in which women exerted authority, that is, those locales that were an extension of women's conventional domestic role as women: in the market, as I said, as well as among shopkeepers and sales clerks, in grocery stores, and in clothing stores (Zukin, 1995, p. 204).

Typing the phrase "gender in public" into an Internet search engine will call up a substantial number of pornographic websites: "Public Porn Videos," "Nude Outdoor Girls, Sex Movies," "Hot Public Sex and Nudity," and so on. Many men find the topic of "gender" (even more so, "sex") in public erotic, sexually stimulating, even pornographic; some even hold the archaic notion that women who appear in public have brought sexual attention upon themselves, and deserve whatever lewd solicitations they receive. This situation is particularly true in less afflu-ent countries. In a study of women in public in India, a team of archi-tects (Phadke, Khan, and Ranade, 2011) found that, because of women's realistic fear of violence, they are less likely than men to use public spaces; this is still true in many parts of the world. For the most part, women choose a path that avoids clusters of men, tend not to dawdle or linger, are likely to move in pairs or other multiples in public, and, after accomplishing their goal, move expeditiously back to a private space. If women are victims of violence in a public space, chances are, some men will reason, they didn't follow the rules that govern female communal appearances, and probably deserved it. The public transportation system in several cities in India, including those in New Delhi, Mumbai, and Kolkata, have recently begun offering "Ladies Specials"—women-only commuter trains. In the United States, the reader probably assumes, matters are very different. Are women at risk here? Naturally, we are interested in how that issue plays itself out in Washington Square. Do women visit the park as often as men? And is it as *safe* an environment for women as for men?

Gender, Crime, and Danger

Demography paints an extraordinarily distinctive picture of women liv-ing in Manhattan. In the United States as a whole, a majority of women age twenty-six to forty-four, just under 60 percent, live with a spouse; for those forty-five to sixty-four, the figure is 63 percent. The compa-rable figures for men are 56 and 70 percent. In Manhattan, however, only a third of women twenty-six to forty-four (35%) live with a spouse, and for those forty-five to sixty-four, the proportion is four out of ten (42%). For men, these figures are 34 and 48 percent, respectively. The difference in living with a spouse, when we compare Americans generally versus Manhattanites specifically, is substantial, even huge, for both men and women.

The fact is, residents of Manhattan are *much* more likely to be single than is true of the country as a whole. It is possible that there are impli-cations of this fact for deviance and crime, with respect to both commission and victimization. On the basis of their domestic status alone, Manhattan women are far likelier to venture out of their residence, and hence, more likely to be in situations that challenge their safety, than women living elsewhere, and that includes the outer boroughs of New York City. Likewise, Manhattan men, again, considering this factor alone, have a higher chance than males elsewhere of engaging in unconventional behavior, including crime—and likewise being victimized by it—all other factors being equal.

Since most of the time that a woman is victimized by a crime, she is victimized by a man, the fact that there are more single men and more single women living in Manhattan than in the country as a whole lends a statistical edge to the possibility of crime by men, as well as the victimization of women, in New York and, potentially, in Washington Square Park. Just as interesting, though less predictive, are the educational and economic factors. Manhattan women are twice as likely to have four years of a college education as women in the United States as a whole, including those living in the other New York boroughs. And they earn about twenty thousand dollars more. How the educational and the socioeconomic factors play out with respect to deviance and crime is difficult to predict. Does this lower their likelihood of criminal victimization? Here, we are interested in whether and to what extent demographics and socioeconomic status contribute to gender-related crime and crime victimization in Washington Square.

City life poses a serious dilemma for the urban dweller. It offers adventure, excitement, and lots of interesting characters and lifestyles, few of which are available in rural areas. But it also poses the possibility of "dangers and personal harm" (Karp et al., 2015, p. 165). This dilemma is exacerbated for women in that a street encounter could result in a woman being followed and brutalized. Women have to devise "reaction strategies" that men often don't contemplate because many males feel invulnerable, feel they could overpower a potential attacker. Adventures that seem exciting to men feel scary and dangerous to women—"two very different definitions of reality and ways of experiencing urban life" (p. 169). With respect to danger versus excitement, urban space is distinctly gendered (p. 170).

As with making public appearances, behavior tends to be gender distributed; for instance, women are substantially less likely to engage in deviance and crime than men. We find only a few exceptions to this rule—shoplifting and prostitution, for example—but they are exactly that: exceptions to an *almost* iron-clad rule. For instance, in 2014, Uniform Crime Report data indicate that, for all homicides in which the offender is known, 88 percent were committed by men, 12 percent by women. This difference is virtually universal in the industrialized West. But in addition, as I just emphasized, men are substantially more likely than women to be the *victims* of crimes. As an example, consider the fact that, according to the FBI's yearly Uniform Crime Reports, consistently, year by year, three-quarters of all murder victims are men. This may be the case because men venture out in public, especially into problematic places, more than women do, and, in so doing, they increase their likelihood of engaging in interaction with others who might do them harm; some of these "others" include their own friends and acquaintances. People are more likely to be the victims of *intimate* violence than stranger violence, though on an *hour-by-hour basis*—given how much time we spend with intimates—stranger contact is more likely to lead to victimization, and quite possibly, even more so for females.

Even today, men also drink in bars more than women, which increases their chances of engaging in and encountering other men who also engage in rowdy, drunken behavior. Men are much likelier to participate in risk-taking behavior—behavior for which there is a definite likelihood of physical danger—and they tend to be more impulsive. Moreover, men interact more *with men* than women do, and in a greater variety of capacities, and hence, spend more time, especially more emotionally charged time, with the more dangerous sex of the species—their own. Men are significantly more likely to tread along virtually all social and psychological paths that lead to their possible victimization by acts of crime and deviance than is true of women.

Still, most of the time that women *are* victimized, they are victimized *by* men; hence, we might reason, other things being equal, the women who spend the most time with men are the ones most likely to be victimized by crime and deviance. When we look at the subject of deviance and gender, we are forced to consider the wrongful things that men do *to* women. As we've seen, serious crimes in Washington Square are rare, and most park visitors feel safe there, but we need to reference crime that takes place elsewhere, especially in public places, to serve as markers or comparisons. In addition, such conditions may tell us something about the assessment Manhattanites are likely to make with respect to when and where they shouldn't venture outside.

Early in adolescence, most females, more acutely than males, develop a *geography of fear*—a sense that certain places are more dangerous than others and should be avoided (Valentine, 1989). Women are statistically more likely to be the victims of crime *in private* than they are in public, true, but they *fear* public spaces more. This is not necessarily paradoxical since it is possible, to repeat, that on an hour-by-hour basis, intimates, in private, commit crimes against women *less* frequently than do strangers, as compared with public places. But the *total volume* of crimes against women is more likely to be committed by intimates, and characteristically in private. In 2010, the overall nonfatal victimization rate *by strangers* for the population at large was 7.1 per 1,000; the rate committed by *intimates* was 10.5 (Harrell, 2012, p. 1).

Roughly three-quarters of all criminal homicides that take place each year are committed by intimates. And with respect to homicide, consistently, men are more likely to *kill*, as well as *to be killed*, than women; likewise, men are more likely to *kill* a man than a woman, and to *be killed by* a man than a woman. When women *kill*, they tend to kill a man; when women *are* killed, they tend to *have been killed* by a man. In other words, men loom much larger than women in the fewer killings that women *commit*, and men loom much larger than women in the fewer killings that women *are the victims of.* Criminal homicide is a tiny (though immensely momentous) fragment of the total edifice of interpersonal crime; however, it may be paradigmatic in that much the same story prevails, with one or another wrinkle, for other crimes where one party victimizes another. And women's role in both crime and criminal victimization is causally related to their use of a public space such as a square or park. However safe the square is, there are few women who do not consider the possible danger posed by their appearance in public, and this thought process is particularly acute at night.

Women in Public

The behavior of men, specifically with respect to how they behave when they are in the company of women—for instance, in bars, on public transportation, and in the college classroom—relates directly to their behavior in a setting such as a public park, and hence, helps explain the distribution of women in and around Washington Square Park. The most desirable and attractive public spaces, says William H. Whyte, "tend to have a higher than average proportion of women. . . . Women are more discriminating as to where they will sit, more sensitive to annoyances, and women spend more time casting the possibilities." Whyte proposes a readily accessible indicator of the desirability of a public space: "If a plaza has a markedly lower than average proportion of women, something is wrong. Where there is a higher than average proportion of women, the plaza is probably a good one and has been chosen as such" (1980, p. 18).

The "something is wrong" dimension to which Whyte alludes is the factor of danger—specifically, danger to women. Unsafe public places tend not to draw the public at large, but they especially discourage women. Women take fewer physical risks than men, and they are *particularly* attuned to the fact that certain spaces put them at risk with respect to male disrespect, harassment, and physical aggression. Hence, to specify Whyte's formulation: If a public space draws large numbers of both men and women, and in more or less equal proportion, then it is almost certainly a *safe* place to be; even more specifically, it is a place where women are not likely to be victimized *as women*. "Women pick up on . . . cues of disorder better than men do," explains Dan Biederman, president of the Bryant Park Corporation; "if women don't see other women, they tend to leave." They "notice homeless people more than men do" and "are more sensitive to foul odors, such as that of urine, which signals that there are no bathrooms nearby." In the seventies, Bryant Park was in a state of "infamous shambles." Renovated, it is now to the point where more than half of its visitors are women (Paumgarten, 2007).

It *almost* does not need to be said (though Whyte does say it) that the sexual composition in a public space also depends on the ecology of the surrounding institutions from which that space largely draws. For instance, if the workforce of nearby offices is more male than female, or more female than male, other things being equal, the composition of the visitors of its closest park will reflect that fact (Whyte, 1980, p. 18). Times Square in the seventies and eighties reflected these principles. When this space was at its seediest, sleaziest, most drug-ridden, blighted, and most dangerous, when prostitutes patrolled the streets in search of customers, virtually everyone there (except the prostitutes) was a man; a study by the Urban Development Corporation revealed that 90 percent of the visitors to Times Square at that time were men (Stern, 1999); today, with the purge of drugs, porn, and prostitution, the sex ratio is more even. Bryant Park, located behind the New York Public Library, between Fortieth and Forty-second streets, is near many offices, and so the composition of their workforce—more women than men—reflects that fact. Lunch hour, for instance, finds many office workers taking their break on the grass in the park.

In almost all societies, the presence of women in certain public spaces, especially at night, is less frequent and their behavior, more cautious than for men, and in large part this phenomenon has its origin in the fear of being the victim of sexual harassment and crime, especially crimes of violence (Koskela, 1999; Schmucki, 2012). The observer may verify this public-private sex distribution by doing some systematic counting. The fact is that, in most places, women are less likely to venture outdoors, especially at night, than men; this is specifically true in urban spaces, though the ratio varies from one specific locale to another. In addition, the fact that women, when they do go out, are more likely to be *accompanied*—and accompanied by particular parties—reveals important features about gender relations and the dynamics of public behavior. Along with local and societal norms, the desirability and safety of a public place may be measured by how *nearly equal* the distribution of the sexes is.

Women in Washington Square

We notice substantial gender patterning in Washington Square, as there is in any public setting. It's not difficult to draw a connection between the public distribution of males and females and engaging in and being victimized by deviance and crime. According to New York's Department of City Planning, during the years relevant to these tallies (2015–2017), both New York City's and Manhattan's populations were 48 percent male and 52 percent female. I conducted my observations throughout the week, that is, both weekdays and weekends; these observations were made during daylight hours. (I tallied male versus female nighttime appearances separately.) Consider the role of propinquity, one of the points stressed by William H. Whyte: The student body of adjacent New York University, almost sixty thousand students, is 57 percent female.

In my counts, during the day, half the people walking into and around the central fountain area of the park during the daytime hours (4,352) were males (2,184) and half were females (2,168). Substantially more of the *singletons*—people who are alone—were men, 57 percent, while only 43 percent were women. But only 48 percent of the people in *dyads*—two people, together—were males, 52 percent were women, and for the triads (three people together), these figures were 44 and 56, respectively. And in the most gregarious social units, four or more people together, the "triads-plus," females made up nearly six in ten (59%) of their membership. In this locale at least, women are significantly less likely than men to appear in public alone, though they are significantly and consistently *more* likely than men to go out accompanied by a companion, whether female or, more often, male. And the predominance of singleton males in public is even more pronounced at night than during the daylight hours.

One of the most interesting findings in the dyad figures is that significantly more than half of them are *heterosocial*, that is, they are specifically a male and a female together; these are the MF dyads. With respect to the homosocial or "homophilous" dyads, slightly more were made up of two females together (24%) than two males together (19%); obviously, the remainder (57%) were heterosocial or heterophilous (MF) dyads. But the most interesting feature of these tallies is the contrast in the sociability of men versus women: To emphasize the point, males are the majority *only for singletons*; for *all* the *social* units, that is, with two or more parties, women make up more than half of the groupings. The daytime female edge in sociality is consistent and uniformly directional: as I said, the female composition of units increased as the size of the unit increased, from 43 percent for singletons to 52 percent for dyads, to 56 percent for triads, to 59 percent for triads-plus. Clearly, in Washington Square, females are the more sociable of the sexes.

The first seven components in table 6.1, from "persons in singletons" to "persons in triads-plus," examine the gender composition of units—how many males versus females are in singletons, dyads, triads,

TABLE 6.1. Gender Units, Washington Square Park, Daytime, 2015–2017

Persons in Singletons

Composition of Singletons	Number	Percent
Males	939	57
Females	697	43
Total	1636	100

Composition of Dyads

Dyads	Number	Percentage
MM Dyads	169	19
FF Dyads	215	24
MF Dyads	512	57
Total	896	100

Composition of Dyads	Total Ns	
Males in MM Dyads	338	
Females in FF Dyads	430	
Males in MF Dyads	512	
Females in MF Dyads	512	
Total	1792	

Persons in Triads-Plus	Number	Percent
Males	144	41
Females	210	59
Persons in Triads-Plus	354	100
Total Number of Triads-Plus	91	

Persons in Dyads	Number	Percent
Males	850	48
Females	942	52
Total	1792	100

Persons in Triads	Number	Percent
Males	251	44
Females	319	56
Total	570	100

(continued)

TABLE 6.1. (*cont.*)

Composition of Triads	Number	Percent
MMM Triads	26	14
FFF Triads	49	26
MMF Triads	58	31
MFF Triads	57	30
Total	190	100

	Totals for Males		Totals for Females		Totals	
	Number	Percent	Number	Percent	Number	Percent
Singletons	939	43	697	32	1636	38
Dyads	850	39	942	43	1792	41
Triads	251	11	319	15	570	13
Triads-Plus	144	7	210	10	354	8
Social Units	1245	57	1471	68	2716	62
Totals	2184	100	2168	100	4352	100
Overall Totals	2184	50	2168	50	4352	100

Source: Observations in Washington Square Park, central fountain area, five afternoons, 2015–2017; percentages are rounded off. These observations overlap with but are not identical to those in table 2.1. I did not count infants and toddlers.

and triads-plus. What percent of males versus females are in each unit? Women visit Washington Square as frequently as men, and when they *do* go out, they are more likely to be accompanied than men are; four in ten of all the men in the square (43%) are alone, while only a third of women are (32%) by themselves; conversely, then, 57 percent of men are in social units, but nearly seven in ten of women (68%) are. Another way of putting this is that males are slightly more likely to be in singletons than in dyads (43% versus 39%), while females are more likely to be in dyads than in singletons (43% versus 32%), but, on a total-person basis, both males and females are more likely to be in social units than alone.

For our interests, other factors being equal, the *comparative* solitude of males makes unconventional behavior more likely, while the sociability of females makes deviance, criminality, and untoward behavior—including victimhood—correspondingly less likely. Alternatively, when solitary males are in the substantial majority, this may be an indication that this is not a safe space, that conventional, female-friendly sociability may have been driven away. Washington Square *is* a safe space, particularly in comparison with those that are even more male populated, partly because it possesses multiple *other* features that discourage untoward behavior. Clearly, women feel welcome in Washington Square, though when they do visit, they are more likely to do so within a social context than males; males are more likely than females to visit the place unaccompanied. None of this is surprising, since, stereotypically—as well as in empirical reality—women tend to be more gregarious than men, girls more than boys. Again, levels of sociability both *cause* and *are caused by* degrees of crime, physical risk, and danger: The safer the place, the more that people visit and socialize there, and the more that people visit and socialize there, the safer it becomes, the point being that in a particular locale, certain *kinds* of gender aggregations foster a tendency toward agreeable sociability in that space. Moreover, the safer the place, the more likely it is that women visit it. When a public place is visited by a high proportion of women, the observer knows that it is a relatively safe space. (Of course, as I said, some locales that are not dangerous specialize in activities that are particularly appealing to men.) When few women go there, one reason is likely to be that it is known to be unsafe. The greater the number who visit the space, the more even the sex ratio is; and the more even the sex ratio, the lower the likelihood of untoward behavior. But there are very few serious felonies in the park, so such equations, though interesting, may be immaterial to begin with in regard to Washington Square, though it is far from irrelevant when we compare the square with more unsafe public spaces.

The results of the interviews I conducted with sixty park-goers add a somewhat different dimension to the gender and public space issue. I asked, "As a woman, do you feel safe in Washington Square Park?" Of the twenty-eight women in the sample, twenty-five gave a simple "Yes," "Yes I do," or, "Oh, yeah" answer to my question. One female respondent said that, the night before the interview, she had come to the park after midnight and felt safe even then. Another explained that since there are so many people around (Jane Jacobs's "eyes upon the street"), it's always safe. But there were three respondents who qualified their answer. One explained that, generally speaking, she feels safe in the park, but in the southwest quadrant, where marijuana dealing is transacted, she has felt unsafe, so she avoids taking the path through that sector. But a second qualifier said that "generally speaking, I don't feel 100 percent safe anywhere. But this [Washington Square] is no different from elsewhere, so, yeah, I feel as safe here as most other places." My third qualifier, Jane, a homeless woman, a former drug abuser and an ex-convict who often slept in the park or on the street, said, understandably, "I don't feel safe anywhere."

In addition to a specific question about how they assessed their safety in Washington Square Park, I also asked my respondents a more generic question: "Are there any specific problems when women appear in public?" Their answers reveal that *feeling safe* and *being vulnerable* are not quite the same thing. Women rendered a realistic and objective assessment of the likelihood—*some* likelihood—that appearing in public *may* subject them to certain physical risks that men do not face. The younger women pointed out that appearing in public subjected them, in the words of a twenty-year-old African American undergraduate, to having "guys coming on to them." "I came on to you," I countered. "That's not the same thing," she responded. "This is OK, that's different." A forty-four-year-old white woman said that whether or not a woman has problems in public "depends on her age. If I were in my early twenties, there would be problems. I might get approached. It's not going to happen anymore." Three women mentioned getting "catcalls" in the park, on the street, anywhere in public. A stereotypically beautiful model, cocktail and beer waitress, and aspiring writer in her late twenties explained the matter in the following words: "Women face the problem that open, public spaces are easy spots for voyeurs and harassers." While no urban locale is completely free of potential danger for women, my female respondents expressed the view that Washington Square is as safe as any public space is likely to be.

Gender and Busking

Busking is not entirely respectable and not entirely safe; it entails certain social and physical risks that are absent in most conventional activities. Few parents raise children with the aspiration that they will entertain passers-by for handouts. In addition, the activity's income stream is not secure or predictable, and it's difficult. It is not for the faint-hearted, the timid, the vulnerable, or the defenseless. Men are more likely than women to feel that they can protect themselves in risky situations; they are more likely to take physical chances than women, they injure themselves more, they get into fights more, and they are more likely to become victims of criminal homicide. They are more likely to rob—and be robbed. Men drink substantially more alcohol and are more likely to take psychoactive drugs for the purpose of getting high. Their tendency toward deviance and crime is greater. They are more likely to fly airplanes recreationally, and to drive cars recklessly and substantially faster than the speed limit. They are more likely to climb cliffs, hang-glide, parasail, parachute jump, to be willing to engage in unsafe sex, have sex with strangers, gamble when the stakes are high, and smoke—in short, to seek exciting, novel, and hedonistic sensations. The literature on gender differences in risk taking, and its obverse, risk aversion, is robust and consistent.

Jed Weinstein, in concert with his brother, a one-time busker, explains the matter of the activity's lack of respectability by describing the reaction, in a bar, of a young woman he wished to date, to whom he had just revealed what he did for a living. "Hey," she told him, "I'm sorry but I could never be with someone who performs on the streets. What would I tell my friends?" With that, she gulped the remainder of her appletini and "bolted" from the room. Jed got the picture. "I briefly entertained the notion that busking might be a shameful disorder. . . . When I went out with new women, I wrestled with whether I had to divulge my dark secret right away, or if I could wait a few dates first." He "practiced" his speech in front of a mirror. "Busking is not begging," he explained to his reflection. "Our hands are not simply outstretched. It's a trade, as in we trade our music for money." He reconciled himself to recognizing that "we'd hover forever just below the threshold of general acceptability." A performer with whom he had previously worked asked him, "You guys aren't homeless, are you?" He told the guy, no, he was simply "promoting the band" (Weinstein and Weinstein, 2011, p. 151).

What men feel is acceptable, in comparison with women, along with a host of other factors, leads me to the conclusion that they are more likely to engage in busking in a public space. Not all buskers are men—not by a long shot—but most are, and a substantial proportion of the women who do perform in public work with a man. Female buskers tend to be the exception rather than the rule. There are many reasons for this propensity, but it seems to be that the strongest factors here are several: the greater male tendency toward the chancy proposition, the higher likelihood that males will violate conventional norms, and the male willingness to make fools of themselves. All of the major performers Sally Harrison-Pepper discussed in her book on busking a generation ago in Washington Square Park, *Drawing a Circle in the Square* (1990)—the fire-eater, the mime, the turtle racer, the juggler, the puppeteer—were men. Is this tendency changing? Not now, and not yet.

In the park, there's a guy who carries around a cardboard sign that reads, "FREE HUGS," which, in spite of what his sign says, are not free; this is how he earns a living—by "busking" nonfree "free" hugs. He hugs unsuspecting prospective customers who aren't aware that the hugs aren't exactly "free." After hugging someone, he backs off, pulls his wallet out of his back pocket, then withdraws and displays a dollar bill, indicating what he wants from the transaction. Often, the customer is flustered and refuses to go along with the bait-and-switch, but some take out a bill and hand it to him—from his point of view, mission accomplished. Sometimes, from the point of view of the officers who patrol the park, however, he is a little too persistent. After he follows one of his reluctant clients too closely, an NYPD officer warns him, "Next time you do it, you get banned from the Park. You'll have to go to Tompkins Square."

The hugger looks downcast. "I don't want to be banned from this park. And I don't want to go to Tompkins Square."

After the officer leaves, I approach the hugger and ask, "What did that NYPD say you were doing wrong?"

"Harassing people." He replies. "But that's in the past. It's not going to happen again. I'm going to stay right here." A week later, I saw him with his sign; he hugged me and it was actually free. Since we're considering the role that gender plays in busking, consider how a woman who offers "free hugs" in the park would be treated. Solicitation, anyone?

A man who calls himself Kyler and wears a pointed wizard's cap gives astrology readings with Tarot cards; that's how he earns a living. Joe Mangrum, the sand painter, is likewise doing his thing; he's just begun sand painting an image immediately south of the Arch. He receives donations in a white plastic bucket. In the southwest corner of the park, the chess players—more in the way of hustlers than buskers—are doing their thing; on this occasion, the tables are full, all of the chess entrepreneurs are men, all are black, all except one of their opponents is a man, and all the opponents except one are white. Johan Figueroa, the human statue, is posing in the fountain circle. Rasheed and the Jazz Collective, all male, is performing "After Dark." There's a guy who's spinning a gold-colored spool on a string; he has placed an overturned Asian straw hat on top of a cardboard box with several dollar bills inside, into which he'd like passersby to place more. Tic and Tac Barnes, an athletic tumbling act, have drawn a crowd of nearly a hundred southwest of the Arch, near the stone benches. Separately, there are two guys sitting on stools in front of typewriters, offering to write poems on request. Eddie Rodriguez, a mime with abundant and colorful props, does his Marcel Marceau–type routine but without whiteface. Female buskers here are in the distinct minority.

Many acts are not successful; they are unappealing, and park-goers pass them by, or they gather in minuscule numbers. Performances frequently fall flat; that magical reaction between the performer, the act, and the audience that should ignite often fizzles. A man in his thirties sporting a straw-colored goatee and a cowboy hat is standing next to the fountain, holding a rubber chicken by the neck in one hand and a bullwhip, which he cracks, in the other. A bottle of water and an egg rest at his feet. "I'm about to attempt the world's most dangerous feat," he announces. Pedestrians walk by him with barely a sidelong glance. He puts down the chicken and holds up the egg. "I'm going to crack *this* egg with *this* whip!" A young Asian woman stands in front of him and smiles. "Is no one going to stop me?" he intones. He cracks the whip again. Then he opens his hand and the egg is gone; then reaches behind the young woman's ear and retrieves the egg. She giggles and claps and a young man about to pass by joins her. Eventually his audience reaches a stable size of four. He tries to bunch them together, possibly to attract more viewers; he tries to herd them closer to him—all of his efforts fail. The foursome waits patiently for something to happen. He puts down the egg and holds up the bottle, announcing that he's going to slug down its contents in one gulp; he takes one swallow and says he's changed his mind. "Hm," he grunts, "this isn't happening." It's the kind of act that might work at a four-year-old's birthday party, but not here. The would-be magician needs more props, bigger gimmicks, more flamboyance, charisma, experience, and skill.

What we see in the performances and acts in Washington Square is a decided lopsidedness with respect to gender. During a three-year period, during fifteen visits, I conducted a running census of the gender of the money-seeking acts and performances in Washington Square. From May 2014, when the renovation of the park was completed, until April 2017, I counted 131 male and 17 female buskers. The skewing of the totals should not be surprising. Some endeavors, like busking, place the actor out over the edge with respect to physical risk and social respectability, not to mention appearing foolish. Moreover, busking is both overt and public, on the one hand, and anonymous, on the other; hence, it exposes women to the possibility that men with lewd designs on them have the opportunity to express those designs.

Public Nudity

On the grassy stretch of grass just southwest of the Arch, three young women are taking in the sun's warmth. Two are sitting on a blanket, topless, and the third is wearing a pullover, lying face down. A man walks across the grass and takes their picture; the women seem unconcerned and don't even acknowledge him. From the walkway, about twenty feet away, another man stops and takes their picture. The woman who was lying down sits up and takes off her pullover, then her bra. A police car cruises by along the walkway leading to Washington Place, past the Holley bust. The cops glance at the topless women but they do not stop. Perhaps they got a complaint from a neighbor that there were "naked women" prancing around in the park. The women don't even look at the cops; one of them is texting on her cell.

A tall, angular-looking man, wildly gesticulating, walks onto the grass toward the topless women, stops, stands about eight feet away from them, ogling them for three or four minutes, then he walks away; the whole time, the women completely ignore him. Three more photographers, one from the grass, two from the walkway, take their picture. An organized group of teenagers with badges, probably prospective NYU students, walks by along the pathway, away from the fountain; two of them glance shyly, almost surreptitiously, at the young women. A young man, possibly an NYU student, sitting on the grass about ten feet away from the topless quintet, is staring at them; he begins writing a message on his laptop. The amount of attention the incident attracts would register roughly in the middle of an attention-meter—less than a fight but a great deal more than a homeless man babbling to himself. Recall the rules on staring, ogling, and leering I spelled out earlier: How much staring at naked women in public is warranted? Does being naked in public *invite* staring? Did these women *want* people to stare at them—to make a political point? When does staring become ogling? When does ogling become leering?

Most states outlaw public nudity. New York Statute 245 decrees that a person is guilty of public lewdness when he or she intentionally exposes the "private or intimate parts" of his or her body—for a female, technically, below the tops of the areola. Appearing nude in public (except in a nudist colony or designated nude beach) constitutes a class B misdemeanor. But in 1992, the New York State Court of Appeals ruled that any law that discriminates against women by prohibiting them from exposing their breasts while men are allowed to display theirs cannot be legally justified; in May 2013, the NYPD issued a statement to the effect that women who go topless in public are not violating the law. (Detective Alberici, in my interview with him that follows chapter 4, expresses that position.) A pamphlet for police officers reads, "Witnessing a woman exposing her breasts may lead some men, particularly those under the influence of alcohol, to believe they have permission to pursue sexual activity with her" (Johnson, 2005, p. 11).

To most heterosexual males, the sight of women's bare breasts is sexually arousing, while women tend not to react in nearly the same way to a man's naked chest. Lab experiments on male sexual arousal verify the reasoning, and it works for the tens of millions of men who call up Internet porn daily—but the justice of the prohibition is nonetheless debatable. Evidently, these young women are attempting to redefine the law, as well as the norm, regarding public female toplessness. They're saying, "We have the same rights as men do!" *DNAinfo.com* lists Washington Square Park as one of the five best public spots in New York City for women to go topless. They hope to reconfigure the stereotype of female nudity as conveying an automatic implication of sexuality. Notice: These women are not completely naked—they are merely topless. Men go topless without a sidelong glance, but, as with these women, do not appear nude from top to bottom.

The Outdoor Co-ed Topless Pulp Fiction Appreciation Society holds irregular "meetings" in various parks in Manhattan; Washington Square Park seems to be one of their favorite locales. Judging from the photographs on its website, all of the members of this society are attractive young women, and almost all are white. "It's finally sunny and warm," declares Anonymous on the June 2, 2012, post, "Remember: It's Your Right," adding, "and guys are going merrily shirtless all over town. It's legal for us too, and there is absolutely no reason you shouldn't do it anywhere a man can." As developments unfolded, the issue proved to be somewhat more complicated. An earlier, August 18, 2011, blog post mentions that, in Central Park, several men, one of them supposedly French, ogled and harassed them, so the members of the society decided to move their protests to Washington Square, "where the men were much more respectful." Consider the potential of this manner of protest in both attracting attention and overturning the status quo: On election day, November 8, 2016, two women walked into Republican candidate Donald Trump's voting site at a gym on East Fifty-sixth Street, topless, and began shouting anti-Trump slogans. They were quickly escorted out of the building, but not before they made their point. Absent their toplessness, the protest would not have merited a *Daily News* story.

In my survey of Washington Square Park visitors, respondents regarded the wrongfulness ranking of women appearing topless somewhere in the middle of potential violations I asked about—more serious than feeding squirrels, less so than feeding pigeons. Women respondents were slightly more likely to judge female public toplessness as wrong than men (43% versus 35%), but given the small sample, a difference of less than 10 percent would be unlikely to survive a statistical test. Half the respondents adopted a live-and-let-live attitude, and even the nay-sayers objected to topless women appearing in the park mainly because they didn't want children to be exposed to nudity. Several of my interviewees raised the cultural relativity issue—it's accepted in Western Europe, why not here?

On the other hand, aside from the Outdoor Co-ed Topless Pulp Fiction Appreciation Society demonstration, I have never seen a woman sunbathing topless on a blanket on the grass in Washington Square. (In roughly a thousand hours of observation, just north of the fountain, I saw one non-sunbathing topless woman, who was casually chatting with a male companion. One.) Toplessness has not caught on in New York City, and both the dense, congested nature of the park—and the fact that it is, after all, a park that attracts many families—ensures that the custom will be judged as at least mildly deviant; if a woman were to appear topless in this location, it would stir up commentary, and the woman would be regarded as an eccentric. But the protesters are making a point: Men do it frequently, and with little comment—why raise such a fuss when women do it? This is the twenty-first century; why aren't women allowed the same rights as men? Alternatively, the implications of normatively overlooking women going topless are substantial. Men and women appear before one another, accompanied by children, completely naked in nudist camps. Such an act would be predicated on an entirely different set of gender roles for both men and women. What would it take for us to achieve that goal? These women hope to socialize the society into fuller gender equality.

During July 2017, New York City experienced a substantial heat wave, with temperatures consistently hovering in the high nineties for a week. Members of the Human Connection Arts, male and female, took all their clothes off, painted one another's bodies, and waded into the central fountain pool, completely nude. A photographer, Milo Hess, captured one middle-aged couple, their arms blue from the body paint, fondling one another's bare bottoms. A young, female member of the organization, kneeling on a towel and surrounded by small paint cans containing a variety of colors, applied pink paint, by hand, to the legs of a sandaled man with a sagging belly. No doubt fun was had by all ("Art Does," 2017). It seems almost unnecessary to point this out, but I shall anyway: Both this event and the one sponsored by the Pulp Fiction Appreciation Society were expressions of an organized group's views—not routine, culturally grounded practices for the community or the denizens of the park as a whole.

The Ecology of Gender in Washington Square

Men and women distribute themselves in somewhat different ways in the park; men are more likely to visit or walk through particular spaces, while women are more likely to frequent different ones. Obviously, their paths cross, their geographies overlap, but there is a pattern with respect to the park's ecological distribution. Most people, when they walk through the square, notice that several sectors west of the fountain seem sketchy—and they are in fact spots where marijuana sellers engage in commerce. After I interview Ann, a retired office worker in her seventies, I decide to look at how women distribute themselves in the park. She tells me that she had decided to avoid specific areas of the park whose denizens seem "suspicious." Because of this seeming menace, I decide, there must be a "gender ecology" within Washington Square Park. And indeed, there is.

I set forth a reasonable hypothesis of gender ecology: Because the central fountain area is so heavily congregated, patrolled, and surveilled, it is the safest; hence, the ratio of women relative to men must be higher than that of men to women. Because the perimeter walkway is darker, less easily observed, planted with an abundance of bushes, and distant from the busy center, the ratio of men to women must be higher. There were two potential flies in the ointment of this theory: One, the perimeter walkways are immediately adjacent to the street—separated only by a bush or two—namely, Washington Square North, South, East, and West, and hence, people are likely to be walking close by to intervene in case of danger. And two, the three playgrounds are all adjacent to the perimeter walkway and hence, those are spots where women—mothers and child caretakers—are likely to congregate, walking in and out and, often, sitting down to talk.

Factors and speculations aside, as we saw in table 6.1, the proportion of women versus men in the fountain circle—walking, standing, sitting, in the fountain itself or perched on its barrier—is close to fifty/fifty—2,184 men and 2,168 women. Promising, I thought. Then I walk clockwise around the outer ring walkway, from the western side of the Arch around to its eastern side; I count everyone who sets foot in the path, sitting, walking in either direction, standing and looking around.

I do not count the adults or children in the playgrounds nor anyone in the dog runs. Along the perimeter pathway, I count 162 men (61%) and 103 women (39%). My commonsensical theory seems to hold up, I thought. Obviously, as with everything else sociological, this is a variable, so the pattern will be somewhat different according to time of day, day of the week, weather, and so on, but the basic observation is a good place to start.

Clearly, the sexes are ecologically distributed in Washington Square. Men and women distribute themselves in somewhat different locations throughout the park, and, in all likelihood, this emplacement is gender related. The central fountain area is well-attended and everyone is visible there. An untoward event—whether directed at a woman specifically or a victim of either gender—is unlikely to take place there because there's nowhere to hide. The PEP and NYPD are more likely to be there than anywhere else in the park, and that's where the surveillance cameras are. As I've said, with respect to victimization, the park itself is extremely safe, though the fountain area gives off the safest *aura* of any spot in the park. The fringe areas are darker, more closed in, less closely surveilled, and offer bushes as concealment, as well as a short route out of the park and onto the streets in case of flight from an offense. The central-fountain-versus-perimeter-walkways contrast in gender distribution offers an obvious explanation: perceived safety.

Women in the Square at Night

I've indicated in several discussions that women tend to be more concerned about their safety in public than men. As I pointed out, women are more likely to congregate in the central fountain area than in the peripheral pathways, they fear being victimized by crime in public more than men do, they are more likely to sense danger in a potentially dicey situation, in most urban areas, women venture out in public less than men, most public locales are regarded as "male" spaces, and so on. Nighttime in the park would seem to be a paradigmatic context to use to illuminate the matter of gender-related safety. As Holley Whyte reminds us, public places where we find few women are not good or safe places; those in which a high proportion of women gather are good and safe (1980, p. 18). This seems an appropriate juncture to move beyond the message conveyed in table 6.1, which looks at the square's *daytime* gender-related units and aggregations, by examining the park's gender-related nighttime sociability. If Washington Square Park is a safe place for women to visit in general, it should be safe at night as well.

Table 6.2 addresses the matter of Washington Square Park at night. I visited the park after 9:00 on three occasions, one weekend and two weekday evenings. (Again, I did not count infants and toddlers.) Note that a very substantial number of females enter the park at night—48 percent of the total—quite a remarkable showing for women at night in an urban area, a very reliable and valid indication of the safety of the park. The same pattern of sociability we see during the day is displayed at night, but with a more substantial edge for male singletons—67 versus 33 percent for females. Well over half of all dyads (59%) are MF (male-female) dyads, just under half of the composition of all dyads (49%) are female, 52 percent of the composition of triads is female, and 56 percent of the persons in triads-plus are women. Again, even at night, women appear in the park in substantial numbers, but, understandably, they appear in sociable units more than men. At the same time, the tendency of women to venture out at night in social units, while substantial during the day, is even greater at night. As we saw, as the size of the social unit increases, women increasingly make their appearance, again emphasizing the point that women are more sociable than men in a public park, and at night even more so than during the day. Though the danger presented by Washington Square Park, even at night, seems slight, clearly the sociability factor plays a role in female patterns of aggregation here, during the evening hours, as well as during the day.

As we saw earlier, the assembly of women versus men in the park raises two points that tie in specifically with deviance, one addressing the factors that make for women and men *coming to the park*—at all, as well as in units of a certain size—and the second raising the matter of what such assembly suggests about the behavior of men and women once they are *in* the park.

TABLE 6.2. Gender Units, Washington Square Park, Nighttime, 2017

Total Number of people		3265	
Total number and percentage of males		1709 (52%)	
Total number and percentage of females		1556 (48%)	
Singletons		586	
Singletons who are male		394 (67%)	
Singletons who are female		195 (33%)	
Of all males, what % are singletons		23%	
Of all females, what % are singletons		13%	

Dyads		Males	Females
Total N of people	1486	765	721
Total N of dyads	743		
M-M dyads	165 (22%)	330	
F-F dyads	143 (19%)		286
M-F dyads	435 (59%)	435	435
Total N of dyads with males		600	
Total N of dyads with females			578
Percent composition of dyads		51%	49%
Of all males and females, what % are in dyads		45%	46%

Triads (N=174)		Males	Females
MMM Triads	29 (17%)	87	
FFF Triads	36 (21%)		108
MMF Triads	57 (33%)	114	57
MFF Triads	52 (30%)	52	104
Total people	522	253	269
Percent composition of triads		48%	52%
Of all males and females, what % are in triads		15%	17%

Triads-Plus		
Number of units	145	
Number of people in triads-plus	668	
Males in triads-plus	297 (44%)	
Females in triads-plus	371 (56%)	
Of all males, what % are in triads-plus	17%	
Of all females, what % are in triads-plus	24%	

Source: Three summer, nighttime observations (after 9:00 p.m.) of gender-related units in Washington Square, one weekend and two weekday evenings, fountain area; I did not count infants or toddlers. Percentages are rounded off.

To reiterate the point, as a general rule, women are more likely to socialize with others than men, with men as well as with women; they are more social creatures than men, they engage in more social activities—and are more likely to be motivated and socially pressured to do so—than is true of men. More specifically, women are more likely than men to feel that they should be accompanied when they enter public spaces, and they are more likely to feel uncomfortable alone in public. They are half as likely to comprise singletons as is true of men. To put the matter another way, women have to overcome more formidable barriers to venture out on their own than men do, especially in urban spaces, and yet, the nighttime presence of women in the park is substantial—in my count, 1,556 women versus 1,709 men. Again, Washington Square is an extremely safe public space, even at night; as we've seen, for the most part, women *feel* safe there, and they are more likely to go there than to other public places, everything else being equal. Social aggregation, as with everything else we've seen in the park, is sociologically patterned, and it falls on the side of minimizing differences between males and females, especially in public, and most especially at night.

But there's a second point at issue here as well. The percentage of males and females overall, and the percent in particular of the gender configurations of units, lend a certain likelihood that, once there, park-goers will engage in specific forms of behavior. A likelihood is not a certainty; we all know that. But likelihood is what it is, and the higher the percentage of males, and of single males in particular, increases the chance that unconventional behavior will take place in a public space. As police records show, and as I've pointed out multiple times, Washington Square is far from a crime-ridden locale; felonies are extremely rare there, and males hugely outnumber females among the perpetrators of these few offenses. In the park, numerous less serious offenses are common, notable among them, marijuana selling, and far less commonly, crack use. In addition, eccentricities of all kinds abound. Again, males are the typical offenders of the more serious of these offenses, and, though females continue to come to the park, they are more likely to congregate in the central fountain area than gravitate to the peripheral pathways. Of necessity, many females walk along the pathways leading in and out of the fountain area, but most are expeditious about it. The one anomaly is the playground located in the southwest quadrant of the park, which is occupied only during the day. As with daytime foot traffic, at night, social units are more common than singletons, and for both females and males, dyads are the most common *social* unit in the park. Even at night, male-female dyads, the most conventional social unit, outnumber all others. A more detailed and formidable study might very well trace out the intricate lines of causality here, but in advance of that study, I'd speculate that male-female aggregation patterns both reflect and play a role in the park's relative safety and its low crime rate. The fact that this plays itself out in an atmosphere of tolerance for diversity and milder forms of deviance is noteworthy.

* * *

Interview with Jane, a Homeless Woman

When young, Jane must have been an attractive, lively woman. Now, at forty, her eyes have a haunted, apprehensive look, as if she were scanning her surroundings for assailants. Her hair is brown and straight and appears to have been recently brushed, but her mouth is missing most of its teeth. Three years ago, she tells me, she supported herself as an assistant super of a small, less-than-respectable building, and it gave her a place to live, a roof over her head—a domicile. Today, Jane is homeless. It almost goes without saying but it's worth reiterating: Homelessness is a difficult and potentially dangerous way to live; it is especially so for women.

"Do you live in a shelter?" I ask her.

"I avoid the shelters. There are a lot of crazy people in shelters. You can get hurt if you live in one. I live on the street."

"Why? How did it happen?"

"I lost my job. I lost everything. The owner moved two guys into the building. They were dealers. I couldn't stop what was going on even if I tried—I'd get hurt. The landlady asked me to move out. But I was arrested. An undercover cop said I tried to sell him drugs, which was BS. I did two years in prison. Now, I have one blanket and one sleeping bag, which I have tucked away somewhere. I hope they haven't gotten wet in this rain. I sleep [names a location] where there are grates that keep you warm."

"It must be dangerous, sleeping out on the street."

"Once, I was sleeping with my purse under my head. Someone must have propped up my head and put a big, fluffy pillow under it when I was sleeping, and they went through my purse. They stole my teeth! When I woke up, I looked in my purse and my teeth were gone. Can you imagine that?"

For me, her story lacks the details that pull a narrative together. I press on, yearning to know more about her inability to reintegrate herself back into the world of the more-or-less housed, but she seems emotionally fragile, and so I don't want to become overly intrusive or verbally pushy. Still, something's not quite right in her narrative. "Jane, what do you think caused your problems? Why the difficulty with getting a job? How exactly did you end up on the street? Why this spiral downward? What's behind it all? Did you have a drug problem, a drinking problem, some mental difficulty?"

"No, well, I *did* have a drug habit awhile back but I haven't used anything in two years, I've been off heroin, I'm clean, I'm never going back to using again. I did my time in prison, I was in prison for two years, but I've gotten myself straightened out. I get depressed about some of the things I've done, maybe the depression has helped bring me down, I don't know . . ." Her voice trails off and she looks away, off somewhere, through the trees. Jane's mind was elsewhere. I decided not to pursue the matter.

Two days after our interview, I run across Jane near the bench where we had talked earlier, so I sit down and we chat. She tells me that during the previous night, someone stole her sleeping bag and blanket. "Oh, no, that's terrible!" I respond. "So how and where are you going to sleep?" She says she'll figure something out. I reply, "Listen, my wife and I have some sleeping bags and extra blankets, I can give you one of each. I'll be back in twenty minutes. You'll be here when I get back, right?" I ask. Jane nods.

I rush home—my wife is out—and, without asking her permission, grab one of our sleeping bags, stuff it into a Citarella shopping bag, then shove a blanket into a trash bag, and run back to the bench, but Jane is gone, and I can't find her. I try to think of a thousand reasons why she wouldn't be there, but I'm still surprised. I run around, checking one corner, then another, and hang around the vicinity for almost an hour; I finally realize that she hadn't shown up for a reason known only to herself. When I later tell my wife about this, she says, "That's the sort of thing that happens when you deal with mentally disordered, homeless people. Maybe she forgot."

7

The Heterotopia

We are in the epoch of simultaneity; we are in the epoch of juxtaposition, the epoch of the near and far, of the side-by-side, of the dispersed.
—Michel Foucault, 1986

Medicine defines the heterotopia as "a spatial displacement of normal tissue" (Lax, 1998, p. 115); it is a site in which biological material is *out of place*. The etymology of the word "heterotopia," from the Greek, indicates the conjunction of "*hetero*," meaning "another" or "different," and "*topos*," or "place." This peculiar medical irregularity or deviation inspired the French philosopher Michel Foucault to draw parallels with the social world. Perhaps, he reasoned, we may fruitfully apply the notion to gain insight into the workings of social institutions and practices. As with many of Foucault's concepts, as applied to the social world, the heterotopia concept offers intellectual paradoxes, clever literary conceits, and derivations that might seem far-fetched and obscure to the more traditional observer.

The heterotopia is a space that challenges or subverts the hegemonic order, one that valorizes differentness and diversity. Foucault's heterotopia assumes a multiplicity of guises; indeed, the concept itself has inspired a multiplicity of interpretations, the explication of which would fill a substantial shelf of works by authors with a panoply of scholarly, academic, and literary allegiances and practices. Big ideas tend to attract the attention of lots of thinkers and writers from a diversity of traditions and disciplines; weighed by that criterion, the heterotopia is a big idea. And big ideas are usually controversial; thus, multiple scholars have challenged and critiqued the various images and diverse treatments of it. Peter Johnson refers to the concept as "elusive"; Foucault often examines the past to understand the present; his conceptualization of the heterotopia seems a dimension that we can apply, in varying degrees, to all periods of history.

Heterotopias *desanctify* barriers—those between public and private, family and more generic or common social spaces, places of leisure and work, culture and practical utility (Foucault, 1986, p. 23). They represent the "other," set in a context of the "everyday," the ordinary, routine, typical, or expected. There is probably, Foucault declared, "not a single culture in the world that fails to constitute heterotopias" (p. 24). Heterotopias *juxtapose* entities that are "incompatible" or "foreign to" one another within a particular locale or space (p. 25), yet paradoxically they "somehow mirror and at the same time distort, unsettle or invert other spaces" (Johnson, 2013, pp. 790–91).

Rather than tying down his definition to a single species, variety, or interpretation, Foucault offered a bouquet of them—much in the spirit of the concept of the heterotopia itself. *Heterotopias of deviation* are "places in which individuals whose behavior is deviant in relation to the required mean or norm" (Foucault, 1986, p. 25) may be found. Such places include rest homes, psychiatric hospitals, and prisons. The garden is a "microcosm," the "smallest parcel of the world," which embodies a presentation of plant species arranged, side by side, to "symbolic perfection," while, at the same time, offering "the totality of the world." The cemetery, a "heterochronistic" heterotopia, is a place that is both terminal for the deceased—a representation of the loss of life—yet is simultaneously quasi-eternal, an emplacement or representation of perpetuity. Museums and libraries are heterotopic in the sense of offering a shelf-by-shelf collection of cultural archives from all epochs, forms, and tastes—bringing together the full sweep of historical time in a singular, concrete, immobile place. Brothels, bordellos, or houses of prostitution are heterotopias in that they accept customers from all walks of life, customers who, in the absence of paying, would not and could not associate with the women with whom they pay to have sex. Many prostitutes cater to the fantasies of their customers—mostly respectable men who should not be patronizing them in the first place, though clearly engaged in a disreputable activity. They are "there" but "not there"; that is, they may be lying to their wives or girlfriends about where they are going or have been. The same heterotopic designation applies to the motel room, to which the philandering married man "goes with his car and his mistress and where illicit sex is both absolutely sheltered and absolutely hidden, kept isolated without however being allowed out in the open" (p. 27).

The carnival or fairground offers anomalous or "heteroclite" performers or exhibits—"wrestlers, snakewomen, fortune-tellers, and so on" (p. 26). *Temporal* heterotopias embody time "in its most fleeting, transitory, precarious aspects," such as with festivals celebrating the past and vacation villages in which guests may live in bogus primitive huts (p. 26). The boat is a "floating piece of space, a place without a place, that exists by itself, that is closed in on itself and at the same time is given over to the infinity of the sea," which sails "from port to port, from tack to tack, from brothel to brothel" and "goes as far as the colonies in search of the most precious treasures they conceal in their gardens" and hence, offers "the greatest reserve of the imagination. The ship," Foucault declared, "is the heterotopia *par excellence*" (p. 27).

To most observers, this mélange of gaudy specimens is likely to seem incoherent, a mixed bag of gadgets so motley that they scarcely belong together. Moreover, Foucault's notion of the heterotopia gathers unto itself heterogeneous *kinds* of contrasting juxtapositions—one or more features of different and almost random dimensions, aspects, and universes of corporeality. The ability to successfully bridge such enormous conceptual chasms is, again, the sign of a major thinker, and many observers believe that, in devising the notion of the heterotopia, Foucault succeeded in his mission of putting this jagged puzzle together. But other commentators believe that, while imaginative, the notion is half-baked, insufficiently theorized, much in need of sharpening (Harvey, 2008).

It seems to me that Foucault meant his concept of the heterotopia to be suggestive and heuristic, almost symbolic, rather than conclusive, definitive, or precise—more dramatic, literary, and imaginative than scrupulously and literally ethnographic. In any case, the notion has passed out of Foucault's stewardship; it has been customized to multiple uses and contexts. Judging from his typology, we can apply the concept to nearly any locale that either contrasts sharply with society's norms or emplaces diverse occupants in side-by-side juxtaposition. The heterotopia delineates conceptualizations that, according to some observers, offer a "dazzling variety" of "reimaginings" of material-world spaces, including Arabic-Islamic architecture, an off-shore pirate radio station, the shopping mall, the nude beach, Internet pornography, American Chinatowns, and the heroin shooting gallery (Johnson, 2013, pp. 796–97). Here, I'd like to proffer another candidate for inclusion.

Foucault and his followers stress some of the following criteria as defining elements of the heterotopia. *First*, it represents a challenge or at least a counterinstance of the prevailing or dominant normative, social, or political order. *Second*, the heterotopia accepts, tolerates, or exposes parties to a diversity of viewpoints, experiences, and/or parties or participants. *Third*, it offers or serves a *diversity of functions*. *Fourth*, it represents a space that is antimundane, *beyond the quotidian*, the everyday; it personifies, or takes the visitor or occupant to a place that is different from or stretches beyond the familiar, the commonplace—thereby activating one's imagination, enabling one to think about or experience something different, unusual, unconventional. *Fifth*, the embeddedness of "multiple meanings" centers on "spatio-temporal contradictions or ambiguities" in a "social or cultural space that is both in place and out of place" (Johnson, 2013 p. 797). And *sixth*, while heterotopias offer a "sanctuary" from everyday life, they also propose "opportunities and dangers" and enable a place where "unfamiliar aspects of the self and the other" emerge. The heterotopia "mirrors, condenses, and transforms" the surrounding or outside spaces (p. 799).

Jane Jacobs discussed the concept of the heterotopia—*sans* the name—nearly a decade before Foucault coined the term, but the contrast between the two delineations is illuminating. Foucault fires laser beams into a diversity of material-world examples, pinpointing a strange-fruit mixture of quirks, oddities, and jarring conundrums that share the single conceptual feature of incorporated juxtapositions. In contrast, Jacobs paints an idealistic, almost giddy portrait of variegated urban landscapes depicted in the best possible light. What draws or magnetizes people to an urban space? she asks. Such places offer a variety of functions; they are used for multiple purposes, but local residents "are able to use many facilities in common" (1961, p. 196). Dense concentrations of people, especially those "who are there because of residence" (p. 197), are drawn to certain places that are lively and fun. And the presence of people draws even more people, usually more diverse than the locals, attracted by the variety and contrasts of a space's sights, sounds, and happenings; it offers promenades for promenaders, theater for audiences who seek drama, and spectacle for passersby (Jacobs, 1958).

But sadly, during the post–World War II era, one of the reasons so many urban dwellers moved to the suburbs was to flee from the very diversity that Jacobs celebrates. She refers to the "unbelievable dullness" of the suburbs (1961, p. 360), but the goal of the middle-class whites who fled to these suburbs, well in progress when she wrote, was to live in a safer, neater, more manicured, less diverse, and more predictable—and ultimately, more boring—community than the cities they left. What the urban residents who fled to the suburbs did *not* want was the heterotopia; what they *wanted* was to be surrounded by people who looked a great deal more like themselves than was true of the places they left. Of course, the ideal heterotopia should be fun—"carnivalesque." And safe, but with more than a hint of danger. And that is what the new suburbanites gave up in making this transition.

Washington Square is a successful park, Jacobs tells us, because it is intricate and complicated, that is, because it has many features and functions, and there's always lots to do and hence, lots of people are attracted to it and feel charmed by the place. People watching is entertaining, and often, the entertainers and spectators—the people who are watching the entertainers—become indistinguishable and mixed up with them. The park also has a feature that Jacobs feels helps *center* a public space—that is, its fountain (1961, pp. 91, 116, 133–35). The blocks around the square are short and, though the residents who live in buildings surrounding the park are decidedly not diverse, the buildings are as stylistically diverse an aggregation of architectures as can be found anywhere—from low-rise to high-rise, from modernist to Federalist, from small and quaint to grand and imposing. No one could be bored by squaring the square, time traveling as one does through more than a century of American architectural history.

Architecture provides but a metaphor—a stage or set—for social relations. Just as anatomy is not destiny, so a space's physical setting does not dictate the social relations that take place there. The fact is, as we've seen, most of the park's visitors come there from somewhere else. Washington Square, like many urban spaces, has more than its share of undesirables; hence, we become intrigued by the matter of how social order is achieved in Washington Square. Banishment is a common practice elsewhere (Beckett and Herbert, 2009) but, given the substantial visible presence of "undesirables" in Washington Square, the layperson's impression is that keeping out the mentally disordered, the alcoholics, and the homeless does not prevail here. We might be interested in how such parties mix and mingle with the visitors who are more conventional, more mainstream, what the nature of such sociability is, and, further, if it does take place, whether and to what extent such contact transforms parties involved in the interaction. On the surface, it might seem that the powerless, fringier denizens can't do much to challenge the hegemonic conception of proper public behavior, but does the hegemon adapt to the fringe? In short: Is Washington Square Park a heterotopia?

Here's a wrinkle on Foucault's notion of the heterotopia: He suggests that *diversity* is not the same thing as mere *heteronormativity*. Mentally disordered persons do not so much challenge or undermine society's dominant normative structure as emplace themselves next to it, much like the medically abnormal tissue that launched the concept. And yet, in their mentally disordered condition, such people regard their behavior and their rantings as perfectly reasonable. Hence, Foucault's concept harbors a bias or skew—that is, it assumes that no one in his or her right mind would *choose* to act that way or say those things. And yet, here they are, doing and saying things that they consider reasonable and we don't. No matter; the mentally disordered are a fraction of the whole, and enough heteroclite actors do defy the political and cultural orthodoxy to make Washington Square a species of heterotopia. And meanwhile, the mainstream takes in—and perhaps is touched by—the spectacle.

A mime, Eddie Rodriguez, is in the center of the fountain. A video crew, probably NYU film students, all in their early twenties, is setting up in the fountain and an assistant is trying to convince the mime to move his stuff aside, but he gives her a long-winded story about why he refuses—apparently, the man does talk, and effusively! The models are smiling at one another as the female assistant talks for about fifteen minutes to the recalcitrant performer. Her entreaties ("We help the park by paying for a permit to shoot here") are to no avail; Rodriguez stays put, very much in their way. At some point, her face registers exasperation and she walks back to the crew. "I give up," she declares. "Do the best you can," she tells a fellow crew member. The mélange of stuff he has strewn about in the center of the fountain next to the central platform includes a red towel, his rolled-up pullovers and a jacket, what looks like a tall, orange, paperboard Chinese menu with gold scrolling, his big blue rollie, a black half-rollie, a large, silver disc, a Zen-type book (with a Yin and Yang on the cover), a sheaf of papers in a plastic sleeve the top of which depicts a jungle scene, and his shoes. "We'll work around him," one crew member finally declares.

Then the mime begins performing in the fountain basin what seems to be a combination of karate moves, military drill, exercises, improvisation, and yoga. He shouts and grunts, flails his arms, gestures, contorts his face, trots this way and that, spins, gyrates, claps. (Eddie is a fan of Bruce Lee.) Two PEP officers slowly walk by and give him the eye but keep walking. People strolling past him or sitting nearby stare at him, swiveling their heads to follow his movements—but nobody does a full *stop* to stare; he's the usual Washington Square Park curiosity. He holds out his arms, palms upward, as if worshipping the sun, then shields his eyes with his hands *from* the sun. He salutes, puts his hands together as if praying, then sits, then lies down and sticks his legs up in the air and does some sort of rowing exercises—all the while grunting, groaning, and yelping. He bends his head to the ground, stretches his legs, then touches his toes, then does sit-ups. The PEP walk around the fountain, return, and, once again, eye the man suspiciously, but they do not stop or confront him. He emits some karate-type sounds—"Hay-*yah*!" Then, "Whoop! Yah!" and a sharp "HUH!" This unusual activity continues for some time. The fact is, he hasn't done anything illegal, he hasn't violated any park ordinances, he doesn't pose a threat to anybody, nor is he a danger to himself. But he has forced a seemingly well-financed enterprise to alter the way it shot the film.

Two of the crew members hold up a gold, circular reflector about three feet in diameter, another hoists a white fabric reflector about the same size. A female model is standing on the low grate-covered platform in the middle of the fountain, posing, as the cameraman checks his distance from her. Meanwhile, the mime seems to be about to take off his t-shirt, then thinks better of it, but he doesn't pull it back down, so his abdomen is showing. For his age, he is in outstanding shape, with a flat belly and muscular arms. My guess is, at one time, he was a professional performer. He prances around the middle of the fountain area, flapping his arms, gesticulating, holding his hands together as if he's praying, then he jerks spasmodically, steps onto then off of the central stanchion, steps forward then backwards, walks back up the stairs, back down, does a soft-shoe dance routine, rests his arms on a stanchion by the wall, places his hands together by the side of his head, hits his head with the heel of his hand and yells, "Ow!" He takes out of his half-rollie two white plastic bags, holds them up and looks at his stuff, then moves his right hand in a "talking" fashion, then makes a sweeping gesture with his left hand.

Two PEP arrive, a white man and a black woman, and the man asks the cinematographer if the film crew has a permit to shoot a film in the park. He says he doesn't have it with him and the PEP says he has to have a permit to shoot a film in the park. The cinematographer says, "Yes I know, I'm just setting up." The PEP leave. The cinematographer asks two men who are sitting on the rim of the fountain near them if they would mind leaving, as the camera crew has to work in that spot. Unlike the mime, they cooperate, get up, and walk away. "Gracias," the camera man says. But they don't challenge Rodriguez, and he continues his routine. The irony of the episode, one might suppose, is that the film crew, who were challenged by the PEP to present appropriate documentation, are eminently conventional, while the agents of social control ignored the distinctly eccentric and probably mentally disordered mime.

I wonder if the mime would be treated in a different manner in another locale. Would he be hustled away from certain places? Certainly, in the lobby of any building in which he did not live. I can think of any number of different parks, as well as commercial malls and squares in small towns, that would not be nearly so accommodating. The same goes for numerous street corners around the City—say, on the Upper East Side, Beekman Place, Sutton Place. Undoubtedly the man chose Washington Square *because* he knew he'd be left alone. Yes, he's politely ignored; yes, people give him supercilious stares, and yes, some people do walk away from him. But he's allowed to stay and do his thing. A rational choice for a guy who's engaged in such eccentric, even peculiar behavior. Still, he's in the way of this film crew, and he's indifferent to its assistant's entreaties.

Washington Square is a site of contradictions and anomalies. The sight, even the scent, of homeless men should be expected—though not necessarily appreciated. Being importuned by a Hasid of African descent who insisted that I return to my (nonexistent) Jewish roots was an unusual though, for me, not a surprising experience. It is a place where NYU students read Keats, Shelley, and Byron, and men, some of whom sleep nightly on their mother's couch, eke out a meager living by playing some of the best chess in the City; where the ethic of freedom of expression prevails, yet dozens of inconspicuous surveillance cameras spy on every move of park visitors; where elderly Chinese women yank plastic bottles out of trash bins and stuff them into garbage bags attached to a pole, which they hoist onto their shoulders, passing within a hundred yards of some of the most expensive real estate in Manhattan and trundling past Wall Street executives in gray suits carrying briefcases containing contracts spelling out agreements that will earn corporations multiple millions of dollars; a space where rape, murder, and robbery are virtually unknown but, from sunup to midnight, drug transactions never cease. (No "broken windows" here!) Our heterotopia reserves a place for the anomalous and the heteroclite, but closely watched, it gives the impression of being a sketchy, sometimes edgy place where encounters are sometimes awkward and discordant—all of which, taken together, practically operationally define the heterotopia.

To my mind, Johan Figueroa, "The Human Statue," who frequently appears in the square, is a heterotopic figure. He's a statue but *not* a statue, that is, he's *pretending* to be a statue but is of course a human being; he's alive but motionless, he's performing while doing nothing—nothing except posing—he wants onlookers to contribute money to him for *doing* nothing, he's different from everyone else there and hence contributes to the park's diversity, he's very far from our notion of the everyday, he manifests one or more "spatio-temporal" ambiguities and contradictions, he "desanctifies" the barrier between the living and the not-living, he transforms the space he occupies into something very different from what it was before he arrived, he freezes and condenses time, and—did you notice his lantern? Perhaps he is Diogenes, looking for an honest man; perhaps not. He has posted a video of himself being ejected by the police from a park in Puerto Rico, from which he hails, yet he is unmolested, practically a fixture, in Washington Square Park. (In April 2018, Eddie Rodriguez was arrested because he was performing on the Arch and refused to climb down when the NYPD ordered him to do so.)

There's a demonstration assembling in the park. A man holds up a sign, in English, that reads, "Latin Americans for Reform." There are maybe twenty signs on the ground, most in Spanish, a few in English, each expressing the same theme. Perhaps twenty or thirty people are in the demonstration—they pick up a sign and are chanting; two are banging a metal bowl with a drumstick. Perhaps there are not quite that many spectators. There's a sign in English that reads, "Crops can be patented. Who are you gonna pay for the intellectual property rights of Incas, Mayans, Aztecs, Persians, Egyptians that did research for millennia?" The signs are distributed to the protesters. They hold up the signs and chant, with the drummer playing. "End U$ Imperialism in Latin America." "*El Campesino Colombiano No Necessita Ni Limosina Ni Agresiones. Necesita Soluciones.*" "*Colombia Resista El Gobierno Colombia.*" "Latin Americans Support Agrarian Popular Strikes." The chant, in Spanish, is to the rhythm and meaning of "A people united will never be defeated." About six people are photographing the protesters, including two with motion picture cameras.

The protesters march around the fountain, slowly, chanting, and after about twenty minutes, return to their former position and put the signs on the ground, then pick them up, then hold them up. There are others, sitting, who are making new, more, signs. I count about thirty or thirty-five people who are chanting and/or holding signs. A man and a woman are sitting about ten feet away, on a stone bench, and the woman seems to be looking at me and saying something. I get up and sit next to her and she begins talking to me—I guess I seem like a harmless and sympathetic person to her. "Colombia and the U.S. entered into a trade agreement, which is ending the farming community as we know it," she says. She is perhaps forty, wearing a yellow dress, and is speaking with an identifiable Latin American accent, but is fluent in English. "It's too bad that so many of the people here can't understand what the protest is all about." I said that I thought they could read enough of the signs that are in English and get a sense of what the protesters' cause is. "They passed laws that force farmers to buy only Monsanto seeds, and the farmers can't afford to buy the seeds and they're being forced off their land, and the big landowners are buying up their land." She's speaking to me and facing me while the man next to her, whom I take to be her husband, is asking her to help him put on his costume. He seems a little annoyed that she's paying attention to me when he needs help. So, she reaches over and helps him put on a large, full-head, papier mâché mask of an ugly old man—representing American imperialism—with dollar signs painted on his eyeballs, a white plastic suit, and gloves with long, Dracula fingernails. He wears a sign that reads, "Free GMO Sample—Have a Cookie." (The sign refers to "genetically modified organisms.") She puts on a hat made of large stage one hundred dollar bills and goes off with the protest marchers, who are going around the fountain another time. This is a classic Washington Square Park protest, and, heterotopically, it does pit one worldview against another, but it's a far cry from the sixties, when this sort of thing took place monthly or weekly. In the years I visited Washington Square, I saw only two protests, this one, and another that took place in the fall of 2016.

One crisp, bright autumn Saturday, in response to the election of Donald J. Trump as president, a rally assembles in Washington Square Park, chanting anti-Trump, anti-Bannon slogans. Occasionally an organizer delivers a short speech with the same theme. About half of the people there hold up signs, some of which depict Trump's angry face plus a slogan, such as "Bully Culprit." The organizers bill this as a "Love Trumps Hate Rally." It's a peaceful protest against an elected but strongly disliked candidate, a right-wing populist cum elitist, who will shortly assume the presidency of the United States. Some of the signs read "Pussy Grabs Back," "Peace Will Win, Fear Will Lose," "Gay Rights and Human Rights," "Not Our President," "Condemn Hate Now," "Proud to Be a Nasty Woman," "Respect Existence or Expect Resistance." Not only are protests in the Washington Square Park today few and far between; they don't attract the crowds that assembled in the sixties; I count a few hundred here—slim pickings for such an important issue.

All around the park, I observe a heterotopic mélange of happenings taking place at the same time as the anti-Trump rally. A transgender group dances to recorded music in the Holley Plaza. Six people hold a Yeshua (Jews for Jesus) prayer session at a nearby table; a sign rests against their table that reads, "You Must Be Born Again." Kyler, the astrologer, is sitting on one of the stone benches, advising a client about her fate. Tic and Tac are lining up volunteers in the dry fountain so they can do backflips over six of them. Across from the Garibaldi statue, "Share a Smile," which helps people struggling to deal with unemployment, health crises, and natural disasters, is taking pictures of smiling faces. Next to them, the "Orange Project," which addresses architecture and design, collects notes written on orange post-its. Just east of the fountain, the International Youth Fellowship registers volunteers to work in developing nations. Next to the fountain barrier, the Spartacist League distributes leaflets and requests converts to their revolutionary ideology. Southeast of the fountain, a group of men and women in their sixties and seventies sing a potpourri of sixties folk and pop songs. Going from person to person, members of a youth athletic league sell Oreo cookies. In front of the Arch, Joe Mangrum, a sand painter, lays down one of his evanescent works of art, which, to a Buddhist, embody the basic principle of life itself. Colin Huggins, the pianist, plays Chopin's Prelude in E Minor under the Arch. The Abe Lincoln look-alike paces around the park in a top hat and long black frock coat. Just east of the Holley Plaza, a flock of pigeons has alighted on and around Paul the Pigeon Man; they explode into flight when a child's scooter falls and clanks onto the pavement. Standing to the side of the walkway leading south to Thompson Street, Peter May, a guitarist, sings "Good Lovin'," a Rascals song ("I've got the fever and you got the cure") and later, Don McNeil's "American Pie." Just north of the Kovary Small Dog Run, the *pètanque* players toss their steel balls onto the sand-filled court. In the central fountain area, five skateboarders, resting their boards on the ground, keep a tiny rubber ball in the air with their feet. At the opening to the Holley Plaza, the bubble woman dips her circular wand into a soap-filled vat, then lofts compound bubbles three feet across, which small children chase, screeching with delight, swinging their arms in the air in an effort to pop them; in the southwest corner of the park, a dozen chess players study their opponents' moves; at one of the tables, an older black man teaches a white family—a couple in their thirties and a six-year-old boy—how to play chess. And, after forty-five minutes of protest, the anti-Trump, anti-Bannon forces, having completed the Washington Square Park phase of their demonstration, chant "Come and join us!" and march out the walkway that leads through the Holley Plaza, then cross Washington Square West and along the sidewalk adjoining Washington Place, toward Sixth Avenue. Six NYPD officers bring up the rear.

In his examination of the writings of Rabelais and Dostoyevsky, Russian literary critic Mikhail Bakhtin developed the notion of the "carnivalesque" or "carnivalistic" view of life (1981). During carnival, the observance of the Catholic Lent—which was celebrated in much of medieval Europe and is currently most elaborately developed in Brazil and in New Orleans—the participants revel in play-acting a reversal of existing hierarchies. Thus, in such celebrations, fools become wise men and vice versa; commoners become kings; women exert dominance over men, and parties who in their everyday lives practice enormous social distance from one another become intimates; eccentric behavior becomes acceptable; blatantly sensual behavior is celebrated while ecclesiastical protocol is mocked; and the body is depicted as grotesque in size, proportion, and representation. In a carnival atmosphere, a deviation from the usual planes, spaces, shapes, appearances, uses, or layouts prevails. The carnival is open to everyone, no payment or ticket is required, there are no guards, and a release from overweening authority is the rule.

While behavior in Washington Square is not consciously carnivalesque, it is *situationally carnival-like*—or "carnival-lite"—in that it is often entertaining and unconventional, but, unlike Mikhail Bakhtin's carnival, its visitors do not threaten to turn the existing social order on its head. In the park, people whom I rarely encounter anywhere else feel free to approach and talk to me and express views I might usually consider foolish, views that have no credibility in the academy or in any extant educational curriculum, but that I am situationally and interpersonally obliged to take seriously.

Along carnivalistic lines, I have seen a number of men wearing a dress—at least one of them, perhaps impishly, also wearing a beard—and I once saw a man with red hair wearing a *half*-beard. Fartman certainly showcases the human body as grotesque—after all, conventional politeness demands that while we are in the company of our fellow beings, we conceal all evidence of breaking wind. No doubt the young men who brought out the fuck doll, fondled her, and told us about her orifices were acting in a kind of carnivalistic spirit. But homeless men do not "dress up" (or "down") as bums and tramps—that's their everyday garb. Kyler, the astrologer, is not "defying" the scientific establishment by practicing his craft; he is advising clients in much the same way conventional professionals would. When Tic and Tac, a street entertainment act, pick out a blonde boy in their audience, ask his name, and berate his parents for the name they've chosen for him and redub him, "White Chocolate," they are simply entertaining a crowd. When the Positive Bros., a similar act that attracts smaller crowds, tells a mother holding a small child as he mock-grabs the infant, "Gimme your baby!" the audience laughs—it does not shrink back in horror. When a Hasid and a South Asian play chess against one another, they are not making a philosophical or political statement; each is simply trying to outsmart his opponent. All too often, the close observer discovers, literary interpretations of social life, though often imaginative, also seem a trifle forced.

The people who visit Washington Square Park do not explicitly mock, defy, or turn established authority on its head so much as devise a working relationship with one another, and with the more conventional park visitors, that is somewhat unconventional, different from that which prevails in much of the rest of society, knowing that it will be acceptable here. I suspect that these interesting and, to some of us, jarring juxtapositions have a cumulative impact on the park's visitors. No one can walk around or through Washington Square and not be struck by the divergent components that exist and function side by side, as well as celebrate their nonnormativity. Still, it seems to me that the literary, metaphorical, and cerebral significance of carnivalism outweighs its sociological or real-world importance.

Perhaps the most anomalous feature of Washington Square's heterotopia ties in with what psychologists refer to as "theory of mind." Humans not only *live* socially—that is, we interact in a give-and-take fashion with others; we also *think* and *feel* socially, that is, develop a sense of empathy, putting ourselves in the place of others, attempt to think and feel as they do, and act accordingly. We take others into account, often because, we surmise, by pleasing them, that will achieve what we want (Wellman, 2014, p. 6). This approach suggests that empathy—the social self, the difference between the "I" and the "me"—is at the core of human development, an idea that George Herbert Mead generated more than a century ago (1913). To the extent that we interact with others, we develop an empathetic understanding. It follows that we broaden our sensibilities by broadening the spectrum of humanity with whom we interact. By including a diversity of representatives in our empathetic repertory, we expand the diversity of ways that we think and feel. (There's a limit to empathy, however; by definition, an empathetic sensibility that encompasses exploitation, harm, force, or abuse is oxymoronic.) Psychologist Henry Wellman asks us to consider the way in which, as a child, he may have come to develop a naïve theory about how his "exotic Aunt Lib" thought and felt. "To understand her I appealed to beliefs and desires in general; but generic, abstract beliefs and desires won't suffice," he explains. In other words, Aunt Lib was similar to all other humans in certain respects but, in many respects, not at all like other humans. Hence,

Wellman says, "I must, more specifically, home in on her at-times bizarre, iconoclastic beliefs to account for her downright peculiar actions and conversations" (2014, p. 10). In Washington Square, the visitor is likely to encounter a diversity of Aunt Libs. If our visitors are at all empathetic, they are likely to wonder what sort of person would *do* some of the things they observe. Most will recognize that this park is the sort of space where eccentricity is allowed to be expressed; indeed, tourists frequently come there to be entertained by such antics. Surely the appreciation of a divergent sensibility constitutes an essential portion of Norbert Elias's notion of the *civilizing process* (1978/1994). I'd like to think the park has such an impact on its visitors. I suspect it does, though I'm not sure how such a proposition could be empirically verified.

"Diversity" is an overused word, granted, and it means different things to different audiences. In the case of Washington Square and its visitors, denizens, employees, and neighbors, one of the things it should *not* connote is exoticism. To pridefully laud diversity as a virtue for its own sake—to display the heterogeneousness of human specimens in order to sing the praises of a kumbaya exhibition of tolerance—is disrespectful of humanity's rainbow. To understand *how* diversity works and *why* it is a positive thing for all of us should be the mission of its champions. Living, working, playing, and relaxing cheek by jowl with people who are different from oneself in significant ways is important not for bragging rights but to reinforce one's humanity. Rubbing shoulders and mixing and mingling with diverse crowds is likely to add to the store of appreciation for views one might not have considered. It enriches our understanding of who we are, and who the fellow members of our species are, broadens our horizons, and adds to our emotional and cognitive capacity and repertory. People who didn't matter to us before begin mattering a great deal.

Moreover, the purpose of studying people who are themselves, or whose behavior is, nonnormative is not to display freaks, weirdos, the far-out or off-the-wall specimens to revel in their differentness. In fact, such research practice is guided by precisely the opposite motive—the impulse to get closer to the people we are studying than we otherwise could. We need to enter their world, observe them—and recognize that, at the same time, they are observing us—and try to understand and appreciate what they are doing and saying; getting close to people very different from ourselves is one way of achieving that goal. We need to begin thinking, What makes that person tick? What does it feel like to stand in that person's shoes? We need to be overtaken by a very simple yet profound insight: *There but for the grace of God go I.* Rather than place enormous distance between ourselves and our subjects, we want to occupy their mental and psychic space, and let them into ours. Yes, some of them are very different from us—that's one of the reasons why we are studying them. But yes, likewise, *since* that's why we are studying them, and since they are different from us, let's find out what moves them, what similarities we share with them, and let's revel in both our similarities and differences. What we do is the *opposite* of exoticism. Perhaps such a research exercise will enrich us, their researchers. Maybe we'll learn something from them.

Yet an irony or paradox enters when we consider the fact that the parties in these encounters already most receptive to encounters with eccentric Aunt Lib Washington Square Park equivalents are enriched most by them, while those who scurry away from parties who horrify or unsettle them have lost the opportunity for cross-fertilization. Now that the antiglobalist, small-town, America-first populist advocate in the form of Donald J. Trump has become institutionalized into the presidency, we are reminded that the capacity to dialogue with parties different from oneself is an all-too-rare human quality, and so Socrates may very well have died in vain. (Even Socrates—a sly old fox—didn't believe in genuine dialogue; he wanted debaters to come to the conclusions *he* considered reasonable.) But there's a double irony here as well, and that is, partly because of neurological circumstances beyond their control, many of the parties who have failed to make a place for themselves in the general society—the homeless, the indigent, the vagrant, Robert Merton's "double failures" (1957, pp. 153–55)—and end up wandering into and around places such as Washington Square seem incapable of enriching themselves through meaningful exchanges with potentially dialogic others, thus preventing them from achieving their full human potential. We are reminded of how contingent, fragile, and exceptional Elijah Anderson's "cosmopolitan canopy" is (2011), how richly it rewards the able and prepared, and how ill suited many of the parties are who are disaffiliated—who have been beaten down by force of circumstances—to profit from such a place's riches. It seems a rigged system, but it's what there is, it's what we have; in spite of the obstacles, I remain cautiously optimistic. Genuine diversity needs a space in which parties very different from ourselves, and different from one another, can relate in a meaningful fashion so that the hot-house fancy of the heterotopia that works so well on the page and in the minds of the intellectual elite may serve as a kind of template that fosters mutual respect, urbanity, civility, and empathetic understanding.

Some members of the surrounding community feel that Washington Square is *too* accessible. Luther Harris cites a 1973 NYU student study to the effect that Washington Square had become "swamped" with "intoxicated and licentious bums, gamblers, panhandlers, pushers, and weirdos" (2003, p. 279). Matters haven't changed that much since then. City officials once proposed that access to eight of the entrances to the park be controlled by gates, but Village residents opposed the plan, and the whole idea was dropped. With respect to Washington Square Park, the issue of the balance of accessibility versus exclusivity remains. Certainly, the heterotopia should be accessible—a quality, it seems reasonable to assume, that maximizes diversity. Even in substantially "red" or conservative states, such as Texas, Missouri, Iowa, Kentucky, and Louisiana, the residents of counties and cities located on navigable waterways are more likely to come into contact with people who have diverse backgrounds than do residents in landlocked counties and cities, and hence, to hold "bluer," or more tolerant and empathetic social and political views. Accessibility increases diversity and so, fosters the heterotopia; exclusivity and banishment stifle it. But what if the heterotopia admits parties who seek to close down or disrupt diversity?

Foucault did not spell out his notion of an *anti-heterotopia*—or the "un-heterotopia"—nor did he give us what he considered paradigmatic *examples* of the opposite of the heterotopia. If Washington Square is a pretty good example of the heterotopia, what's a *homotopia*? Presumably such a space would stand at the polar end point of all or most of the qualities I just spelled out. The un-heterotopia presumably possesses aspects or features that are internally harmonious with one another, generating a consistency, a homogeneous feel; likewise, it would harmonize with the dominant or hegemonic social or cultural order—offer no challenge to the powers that be or the way the society is arranged. It would expose its visitors or members to a narrow range of parties, participants, or viewpoints and serve relatively few functions; it would offer a conventional, convivial take on culture, politics, and social relations, on the hegemon, and opens its visitors to no threat or risks, few opportunities to explore something surprising, few to encounter people startlingly different from oneself, learn something one didn't know or suspect.

Perhaps the most appropriate candidate among New York's major parks that would qualify as the *least* heterotopian, that is, the space that's *least similar* to Washington Square, to my mind, would be Gramercy Park. It is two acres in extent, irregularly shaped, and lies, approximately, between Third and Park avenues, and between Eighteenth and Twenty-first streets, in Manhattan; privately owned and administered, it is surrounded by a fence and a locked gate. Only residents of the thirty-nine buildings in the neighborhood of the same name who pay an annual fee are allowed to own a key to the gate. Exceptions are the members of several exclusive local clubs, two local religious parishes (one Jewish, one Protestant), the owners of a nearby luxury condo, and guests of the Gramercy Park Hotel, who must be accompanied to the park and be picked up later by hotel staff. Only 383 keys to the park gate exist (Finn, 2012). Hence, with respect to accessibility—and, in comparison with Washington Square Park—it is extremely *exclusive* rather than inclusive. In 2001, one of the local clubs invited forty teenagers, mostly minorities, who were students at a nearby high school for a visit to Gramercy Park; while they were in the park, a trustee called the police and alleged that the children were trespassing. The police refused to take action, and the school sued the park's administration; the lawsuit was settled out of court (Serratore, 2016).

In 2014, while on his honeymoon, Shawn Christopher, a computer programmer, stayed at an Airbnb hotel, which owns one of the keys to the park. He visited the park and took panoramic pictures using Photo Sphere, a Google app, then posted them on Google Maps. Mr. Christopher was apparently unaware that he needed to obtain permission to take pictures in the park. "I just really wanted to share this with other people," he explained. "It's such a beautiful part of New York, and people shouldn't miss out on that" (Chaban, 2014). No pets, no frisbees, no smoking—and no photography. He was surprised when keyholders took umbrage at his photographic revelations.

"What is the most noteworthy feature of Gramercy Park?" I ask Arlene Harrison, trustee and president of the Gramercy Park Block Association, which administers the park. "What's most noteworthy about the park is that it's private," she answers. "But the park is administered in the name of the trustees; no one owns it, no one can sell or transfer it. It's always locked, it's accessible only by key, and there are a limited number of keys in existence." When I mention that one of my reasons for requesting permission to see and walk through Gramercy Park is to contrast it with Washington Square, she replies, "It doesn't make sense to compare Gramercy Park, which is private, with a public park like Washington Square. Why not Union Square? People in Colorado have a view of the Rockies. They pay for that view. The value of your property comes from what you can see. People in this neighborhood see Gramercy Park. It's the only park of its kind in the world. But it's fenced and gated, it's not walled off. People can walk by and look inside and enjoy the park from the sidewalk; they come from other neighborhoods to appreciate the park *through* the fence. And the gates and the fence aren't to keep people out," she explains, "they are to protect the landscaping." I agree that the rambunctiousness and the considerable volume of a Washington Square crowd would trample a smaller, carefully tended park like Gramercy.

Ms. Harrison invites me to walk around the park and take notes as she sits on a bench and talks with a member of the block association. It certainly has a very different look and feel from Washington Square, I note. And it is beautiful. With a red Alexander Calder mobile arching toward the sky, a six-story birdhouse, a stone planter with a Greco-Roman bas-relief frieze ("That used to be a well," Harrison explains), a large metal urn planter, a green gardener's shed, a statue of Edwin Booth—a nineteenth-century actor—a gravel walkway, tastefully designed and carefully tended shrubs and bushes and graceful trees, green benches, each of which conveys a brass plaque that commemorates a person close to the donor, the space exudes an air and feel of serenity and security. The rules of Gramercy Park, posted on a small, shiny metal sign on one of the gates, explain a great deal about its security system: "Keys to the Park may not be loaned, transferred or copied. The use of a key by a person who is not eligible to obtain a key is considered an illegal entry. No more than six guests at a time may be invited by a keyholder." No PEP or NYPD necessary here! Everyone would want to enjoy the park's beautiful landscaping, I think, as I'm walking around the grounds. Not only can someone see much of the park through the fence, as Ms. Harrison explained; the inquisitive para-visitor can also enjoy pictures of the park posted on the Internet.

Gramercy Park does not expose the visitor to clashing values or proclivities, or to visitors very different from the keyholders. It is a calm, serene place, classical in its design and administration, harmonious unto itself, harmonious to its surroundings, and a harmonious experience for its visitors. The park keeps the riff-raff out, its ethos is consonant with the dominant order, with the hegemonic culture, and it serves a few rather than a multiplicity of functions, and a small and relatively homogeneous rather than a large and diverse patronage. To be simple and plain about the matter, Gramercy Park is not unconventional or nonnormative in any way. It is the *ur*-un-heterotopia, more like a utopia—with an extremely limited clientele.

In Gramercy Park, nobody screams, rants, or babbles, or sells bags of weed, nobody's homeless or sleeping on a bench; there are no drunken brawls, topless women, buskers, human statues, or skateboarders, nobody's marching to the beat of a different drummer—in fact, there are no drummers at all, which there sometimes are in Washington Square. But it is a lovely spot, a space where the very activities that Washington Square hosts virtually every day would nullify the tasteful qualities that Gramercy Park possesses. Both are precious dominions, but they are mutually exclusive. The Gramercy Park-ite is allowed to enjoy Washington Square, but it doesn't operate the other way around. The presence of a substantial number of obstreperous people would equal more action, more diversity, more crazy stuff, more chaos and topsy-turvy—and a mandatory police presence. But Gramercy Park will never be edgy, and its administrators will never admit edgy people who engage in edgy *public* behavior; it's not that kind of place, nor should it be. It's Monet's lilies, not Jackson Pollock's scrambled eggs, and therein lies its pristine charm. That very feature, which prevents it from becoming an edgy place, is what defines its character.

As edgy as it is—and as beautiful as Gramercy Park is—I have grown very fond of Washington Square; it attracts a universe of habitués, many of whom, in their everyday lives, do not typically comingle, yet in this space, they seem to get along reasonably well, at least from an undeniable social distance. It is an environment that has earned a deserved reputation for unconventionality, yet that tolerance for unorthodoxy has limits; most decidedly, "anything" does *not* "go." The Washington Square ethic does not embrace, for instance, truly harmful, predatory behavior. And everyone seems welcome here—to reiterate, up to a point. Washington Square is a place where visitors feel welcome, all things considered, but the truce to which everyone seems to have agreed is rickety and potentially unstable, maintained informally by people who are strangers to one another as much as by patrol officers and surveillance cameras. Even the crazy guy who tried to make me stop taking notes is part of the human panorama in this hallowed space.

I'm left to grapple with the matter of accounting for the square's relative harmony. It can't only be the surveillance and the cops alone; other urban spaces have them as well, and most experience more crime, petty and serious, more racial friction, and a greater sense of unease among its visitors. Crime is lower in Washington Square than it is for any of Manhattan's major parks and squares of comparable size. Whites tell me that blacks are welcome, and African Americans back up that assertion, saying that they indeed feel welcome, and all who comment on the matter describe the park as peaceful—a place where everyone can relax and chill. Washington Square Park is set in the middle of an affluent, nearly all-white neighborhood, though with a growing Asian presence. Like Duneier's and Molotch's white subjects, upper-middle-class, mainly liberal, white residents of the Village feel guilty about calling working-class blacks on petty offenses. The ample presence of children and their caretakers certainly puts a damper on conflict and wilder behavior in the square. More specifically, the artificial grass playground is located just across the southwest corner of the park from the chess tables, where mostly black hustlers hang around, waiting for a game, then engage in intense contests with their usually white opponents; whoops and cries emanate from that corner, but no one seems to feel there's anything amiss about the ecology of the arrangement.

The social coupling of men into homophilic and heterophilic dyads and hence, the lower proportion of single men—relative to, say, Union

Square—as compared with elsewhere certainly adds to the gregarious feel of the space. The virtual disappearance of gay cruising and sex in the park has removed a major source of tension that prevailed in earlier eras; no parent with small children wants to peek into the bushes and spy one man sodomizing another. The design and layout of Washington Square—true, after multiple renovations—was masterful from the perspective not only of aesthetics but also of line-of-sight; standing at the fountain and boxing the compass will yield a view of what's going on in major swathes of the entire space. In 2011, a PEP officer spoke off the record to the *Washington Square News* to the effect that he walks in on sexual encounters in the park's men's room "every single day"—the type of behavior that comprised the subject of the classic *Tearoom Trade* (Humphreys, 1970, 1975)—not an appropriate activity in a locale where children are likely to enter. In the 1970s, during drastic budgetary times, New York City laid off every single one of its park restroom attendants—seven hundred in all. Clearly, monitoring public sexual encounters has a low priority for the municipality.

Washington Square is hardly free from conflict. We saw a number of locals complaining to a PEP about an extremely loud and clangorous drummer; as I explained, one of these guys told me he wanted to *stab* the dude, but of course, he did not. One guitarist, whom a PEP told had to disconnect his amplifier, indicated with his fist what he wanted to do to the officer, but again, he restrained the impulse. We saw several performers competing for the prime location for putting on a show—the empty fountain basin—and one of the members of a troupe shoving a solo act away from the spot, even throwing a couple of his props (two oranges) into some nearby trees, but again, no violence ensued. I witnessed two fist-fights (and the aftermath of another), which resulted in a total of one not very hard punch being landed. True, surveillance cameras tell everyone there that their actions are under surveillance by the police; the ever-presence of the PEP, the NYPD, and occasionally, the NYU safety patrol, likewise, reminds visitors, on one side of the law or the other, that serious wrongdoing is likely to lead to apprehension. Conflict is inherent to the human condition, but in a given delimited spot, violence may not be. Add to the mix the substantial presence of mentally disordered individuals, the major ongoing marijuana-selling enterprise a few dozen yards from the central fountain, and a clientele who come from the ends of the earth, and the fact of the relative cordiality of the place is nothing short of remarkable. Located in a country whose leader is doing his very best to keep immigrants out, Washington Square Park seems to embrace everyone who respects the rights of others. To the extent that democracy combines majority rule and minority rights, this space truly is an exercise in democracy.

ACKNOWLEDGMENTS

I'd like to thank an abundance of people for helping me fashion *The Taming of New York's Washington Square* into a better book than I could otherwise have written: Nachman and Etti Ben-Yehuda, whose insights grace these pages, especially their comments in chapter 4, and Nachman, whom I must thank a second time, for a critical reading of the manuscript, and a third time as well, for accompanying me on some of these expeditions that my observations entailed (he is often the "friend" I don't identify); Jeffery Dennis and Marty Weinberg, who kept me up to date regarding the matter of gay people in Washington Square Park and in Greenwich Village; Paul Hond, who interviewed me for *Columbia* magazine (2017) and so, gave me some sensitivity about the matters an interested, educated layperson might want to know about the park and what goes on there; Harvey Molotch, who gave me a substantial dose of editorial assistance, and Ilene Kalish and Maryam Arain at NYU Press, who likewise helped me fashion the manuscript into more readable form; Arlene Harrison, who graciously discussed and granted me access to Gramercy Park and permitted me to wander around that urban paradise and take notes; Hakim Hasan, who critically read chapter 5 and contributed the account that follows it, on race in Washington Square; Bill Nelson for supplying me with a beautifully simple and elegant map of Washington Square Park; Andrea Swalec and Linda Massarella, reporters who advised me on points of park behavior; David Kraiker, of the U.S. Census Bureau, for supplying me with crime statistics in New York's Sixth Precinct; Aisha Khan, who gave me her experienced opinion about a particular ethnographic matter; Phillip Scarboro, who demonstrated that Greenwich Village denizens may not be as politically correct as I had thought; Linda Gordon, who raised a question about women's role in the park I hadn't considered; my fabulous wife, Barbara Weinstein, who kept me alive and relatively happy during the period of time I worked on this book; readers who contributed helpful suggestions for improving earlier versions of the manuscript; several officers at the Sixth Precinct of the NYPD, who expressed their views about their enforcement protocol, especially James Alberici, Communications Officer, who granted me the interview that appears at the end of chapter 4.

I'd also like to thank the anonymous souls whose behavior I observed and statements I've overheard and written about here. It seems superfluous to say this, but as per widely accepted research methodology, I've altered interviewees' names, along with identifying details about them, to ensure their anonymity as best I could. In the view of copyright and fair use experts, journalists and social scientists have the right to quote overheard conversations, as long as the speakers cannot be identified, and I've done that, and so, I thank Washington Square Park denizens for expressing themselves in the park. I've adapted four paragraphs from two prior publications: two from my book *Deviant Behavior* (2016) and two from "Ethical Issues in the Qualitative Study of Deviance and Crime" (2015). Acknowledgment of this adaptation is duly noted. I took all the photographs that appear in the book, making sure that most of my subjects cannot be personally identified; Anil Kumar of Bleeker Digital Solutions skillfully printed my photographs. I've obtained signed model releases from those parties whose identity can be determined from their images, including Dusty Rhodes, Matthew Silver, and Johan Figueroa. The current political regime, headed by our commander-in-chief, began leading me to believe that Socrates was dead, but the people in the square have enabled me to see the opposite: that he is alive and well—and this makes me happy.

APPENDIX

A Note on the Ethics of Research Methods

The two research methods I used to gather the information I recorded and analyzed in this book are fairly straightforward, as well as widely accepted among most sociologists. First, I observed. I sat in the park, watched behavior relevant to my topic—that is, normative violations—or overheard what park visitors were saying, and wrote in notebooks what I saw and heard. This method is not truly ethnographic—the social components of the park-going individuals, sectors, and interest groups are too vast, too diffuse, too scattered for that; what I've done is mainly observational. Typically, the park's visitors and habitués do not intermesh with one another in the manner of persons living in a village or a community or working in a factory. Ideally, simple observation is *unobtrusive* and *nonreactive* (Webb et al., 1966); the researcher does not alter the social landscape at all. I tried to write my observations as they unfolded, but sometimes this was impractical—on occasion, I became a coparticipant in the activity in question—and then I held the sequence of events or the words in my mind, and later wrote as much as I could recall. One aspect of the observational phase of the study entailed recording units of people of certain sizes (singletons, dyads, triads, and triads-plus), whenever units were more or less clearly discernable. I did not count infants or toddlers in units.

Second, I conducted interviews, which were of two types. I talked informally and in an unstructured fashion to participants and bystanders about the behavior I observed or statements I overheard, though most of the time, I wasn't able to do this. In addition, I drew an unsystematically selected "convenience" sample of park visitors and interviewed them regarding their attitudes about twenty-two violations of park rules or other ordinary infractions ("park rules–plus"). Webb et al. (1966) refer to the use of multiple methodologies as "triangulation"; as we saw, Whyte (1980, pp. 94–101) uses the term in a different way.

I selected my sixty interviewees (out of the seventy I approached—ten refused to talk to me, including one impeccable-looking elderly gent, who responded to my request by stating, "I want my life to remain *completely* silent") simply by walking up to someone sitting on a bench, holding up or handing him or her my business card, briefly explaining my research mission, and requesting an interview. I did not mention that I was studying mainly or specifically nonnormative or *deviant* behavior. What I said was, "Hi, I'm a sociologist doing a study of behavior in Washington Square. I wonder if I might ask you a few questions about your views on the subject. I'm writing a book and it's possible I may quote you in the published book. I'll keep your name and identity anonymous. Do you agree to talk to me under these conditions?" The interviews usually lasted no more than seven minutes, though sometimes they were as long as twelve. I selected my respondents pragmatically: They should be sitting on a bench, alone, not engaged in an electronic activity (listening with earbuds, texting, talking with someone on a cell), and they must not seem to be psychiatrically disordered, or hostile. I aimed for a reasonable mix of people with respect to gender (twenty-eight females, thirty-two males) and race and ethnicity (see the note at the bottom of table 3.1, as well as table 5.4), and I interviewed only adults; all respondents were eighteen and older, which I determined when I approached them. I also conducted ten briefer, more specialized interviews of dog walkers, and ten interviews of park-goers about how they felt regarding the homeless.

I believe, as do John Lofland, David Snow, Leon Anderson, and Lyn Lofland (2005, pp. 36–39; L. Lofland, 1973), that covert observation of manifest behavior—and, by implication, the talk I overheard—which is enacted or spoken *in a public place to which any person has legal access,* and describing said behavior for publication, is acceptable and does not require anyone's formal or signed permission. I was not conducting research in a closed, private, or quasi-private place, and as long as I followed ethical procedures and revealed no one's identity, I had the right to observe and eavesdrop (or "snoop") and publish narratives of what I saw and overheard. I also did not inform people whose behavior I covertly observed and wrote about *that* I was conducting research, or that they had been unwitting participants in this research project.

Most of the incidents I describe in this book I observed by means of the techniques described in Adler and Adler (1994). Lyn Lofland describes the research methods that she used in a personal communication to the Adlers by saying that she was "passing . . . as someone who is simply hanging about in public" (Adler and Adler, 1994, p. 379). In Washington Square, to the people to whom I did *not* administer a formal interview, I was in public, pretending to be an ordinary park-goer (which I was, and continue to be, though *at that time*, I was principally a researcher). Although some of these interactions took place *in* public, they were of an intimate nature, within an imaginary "bubble" that its inhabitants felt they had created, a kind of self-defined (in fact, pseudo) shield of privacy. Was overhearing and recording conversations taking place in such bubbles *ethical*? Some think not.

Consider the outraged reaction of Carol A. B. Warren, a sociologist, in a personal communication to the Adlers (1994, p. 388), about *her* becoming an inadvertent research subject for *another* ethnographer. As she was sitting in a coffee shop talking with a friend, a man walked to a bench close to theirs, sat down, and began writing on a pad of paper. "It occurred to me then," Warren wrote, "that he was an ethnographer taking notes on this public setting. As soon as I had this thought I became furiously indignant, and felt invaded." Although the coffee shop was technically a public space, she said, "it was also a privatized one, in which each separate unit in that space had [its] own focus of attention and interaction" (p. 388). Hence, the notion of a certain kind of space as being *strictly* public, some feel, is misleading; the "bubbles" that interacting parties create become spontaneous private realms—readily observable, some within earshot, but *impermissibly accessible*. Warren's surreptitious observer clearly considers concealed public research legitimate; she does not. Kenneth Vogel, a *New York Times* reporter, describes breaking a major story that he obtained by overhearing a conversation at a restaurant between two Washington lobbyists; he even secretly snapped a photograph of them talking. No sin in that, Vogel implies (2017), and the importance of the story ("proof of the pudding") confirmed its validity.

Like Vogel and Warren's covert ethnographer, in this study I too was overhearing conversations the speakers didn't necessarily want me to hear, as well as observing behavior to which (I'm sure they felt) I shouldn't have paid attention—and if they didn't want me to overhear their conversations or pay attention to their behavior, they *certainly* didn't want me to reproduce them in print. But I do not share Warren's outrage, nor do I believe the behavior of the snooping ethnographer who observed and took notes on her behavior to have been unwarranted. To me, anonymity is the crucial factor. In this case, Warren outed herself as the subject of the research.

Though covert or disguised observation *in public* seems acceptable to me, a number of sociologists feel it is decidedly unethical (Erikson, 1962; Bulmer, 1982); it is also considered unethical to most members of contemporary human subjects committees, or IRBs (institutional review boards). I disagree emphatically and wholeheartedly with this judgment; I believe that sociologists have the right to overhear conversations, observe behavior, and describe what they hear and see, without being granted informal access to do so, as long as they protect the identities of the parties speaking and acting. I feel that the rights of sociologists are no different from those of journalists, who have had such privileges for more than a century.

Still, a major part of what I was doing in this research enterprise is conventionally known as "snooping" (Allen, 1997). I didn't deceive anyone, but, like Laud Humphreys when he observed tearoom sex (1970, 1975), I didn't announce that I was conducting a study of deviance and social control, "and so everyone should be careful about what they say and do!" But snooping is what it is, and snooping was what I had to do to hear what was being said and see what was taking place. Unobtrusive snooping in a public place is, to my way of thinking, a legitimate research methodology; "snooping" is simply observing behavior in public without the observed being aware that they *are* being observed. Of course, as all sociologists know, Laud Humphreys committed multiple ethical sins *aside from* "snooping."

Following the norm of confidentiality, I have altered the names and specific biographical details of my interviewees or parties whose designations I learned and behavior I described or statements I quoted; hence, the relevant parties cannot be identified by name. Lofland et al. state that "the practice of assuring informant confidentiality is such a cardinal principle of naturalistic fieldwork that it has long been taken for granted within this research tradition" (2005, p. 51).

In small communities or settings, where many of the residents or parties know one another, even broad, sketchy details can identify a known participant. They cite the case of the study that resulted in the book *Small Town in Mass Society* (1958) by Arthur Vidich and Joseph Bensman, in which the residents of the pseudonymous town of "Springdale" (Candor, New York) were able to identify a virtual "who's who" of the persons who constituted the actors described in the volume, "even though the authors did not refer to any of the central characters by their given names" (p. 51). The residents of "Springdale" were so outraged about what they considered breaches of ethics by the researchers that they hanged one of the authors (Vidich) in effigy and depicted him on a Fourth of July parade float spreading manure (Allen, 1997, p. 35). In short, the "veils of disguise used to camouflage the groups or communities [or individuals] to which they are applied can often be seen through or lifted by those interested in doing so" (Lofland et al., 2005, p. 51). Negative portraits lend a special urgency to the persons under scrutiny to actually *make* this sort of identification and *denounce* the parties responsible for the portraits. What outraged the residents of "Springdale" about *Small Town in Mass Society* was the bad, but invariably true, things the authors said about them—a sin that the authors compounded by making these remarks public. In my case, *some* park denizens will be able to identify some of the actors who engaged in the described behaviors, or even the speakers of the words I narrate, through the vague, sketchy details I supply. This may be unavoidable.

Many knowledgeable observers consider *informed consent* as another basic and essential ethical criterion of social research. According to a strict reading of this principle, everyone the researcher investigates must *know* that he or she is being studied, and must grant *consent* to be studied. But in field research, this criterion is even more problematic than confidentiality. Qualitative research, such as the protocol I followed to produce this book, is spontaneous, unpredictable, evanescent, and substantially sub rosa—there's no predicting what might be necessary to obtain information. Qualitative researchers face challenges and dilemmas that more conventional social science researchers, such as pollsters or experimental social psychologists, don't have to think about. Informed consent is virtually impossible in a study like the one I conducted. What on earth could "informed consent" possibly mean in a public place where hundreds of people act out behavior and make statements within the researcher's eyesight or hearing, then vanish as quickly as they came? With respect to making and recording my observations, the principle of informed consent is an absurdity; it simply can't be done.

Regarding the process of observation itself—as opposed to the formal interview—I conveyed no indication to anyone in my presence that I was conducting a study; hence, no consent was requested, or granted, or, to my way of thinking, necessary. As Lyn Lofland did, I just walked into a public site, sat down, and observed what was going on. I was in fact conducting *covert* observation, a practice, to stress the point, that some sociologists believe to be, by its very nature, unethical. I agree with Lofland et al., who state that the "more adamant calls for the pristine purity of openness" are disingenuous and unrealistic because "the distinction between covert and overt research is often blurred and clouded in actual practice" (2005, pp. 34–35).

Ethnographic researchers may "present themselves in one manner or another," according to Richard Mitchell, "but subjects can and usually do reinterpret, transform, or sometimes altogether reject these presentations in favor of their own" (1993, p. 12). In addition, blanket arguments against covert research are "naïve and problematic" because field research proceeds in hesitant steps, the researcher withdrawing some plans and elaborating some strategies that were originally unanticipated; the researcher may not be committed to a definite, preconceived plan, but may change strategies during the course of the research. In addition, to announce one's research interests and program to potential research participants upon entering the setting is likely to result in their withdrawing from participation altogether.

In short, "the ethically sensitive, thoughtful, and knowledgeable investigator is the best judge of whether covert research is justified" (Lofland et al., 2005, p. 39). I agree. When I was in the observation mode of the research, what I did entailed keeping my eyes open and my mouth shut—until I interviewed someone. To have revealed to anyone I observed that I was conducting research for the purpose of publication would have been pointless and could have short-circuited the research process. A fly on the wall I was—in any case, a fly on a bench—and a fly on the wall I tried to remain. But not quite. Toward the end of my observations, in the fountain area, as I took notes while I walked, two young women—NYU graduate students in public health, as it turned out—called me over and asked me what I was doing, so I explained my mission to them. A bit chagrined, I said, "I thought I was invisible." Clearly, I wasn't.

What about deception? Social psychology and psychology researchers have used deception for generations, but, for the most part, sociologists place it off-limits for their investigations. I used deception in a previous research project, by placing bogus personal ads in newspapers and then, after receiving the replies, from men and women expecting to communicate and get in touch with a potential date, analyzing the responses (Goode, 1996). The IRB at the university at which I was affiliated rejected my application for approval (I was in fact a member of that committee!), but I conducted the study anyway. (One of the members of the committee told me, "I can't believe you asked us to review this research protocol!") Yes, I used deception, but no, I did not reveal anyone's identity, everyone remained anonymous, and I felt then and still feel I could not have obtained the information I got in any other way *except* through deception. In any case, I did not *knowingly* use deception in the research on which this book is based.

Charlotte Allen, who clearly disapproves of the practice, accuses practitioners of deception, including myself, of using a kind of cost-benefit analysis: "If the deception doesn't hurt anyone very much and the payoff in data is high, covert research is worth doing" (1997, p. 33)—the distinction between consequentialist and deontological ethics in a nutshell. The consequentialist says, "no harm, no foul." In contrast, the deontologist researcher holds an idealistic, utopian notion of research protocol. Snooping is a form of spying, Allen charges, and she feels it's wrong. Ethically speaking, when it comes to research ethics, Allen is an idealist, a utopian, not a consequentialist. And yes, snooping entails observing people in public without their awareness that they are being studied, then writing about them—and frankly, to me, it's fine; I don't disapprove of it. Our job is difficult enough as it is, and, if it is a sin, I feel, it is a tiny one.

Again, what about deception? For decades, critics have leveled the charge against researchers who deceive subjects. Such accusations are rhetorical devices to win an argument without having to construct a cogent justification for it. Some deception is necessary in virtually all social research, and this is especially true of qualitative work. As Maurice Punch has said, "Many participant-observers cannot escape the realization that deceit and dissemblance are part of the research role and may not feel comfortable with that insight" (1986, p. 72).

Perhaps the most well-known—and one of the most notorious—research project that exemplifies putatively unethical qualitative methods is Laud Humphreys's *Tearoom Trade* (1970, 1975). Humphreys observed homosexual encounters in public restrooms and interviewed the men who engaged in such behavior. Humphreys's research was, and still is, widely considered unethical. He observed tearoom sex taking place, posing as a "watch-queen" or look-out to warn the men engaging in oral sex in public urinals that intruders were approaching, thereby *implicitly* misrepresenting his true purpose. Humphreys did not offer informed consent to his subjects—nor could he have. So far, I don't feel anything he did was an ethical lapse. But Humphreys went much further: He recorded the license plates of the cars on the street adjacent to the park in which the public urinals he monitored were located and got in touch with an acquaintance at the motor vehicles bureau, who tracked down their owners' addresses and revealed them to him, and then he contacted his subjects at their homes, claiming to them that they were members of his sample in a "public health" survey, thereby engaging in both covert and overt deception. The chancellor at Washington University, where Humphreys received his PhD, informed him that, because of the unethical research procedures he followed, his degree "may have to be revoked." This administrator also attempted to prevent the publication of his book by contacting its publisher, informing its executives of Humphreys's dishonest practices. Both attempts failed. And though *Tearoom Trade* ignited a firestorm of controversy and criticism, and textbooks on qualitative research often criticize the author for pursuing this line of research, the volume won the prestigious C. Wright Mills award, and it remains an extremely frequently cited work. (Again, the consequentialist argument in a nutshell.) In contrast, most research based on meticulously ethical methodologies are inoffensive and uncreative, and pass into instant oblivion.

I do not believe that social researchers should coerce, pressure, browbeat, or force anyone to become a research subject, respondent, interviewee, or informant; in principle, the decision to knowingly become a research participant should be made by the individual. But to emphasize the point, *if* the research can be conducted *only* by covert means *and* the unwitting participant is not harmed or seriously discomfited by the research experience, as I see it, stealthy protocol is acceptable. In fact, in many covert research endeavors, the unknowing participant is not even *aware* of being studied, and never learns this fact. To deny the researcher the use of information that is accessible to virtually everyone surveying a scene is to close off potentially productive lines of inquiry about which all of us will remain ignorant.

I believe that the researcher should think seriously about the implications and consequences of paying informants for participation in his or her study, but that, on the whole, modest, judicious, and pragmatic payment of some informants may achieve the goals of the project without compromising its integrity. Mitchell Duneier paid his *Sidewalk* informants a flat sum of money for their ongoing interviews (1999, p. 12), and I think that was a wise decision. As the reader already knows, I paid roughly a dozen informants small sums of money for their time, for sharing their thoughts, beliefs, and feelings; I am completely unapologetic about it. Using their words to create a work that could conceivably result in royalties for me (even for a book published by an academic press) seems to call for some compensation for them, and if they are working while I talk to them (begging, for instance, or busking), and I take up their time, that's time during which they could be earning money—again, which seems to warrant compensatory payment. In any case, the sums were modest. I did not pay any of my "park rules–plus" interviewees.

Researchers of crime and deviance may have to *observe* and hence, *condone*, illegal behavior in order to conduct their data gathering. Hence, they challenge, subvert, or overturn the commonly cited ethical criterion of legality. Patricia Adler (1993) observed "wheeling and dealing" among drug sellers, and wrote a book about it (taking the usual precautions against revealing her subjects' identities); she had made an informal pact with her subjects that she would not report their crimes to the police—which is, itself, a crime. Carl Klockars, a criminologist, investigated the multiple illegal transactions of his subject, a professional fence, that is, a receiver and seller of stolen goods; his book, *The Professional Fence* (1974), could not have been published had the author not witnessed and then concealed these crimes—again, writing up his results by protecting the violator's anonymity. Laud Humphreys observed and kept secret hundreds of acts of sodomy (mainly, oral sex) that were then illegal in the state of Missouri, the site of his tearoom trade research (1970, 1975). The list of participant observers of illegal behavior is long, and some of it has resulted in distinguished work, and these researchers do not—and cannot—report the crimes they have witnessed to the police. I shudder to imagine what kind of society we would have if researchers of crime, along with journalists, were not protected by the practice of confidentiality.

In my estimation, the intellectual, theoretical, and empirical value of such books and articles hugely outweighs the sin of looking the other way in the face of criminal behavior. Indeed, some researchers of deviance and crime have taken even more extreme steps by actually engaging in the behavior itself. Consider only Jeff Ferrell, who, during the course of his research and with members of the groups he studied, engaged in—and survived on—dumpster diving (2006), along with shoplifting and spraying graffiti on public surfaces (1996), and took part in skirmishes against the police to "take back urban spaces" (2001). He urges criminologists to engage in "criminological *Verstehen*," to get inside the immediacy of crime, to immerse themselves in the criminal experience itself (1998, pp. 26–28)—in other words, to study crime, the criminologist should violate the law. Many of criminology's "respected figures," he tells us, "could well be considered a rogue's gallery of common criminals" (p. 24). I don't necessarily agree with everything Ferrell says, but I do agree with the necessity of keeping mum to the police crimes that the researcher discovers during the course of the study. Up to a point.

Of course, I observed crimes taking place, though nearly all of it was marijuana selling, acts that were also readily observable by the police. But what about crimes that are much more serious than fencing, theft, drug possession and sale, and the like? Researchers have to draw a line— but where? What about rape and murder? Child pornography? What about terrorism—for instance, the threat to blow up the Empire State Building? I would not condone (nor did I observe) any such actions nor, in my estimation, would virtually any researcher who is known to me. Every researcher has to draw a line somewhere, and where he/she does is, to a certain extent, a matter of individual choice, but some actions are so heinous that virtually no participant-observer would study it directly or condone its enactment. In any case, I did not observe any such actions, and, I'd guess, few sociologists or criminologists have.

But consider an exception, the ethical lapse Erving Goffman describes, which provides us with an even more extreme, even shocking, example of a normative violation in which he seems to have colluded, apparently in the guise of ethnographic impartiality. "I have seen patients watch, passively, from a few feet away, a young male psychotic rape an old, defenseless mute man, the event occurring in a part of the day-room that was outside the view of the attendant" (1963, p. 207). In noting that the mental patients he was observing were engaged in "the practice and norm of disattending to many immediate stimuli," he admits that, while paying attention to this "disattending," *he himself* tolerated the very crime that took place. Goffman conducted his study well before institutional review boards (IRBs) were instituted, but the sociological observer might speculate whether such behavior represented an instance of an extremely and *inexcusably* unethical research practice.

In an interesting twist of fate, the issue of research ethics exploded with the appearance of the work of Erving Goffman's daughter, Alice—born in 1982, the same year that Goffman died—as a result of her "on the run" study of African American fugitives from the criminal justice system, its first iteration as an article in the *American Sociological Review* (2009), the second, as a PhD dissertation at Princeton University, in 2011, and finally, as a book (2014, 2015). Goffman, the daughter, took the ethical lapse a step further than did Goffman, the father, in that Erving only *ignored* the commission of a felony—a rape—while Alice admitted to *committing* a felony, that is, arguably, conspiracy to commit murder.

The attention paid to and the controversy over Alice Goffman's work is virtually unprecedented for an academic treatise; although her book initially attracted mostly supporters, after a time, multiple critics lodged devastating charges against the researcher, including not only possible conspiracy to commit murder but also embellishment, exaggeration, fabrication, and the inability to keep basic details straight (see Campos, 2015; Schuessler, 2015; Neyfakh, 2015). The most unusual of these critiques was a fifty-page anonymous blog sent to select scholars listing her 670 putative ethical and methodological sins, one by one; the document, and its author, would have the profession dispatch Ms. Goffman to research hell. (Jesse Singal's online *New York* magazine defense, released June 18, 2015, largely exonerates her of these charges.) Among these multiple criticisms by this horde of social science and journalistic scholars, *participating in felonious acts* stands out as most serious; she joined a group of young men with guns who were looking for the alleged killer of a friend named Chuck. "I got into the car because," she tells her readers, "I wanted Chuck's killer to die" (Goffman, 2015, p. 262). Is this ethical? Very few sociologists, myself included, would give this action an ethical pass. (Subsequently, Alice Goffman has affirmed, then rescinded, the veracity of some of her more distressing statements.) Presumably, all social scientists agree that the researcher should *not* join an expedition that has as its intention the killing of a human being, however culpable the target—who was not, as fate unfolded, actually located.

With respect to the ethical guidelines I followed in conducting this investigation, my own ethics are fairly straightforward. Don't invent anything, don't fabricate or falsify data. Everything that's described and quoted in the pages of this book actually took place, though not necessarily in the sequences described here. Though I began observing behavior in Washington Square as early as 2007, when I moved to New York City, I took a break in 2009 to tend to other matters and did not return to my observations until 2013; the renovation of the park was not completed until 2014, and so, the activities I narrate here unfolded mainly between 2015 and 2017. I admit to some fallibility in recording dialogue exactly as it is spoken, especially if I could not write it down at the time it occurred, but I believe that what appears on the pages of this book is very close to what my informants said in real life—if not word for word, at least it is accurate for meaning. (Of course, I have edited the prose I heard somewhat for continuity, compactness, and clarity.) I invented nothing. There are no composite characters in this book and no composite events. I wrote as much down as I could in the form of on-the-spot fieldnotes, and then, after I came home, I typed them up. In fact, as I explain above, several subjects didn't allow me to write down our interviews into notes as I was speaking to them, so that, in those cases, I had to rely on my memory to reconstruct the conversation. I think I managed to record most of the pertinent action and dialogue, and, I believe, distorted nothing.

A few other guidelines: Keep your promises. Try to do more good deeds than harmful ones. Try to feel empathy toward your informants:

How do *they* feel? Why do they do what they do? Whether they do monstrous or virtuous things, if you put yourself in their place, think about what impels them to engage in the behavior they enact. They are part of the human spectrum, they contributed to your understanding of humanity; you owe them at least a shred of empathy.

As a sociologist, a social scientist, and an author, to reiterate, I make the assumption that I have the right of access to virtually any public space everyone else has, that I have the right to study and write about behavior that is taking place in my research site, that I have the right to describe what I see and hear and publish these descriptions, and that knowledge is better than ignorance, as long as ethical guidelines are followed. Every author, I further assume, is under an obligation to demonstrate, through the power of his or her written work's analysis, whether and to what extent descriptions of behavior in that public scene warrant publication. I make the assumption that the strength of my investigation will address the matters of triviality and competence; if not, critics may have a go at it—or the field will ignore it altogether. Moreover, if the work does make a contribution to the literature, I assume that if the research on which it is based does not constitute or contribute to exploitation or oppression, and does not harm anyone or put participants at risk of harm, by their very attention to it, my colleagues will agree that whatever evasion or deception in which I engaged was warranted.

All of that said, in my opinion, researchers make a bigger issue about the ethics of research than subjects and informants do. Extreme cases of harm and exploitation aside, most studied people are not concerned about the nuances of most of the principles that dictate how ethnographers and field researchers ought to go about their work. In the past generation or so, however, *interest groups* have gotten into the act of complaining about procedures when research findings seem to challenge the goals they seek. Moreover, parties may object to a researcher's practices simply because their personal interests are infringed upon by them. All in all, what's most important here is the physician's Hippocratic oath: "First, do no harm." But—and there's always a *but*—as any researcher of problematic settings knows, danger to the investigator is typically greater than danger to the researched. There is no universal consensus about research ethics; no one endorses *exploiting* one's subjects, but constructs of what that entails vary from one researcher to another. *Abusing* one's research participants has a much harsher ring—no researcher would admit to doing such a thing— but fellow social scientists might disagree.

In January 2017, the Office for Human Research Protections, a subdivision of the Department of Health and Human Services, which sets research guidelines that all researchers applying for federal grants must address, revised its long-standing protocols. The new guidelines seemed to relax regulations that investigators must follow, exempting from oversight research that entails "benign behavioral interventions" (Murphy, 2017). The guidelines went on to state that a "substantial number" of social science research activities "should be allowed to proceed without IRB review." In a commentary in the *Chronicle of Higher Education*, two social scientists state that the exempted research activities "include surveys, interviews, and other forms of communication between researchers and human adults," along with observations of behavior in public places, "benign behavioral intervention," secondary analyses of data, "and other low-risk research procedures" (Shweder and Nisbett, 2017). These developments regard a hands-off, self-regulatory policy of the government, as well as universities—and IRBs—toward social science research as a kind of academic freedom. "This is a moment of truth for academe. American universities know how to talk the talk of academic freedom. Yet after so many years of overregulation do we still have the will, and the courage, to walk the walk?" (op. cit.). Time will tell if the federal government, and the academic IRBs that, for the most part, have obeyed its regulatory dictates intend to hew to this deregulation; I certainly hope so. My Washington Square Park observations and interviews clearly fall into the "hands off" territory.

I received no grant support for this investigation, and no colleagues or assistants worked with me; I conducted the study entirely on my own. I had to report to no committees or academic departments or government agencies, and there was no institutional or hierarchical entity, no IRB, that had the responsibility of evaluating the ethical or methodological niceties of the project. If I committed ethical lapses, it's on my own head, though I don't believe that I did anything wrong, at least with respect to ethics. Still, I wish I had been a more skillful ethnographer and a more competent methodologist, and in this report, this book, I explicate my inadequacies, warts and all. In the end, each reader decides on the value of the job the researcher has done, and I'll leave the matter at that.

REFERENCES

Adler, Patricia A. 1993. *Wheeling and Dealing: An Ethnography of an Upper-Level Drug-Dealing and Smuggling Community* (2/e). New York: Columbia University Press.

Adler, Patricia A., and Peter Adler. 1994. "Observational Techniques." In Norman K. Denzin and Yvonna S. Lincoln (eds.), *Handbook of Qualitative Research*. Thousand Oaks, CA: Sage, pp. 377–92.

Alden, Robert. 1959. "'Village' Tension Upsets Residents." *New York Times*, September 29, pp. 1, 42.

Allan, Matthew, Abigail Gepner, and Linda Massarella. 2016. "Cops Finally Take on Washington Square Park Crackheads." *New York Post*, August 5.

Allan, Matthew, and Bruce Golding. 2016. "Crackheads, Bums, and Hookers Rule Washington Square Park." *New York Post*, August 4.

Allen, Charlotte. 1997. "Spies Like Us: When Sociologists Deceive Their Subjects." *Lingua Franca*, 7 (November): 31–39.

Anderson, Elijah. 2011. *The Cosmopolitan Canopy: Race and Civility in Everyday Life*. New York: Norton.

Anderson, Elijah. 2013. "Emmett and Trayvon: How Racial Prejudice in America Has Changed in the Last Sixty Years." *Washington Monthly*, January/February, pp. 32–34.

Anderson, Elijah. 2015. "The White Space." *Sociology of Race and Ethnicity*, 1 (1): 10–21.

Anderson, Lincoln. 2012. "Hot Stuff! Park Benches Are Unfit to Sit, as They Hit 125 degrees F." *Villager*, August 16, pp. 1ff.

Annese, John, and Thomas Tracy. 2017. "Regular at Washington Square Park Chess Tables Nabbed for Man's Shooting Death." *New York Daily News*, February 9.

Anonymous. 2011. "Sex, Drugs & Indecent Exposure in Washington Sq. Park Bathroom," *A Walk in the Park*, awalkintheparknyc.blogspot.com.

"Art Does a Body Good during Heat Wave." 2017. *Villager*, July 27, www.thevillager.com.

Baird-Remba, Rebecca, and Gus Lubin. 2013. "21 Maps of Highly Segregated Cities in America." *Business Insider*, April 25.

Bakhtin, Michael. 1981. *The Dialogic Imagination: Four Essays* (trans. Michael Holquist). Austin: University of Texas Press.

Becker, Howard S. 1963 & 1973. *Outsiders: Studies in the Sociology of Deviance*. New York: Free Press (1st & expanded eds).

Becker, Howard S., and Irving Louis Horowitz. 1970. "The Culture of Civility." *Transaction*, 7 (April): 12–19.

Beckett, Katherine, and Steve Herbert. 2009. *Banished: The New Social Control in Urban America*. New York & Oxford, UK: Oxford University Press.

Ben-Yehuda, Nachman. 1985. *Deviance and Moral Boundaries: Witchcraft, the Occult, Science Fiction, Deviance Sciences and Scientists*. Chicago: University of Chicago Press.

Ben-Yehuda, Nachman. 1990. *The Politics and Morality of Deviance: Moral Panics, Drug Abuse, Deviance Science, and Reversed Stigmatization*. Albany: State University of New York Press.

Ben-Yehuda, Nachman. 2013. *Atrocity, Deviance, and Submarine Warfare: Norms and Practices during the World Wars*. Ann Arbor: University of Michigan Press.

Bernard, Murrye. 2011. "NYU 2013: Six Million Square Feet in 20 Years." *Buildipedia*, September 23.

Beveridge, Andy. 2017. *Gotham Gazette*, www.gothamgazette.com.

Blumer, Herbert. 1972. "Action vs. Interaction." *Trans-Action*, 9 (January): pp. 50–53.

Bogdan, Robert. 1988. *Freak Show: Presenting Human Oddities for Amusement and Profit*. Chicago: University of Chicago Press.

Borer, Michael Ian. 2006. "The Location of Culture: The Urban Cultural Perspective." *City & Community*, 5 (June): 173–97.

Bulmer, Martin. 1982. "When Is Disguise Justified? Alternatives to Covert Participant Observation." *Qualitative Sociology*, 5 (4): 251–64.

Camp, John MacK. II, and Craig A. Mauzy. 2015. *The Athenian Agora: Site Guide*. Athens, Greece: American School of Classical Studies.

Campos, Paul. 2015. "Alice Goffman's Implausible Ethnography." *Chronicle of Higher Education*, August 21.

Casey, Rionach, Rosalind Goudie, and Kesia Reeve. 2008. "Resistance and Identity: Homeless Women's Use of Public Spaces." *Housing Studies*, 23 (November): 899–916.

Chaban, Matt A.V. 2014. "Peek in Gramercy Park, Key No Longer Required." *New York Times*, December 1.

Chauncey, George. 1994. *Gay New York: Gender, Urban Culture, and the Making of the Gay Male World, 1890–1940*. New York: Basic Books.

Cohen, Stanley. 1972 & 2002. *Folk Devils and Moral Panics: The Creation of Mods and Rockers*. London: MacGibbon & Kee/London: Routledge.

Cohen, Stanley. 1985. *Visions of Social Control*. Cambridge, UK: Polity Press.

Davey, Monica. 2017. "Drop in Violence Gives a City Hope." *New York Times*, May 11, 2017, pp. A1, A16.

de Konig, Anouk. 2009. *Global Dreams: Class, Gender, and Public Space in Cosmopolitan Cairo*. Cairo: American University in Cairo Press.

Delph, Edward William. 1978. *The Silent Community: Public Homosexual Encounters*. Beverly Hills, CA: Sage.

Duneier, Mitchell. 1999. *Sidewalk*. New York: Farrar, Straus & Giroux.

Duneier, Mitchell, and Harvey Molotch. 1999. "Talking City Trouble: Interactional Vandalism, Social Inequality, and the 'Urban Interactional Problem.'" *American Journal of Sociology*, 104 (March): 1263–95.

Durham, Minerva. 2015. "Flirting and Fighting on the Real Mean Streets." *Villager*, January 15, p. 15.

Durkheim, Emile. 1893/1984. *The Division of Labor in Society* (trans. W.D. Halls). Glencoe, IL, & New York: Free Press.

Durkheim, Emile. 1895/1938. *The Rules of the Sociological Method* (trans. Sarah A. Solovay & John H. Mueller; ed. George E.G. Catlin). Chicago: University of Chicago Press.

Durkheim, Emile. 1897/1951. *Suicide: A Study in Sociology* (trans. John A. Spaulding & George Simpson; ed. George Simpson). Glencoe, IL, & New York: Free Press.

Elias, Norbert. 1978/1994. *The Civilizing Process: The History of Manners and State Formation and Civilization* (2/e; trans. Edmund Jephcott). Oxford, UK, & Cambridge, MA: Blackwell.

Ellickson, Robert C. 1996. "Controlling Chronic Misconduct in City Spaces: Of Panhandlers, Skid Rows, and Public Space Zoning." *Yale Law Review*, 105 (5): 1165–1248.

Erikson, Kai T. 1962. "A Comment on Disguised Observation in Sociology." *Social Problems*, 14 (4): 366–73.

Felson, Marcus, and Erika Poulsen. 2003. "Simple Indicators of Crime by Time of Day." *International Journal of Forecasting*, 19 (4): 595–601.

Ferrell, Jeff. 1996. *Crimes of Style: Urban Graffiti and the Politics of Criminality*. Boston: Northeastern University Press.

Ferrell, Jeff. 1998. "Criminological *Verstehen*: Inside the Immediacy of Crime." In Jeff Ferrell and Mark S. Hamm (eds.), *Ethnography at the Edge: Crime, Deviance, and Field Research*. Boston: Northeastern University Press, pp. 20–42.

Ferrell, Jeff. 2001. *Tearing Down the Streets: Adventures in Urban Anarchy*. New York: Palgrave.

Ferrell, Jeff. 2006. *Empire of Scrounge: Inside the Urban Underground of Dumpster Diving, Trash Picking, and Street Scavenging*. New York: NYU Press.

Findlay, Eileen J. Suárez. 1999. *Imposing Decency: The Politics of Sexuality and Race in Puerto Rico, 1870–1920*. Durham, NC: Duke University Press.

Finn, Robin. 2012. "That's Some Key." *New York Times*, September 30.

Folpe, Emily. 2002. *It Happened on Washington Square*. Baltimore, MD: Johns Hopkins University Press.

Foucault, Michel. 1979. *Discipline and Punish: The Birth of the Prison* (trans. Alan Sheridan). New York: Vintage Books/Random House.

Foucault, Michel. 1986. "Of Other Spaces" (trans. Jay Miskowiec). *Diacritics*, 16 (Spring): 22–27.

Friedman, Matthew, Ames C. Grawert, and James Cullen. 2017. "Crime Trends: 1990–2016" (pamphlet). New York: Brennan Center for Justice at New York University School of Law.

Gardner, Carol Brooks. 1989. "Analyzing Gender in Public Places: Re-thinking Goffman's Vision of Everyday Life." *American Sociologist*, 20 (1): 42–56.

Garland-Thompson, Rosemarie. 2009. *Staring: How We Look*. Oxford, UK, & New York: Oxford University Press. (See also: Thompson, Rosemarie Garland.).

Ghaziani, Amin. 2015. *There Goes the Gayborhood?* Princeton, NJ: Princeton University Press.

Goffman, Alice. 2009. "On the Run: Wanted Men in a Philadelphia Ghetto." *American Sociological Review*, 74 (3): 339–57.

Goffman, Alice. 2014 & 2015. *On the Run: Fugitive Life in an American City*. Chicago: University of Chicago Press/New York: Picador.

Goffman, Erving. 1959. *The Presentation of Self in Everyday Life*. Garden City, NY: Doubleday Anchor Books.

Goffman, Erving. 1963. *Behavior in Public Places: Notes on the Social Organization of Gatherings*. New York: Free Press.

Goffman, Erving. 1971. *Relations in Public: Microstudies of the Public Order*. New York: Basic Books.

Goode, Erich. 1996. "The Ethics of Deception in Social Research: A Case Study." *Qualitative Sociology*, 19 (1): 11–33.

Goode, Erich. 2015. "Ethical Issues in the Qualitative Study of Deviance and Crime." In Heith Copes and J. Mitchell Miller (eds.), *The Routledge Handbook of Qualitative Criminology*. New York & London: Routledge, pp. 49–59.

Goode, Erich. 2016. *Deviant Behavior* (11/e). London & New York: Routledge.

Gottdiener, Mark, and Leslie Budd. 2005. *Key Concepts in Urban Studies*. London & Thousand Oaks, CA: Sage.

Gregory, Kia. 2014. "Bloom Returns to Washington Square after Years of Renovation." *New York Times*, May 9.

Gross, Michael. 1993. "The Village under Siege: The Struggle to Save a Neighborhood." *New York*, August 16, pp. 30–37.

Harrell, Erika. 2012. "Violent Victimization Committed by Strangers, 1993–2010." *BJS Special Report*, U.S. Department of Justice, December.

Harris, Leslie M. 2003. *In the Shadow of Slavery: African Americans in New York City, 1626–1863*. Amherst & Boston: University of Massachusetts Press.

Harris, Luther S. 2003. *Around Washington Square: An Illustrated History of Greenwich Village*. Baltimore, MD: Johns Hopkins University Press.

Harrison-Pepper, Sally. 1990. *Drawing a Circle in the Square: Street Performing in New York's Washington Square Park*. Jackson: University Press of Mississippi.

Harvey, David. 2008. "The Right to the City." *New Left Review*, 53 (September–October): 23–40.

Hilborn, Jim. 2009. *Dealing with Crime and Disorder in Urban Parks*. Washington, DC: U.S. Department of Justice, Center for Problem-Oriented Policing (COPS).

Hond, Paul. 2017. "Parks and Recreation: A Sociologist Contemplates a Human Ecosystem." *Columbia*, Spring, p. 48.

Horowitz, Craig. 1995. "The End of Crime as We Know It." *New York*, August 14, pp. 20–27, 82.

Horwitz, Allan V. 1990. *The Logic of Social Control*. New York: Plenum Press.

Humphreys, Laud. 1970 & 1975. *Tearoom Trade: Impersonal Sex in Public Places* (1st & enlarged eds.). Hawthorne, NY: de Gruyter.

Jacobs, Jane. 1958. "Downtown Is for People." *Fortune*, 57 (April): 133–40, 236, 238, 240–42.

Jacobs, Jane. 1961. *The Death and Life of Great American Cities*. New York: Random House.

Jaynes, Gregory. 1978. "6 Guilty in Attack at Washington Square." *New York Times*, March 16.

Johnson, Kelly Dedel. 2005. *Illicit Sexual Activity in Public Places*. Washington, DC: U.S., Department of Justice, Office of Community-Oriented Policing (COPS), Problem-Oriented Guides for Police.

Johnson, Peter. 2013. "The Geographies of Heterotopia." *Geography Compass*, 7 (11): 790–803.

Karp, David A., Gregory P. Stone, William C. Yoels, and Nicholas P. Dempsey. 2015. *Being Urban: A Sociology of City Life* (3/e). Santa Barbara, CA: Praeger.

Kelling, George L., and James Q. Wilson. 1982. "Broken Windows: The Police and Neighborhood Safety." *Atlantic*, March, pp. 29–37.

Kerr, Peter. 1987. "Crushing the Drug Dealers of Washington Square." *New York Times*, November 9.

Klockars, Carl B. 1974. *The Professional Fence*. New York: Free Press.

Knightly, Annabel. 2015. *P.D.A., Public Displays of Affection*. N.p.: Kindle edition.

Koskela, Hillie. 1999. "'Gendered Exclusions': Women's Fear of Violence and Changing Relations to Space." *Geografiska Annaler*, Series B, *Human Geography*, 81 (2): 111–24.

Kotlowitz, Alex. 2014. "Deep Cover: Alice Goffman's *On the Run*." *New York Times Book Review*, June 26.

Krauss, Clifford. 1995. "Crime Lab: The Suddenly Safer City." *New York Times*, July 23.

Kusisto, Laura. 2014. "Population Shift Sees Fewer Affluent Blacks." *Wall Street Journal*, November 4.

Lax, F. Sigurd. 1998. "Heterotopia from a Biological and Medical Point of View." In Ronald Ritter and Bernd Knaller-Vlay (eds.), *The Affair of the Heterotopia*. Graz, Austria: Haus der Architektur, pp. 114–23.

Le Bon, Gustave. 1895/1960. *The Crowd: A Study of the Popular Mind*. New York: Viking Press.

Lemert, Edwin M. 1951. *Social Pathology: A Systematic Approach to the Theory of Sociopathic Behavior*. New York: McGraw-Hill.

Lennard, Suzanne Crowhurst, and Henry L. Lennard. 2008. *Genius of the European Square*. Carmel, CA: Gondolier Press.

Lewis-Kraus, Gideon. 2016. "The Trials of Alice Goffman." *New York Times Magazine*, January 7, pp. 31–37, 56–60.

Lichtenstein, Grace. 1970. "McSorley's Admits Women under New City Law." *New York Times*, August 11.

Lofland, John, David Snow, Leon Anderson, and Lyn H. Lofland. 2005. *Analyzing Social Settings: A Guide to Qualitative Observation and Analysis* (4/e). Belmont, CA: Wadsworth.

Lofland, Lyn H. 1973 & 1985. *A World of Strangers: Order and Action in Urban Public Spaces.* New York: Basic Books/Prospect, IL: Waveland Press.

Lofland, Lyn H. 1984. "Women and Urban Public Space." *Women and Environments*, 6 (April): 12–14.

Lofland, Lyn H. 1998. *The Public Realm: Exploring the Quintessential Social Territory.* New York: Aldine de Gruyter.

Logan, John R., and Brian J. Stults. 2011. "The Persistence of Segregation in the Metropolis: New Findings from the 2010 Census." Census Brief prepared for Project U.S. 2010, pp. 1–25.

Loukaitou-Sideris, Anastasia, and Renia Ehrenfeucht. 2009. *Sidewalks: Conflict and Negotiation over Public Space.* Cambridge, MA: MIT Press.

Low, Setha. 2003. *Behind the Gates: Life, Security, and the Pursuit of Happiness in Fortress America.* New York & London: Routledge.

Low, Setha M., Dana Taplin, and Suzanne Scheld. 2005. *Rethinking Urban Parks: Public Space and Cultural Diversity.* Austin: University of Texas Press.

Lowman, John, Robert J. Menzies, and T.S. Palys (eds.). 1987. *Transcarceration: Essays in the Sociology of Social Control.* Aldershot, UK: Gower.

Mangual, Rafael. 2017. "Sub-Chicago and America's Real Crime Rate." *City Journal*, Summer.

May, Reuben A. Buford. 2014. *Urban Nightlife: Entertaining Race, Class, and Culture in Public Space.* New Brunswick, NJ: Rutgers University Press.

McFarland, Gerald. 2001. *Inside Greenwich Village: A New York City Neighborhood, 1898–1918.* Amherst & Boston: University of Massachusetts Press.

McPhail, Clark. 1991. *The Myth of the Madding Crowd.* New York: Aldine de Gruyter.

McRobbie, Angela. 1994. "Folk Devils Fight Back." *New Left Review*, January–February, pp. 107–16.

Mead, George Herbert. 1913. "The Social Self." *Journal of Philosophy, Psychology, and Scientific Methods*, 10 (July 3): 374–80.

Melbin, Murray. 1987. *Night as Frontier: Colonizing the World after Dark.* New York: Free Press.

Merton, Robert K. 1938. "Social Structure and Anomie." *American Sociological Review*, 3 (October): 672–82.

Merton, Robert K. 1957. *Social Theory and Social Structure* (rev. ed.). Glencoe, IL: Free Press.

Merton, Robert K. 1976. *Sociological Ambivalence and Other Essays.* New York: Free Press.

Miller, David L. 2014. *Introduction to Collective Behavior and Collective Action* (3/e). Long Grove, Il: Waveland Press.

Miller, Terry. 1990. *Greenwich Village and How It Got That Way.* New York: Crown.

Mitchell, Richard G., Jr. 1993. *Secrecy and Fieldwork.* Newbury Park, CA: Sage.

Morrone, Francis, with photographs by James Iska. 2002. *The Architectural Guidebook to New York City* (rev. ed.). Layton, UT: Gibbs Smith.

Mumford, Lewis. 1938. *The Culture of Cities.* New York: Harcourt, Brace.

Murji, Karim, and John Solomos (eds.). 2005. *Racialization: Studies in Theory and Practice*. Oxford, UK & New York: Oxford University Press.

Murphy, Kate. 2017. "Less Scrutiny for Social Sciences." *New York Times*, May 23, p. D3.

"New Amsterdam—Origins: African Immigrants." 2018. *Geni*, www.geni.com.

Neyfakh, Leon. 2015. "The Ethics of Ethnography." *Slate*, June 18.

Parsons, Talcott. 1951. *The Social System*. Glencoe, IL: Free Press.

Paumgarten, Nick. 2007. "Girl-Counter: Counting Visitors to Bryant Park." *New Yorker*, September 3.

Peyser, Andrea. 2015. "Bums Are Running Amok in New York City and It Needs to Stop." *New York Post*, July 19.

Phadke, Shilpa, Sameera Khan, and Shilpa Ranade. 2011. *Why Loiter? Women and Risk on Mumbai Streets*. New Delhi: Penguin India.

Phelen, Jo, Bruce G. Link, Robert E. Moore, and Anne Stueve. 1997. "The Stigma of Homelessness: The Impact of the Label 'Homeless' on Attitudes toward Poor Persons." *Social Psychology Quarterly*, 60 (4): 323–37.

Potok, Mark. 2010. "Gays Remain Minority Most Targeted by Hate Crimes." *Intelligence Report* (Southern Poverty Law Center), Winter: 1–6.

Punch, Maurice. 1986. *The Politics and Ethics of Fieldwork*. Newbury Park, CA: Sage.

Ramirez, Jan Seidler. 1990. "Interpretive Script Accompanying *Within Bohemia's Borders: Greenwich Village 1830–1930*." Exhibition at the Museum of the City of New York.

Renee, Dana. 2015. *Public Displays of Affection*. N.p.: Kindle edition.

Riis, Jacob. 1890. *How the Other Half Lives: Studies among the Tenements of New York*. New York: Scribner's.

Rosenzweig, Roy, and Elizabeth Blackmar. 1992. *The Park and the People: A History of Central Park*. Ithaca, NY: Cornell University Press.

Ross, Edward Alsworth. 1902. *Social Control: A Survey of the Foundations of Order*. New York & London: Macmillan.

Rotroff, Susan I., and Robert D. Lamberton. 2006. *Women in the Athenian Agora*. Athens, Greece: American School of Classical Studies.

Rudofsky, Bernard. 1969. *Streets for People: A Primer for Americans*. Garden City, NY: Doubleday.

Ryan, William. 1976. *Blaming the Victim*. New York: Random House.

Salusbury, G.T. 1948. *Street Life in Medieval England* (2/e). Oxford, UK: Pen-in-Hand.

Schmucki, Barbara. 2012. "'If I Walked on My Own at Night I Stuck to Well Lit Areas': Gendered Spaces and Urban Transport in 20th-Century Britain." *Research in Transportation Economics*, 34 (1): 74–85.

Schuessler, Jennifer. 2015. "Heralded Book on Crime Disputed." *New York Times*, June 6, p. C1.

Scull, Andrew. 1988. "Deviance and Social Control." In Neil J. Smelser (ed.), *Handbook of Sociology*. Thousand Oaks, CA: Sage, pp. 667–93.

Serratore, Angela. 2016. "How to Get into Gramercy Park." *Curbed New York*, October 12.

Sestina, Nina. 2015. *Naughty Brat Taboo: Public Display of Affection*. N.p.: Kindle edition.

Sherman, Lawrence B., Patrick R. Gartin, and Michael E. Buerger. 1989. "Hot Spots of Predatory Crime: Routine Activities and the Criminology of Place." *Criminology*, 27 (1): 27–55.

Shweder, Richard A., and Richard E. Nisbett. 2017. "Long-Sought Research Deregulation Is upon Us: Don't Squander the Moment." *Chronicle of Higher Education*, March 12.

Sibley, John. 1964. "'Village' Angered by Rising Number of Derelicts in Washington Square." *New York Times*, September 21, p. 33.

Silver, Nate. 2015. "The Most Diverse Cities Are Often the Most Segregated." *FiveThirtyEight*, May 1, fivethirtyeight.com.

Smith, Philip, Timothy L. Phillips, and Ryan D. King. 2010. *Incivility: The Rude Stranger in Everyday Life*. Cambridge, UK, & New York: Cambridge University Press.

Stern, William J. 1999. "The Unexpected Lessons of Times Square's Comeback." *City Journal*, Autumn, pp. 1–13.

Suttles, Gerald D. 1968. *The Social Order of the Slum: Ethnicity and Territoriality in the Inner City*. Chicago: University of Chicago Press.

Suttles, Gerald D. 1972. *The Social Construction of Communities*. Chicago: University of Chicago Press.

Swalec, Andrea. 2011. "Washington Sq. Park Bathroom Hours Cut amid Concerns of Sex, Drugs." *DNAinfo*, September 22, www.dnainfo.com.

Taylor, Dorceta E. 1999. "Central Park as a Model for Social Control: Urban Parks, Social Class, and Leisure Behavior in Nineteenth-Century America." *Journal of Leisure Research*, 31 (4): 420–77.

Thompson, Rosemarie Garland. 2009. *Staring: How We Look*. Oxford, UK, & New York: Oxford University Press.

Tönnies, Ferdinand. 1887/1957. *Community and Society* (trans. Charles P. Loomis). Lansing: Michigan State University Press.

Treaster, Joseph B. 1976. "White Youths Attack Blacks in Washington Sq." *New York Times*, September 9.

Turner, Ralph H., and Lewis M. Killian. 1987. *Collective Behavior* (3/e). Englewood Cliffs, NJ: Prentice Hall.

Valentine, Gill. 1989. "The Geography of Women's Fear." *Area*, 21 (4): 385–90.

Valentine, Gill. 1990. "Women's Fear and the Design of Public Space." *Built Environment*, 16 (4): 288–303.

Vidich, Arthur, and Joseph Bensman. 1958. *Small Town in Mass Society: Class, Power, and Religion in a Rural Community*. Princeton, NJ: Princeton University Press.

Vogel, Kenneth P. 2017. "A Reporter's Accidental Scoop." *New York Times*, September 20, p. A2.

Wade, Lisa. 2012. "Norm Breaching: Social Responses to Mild Deviance." Videoreport. Los Angeles: Occidental College.

Webb, Eugene J., Donald T. Campbell, Richard D. Schwartz, and Lee Sechrest. 1966. *Unobtrusive Measures: Nonreactive Research in the Social Sciences*. Chicago: Rand McNally.

Weber, Bruce. 1995. "Town Square of Midtown: Drug Dealers' Turf Is Now Office Oasis." *New York Times*, August 25.

Weinberg, Martin S., and Colin J. Williams. 1974. *Male Homosexuals: Their Problems and Adaptations*. London & New York: Oxford University Press.

Weinstein, Heth, and Jed Weinstein. 2011. *Buskers: The on-the-Streets, in-the-Trains, off-the-Grid Memoir of Two New York City Street Musicians*. Berkeley, CA: Soft Skull Press.

Wellman, Henry M. 2014. *Making Minds: How Theory of Mind Develops*. New York & Oxford, UK: Oxford University Press.

Whyte, William H. 1979. *The Social Life of Small Urban Spaces: A Film by William H. Whyte*. New York: Municipal Art Society of New York.

Whyte, William H. 1980. *The Social Life of Small Urban Spaces*. New York: Project for Public Spaces.

Wirth, Louis. 1938. "Urbanism as a Way of Life." *American Journal of Sociology*, 44 (July): 1–24.

Wynn, Jonathan R. 2010. "City Tour Guides: Urban Alchemists at Work." *City & Community*, 9 (June): 145–64.

Wynn, Jonathan R. 2011. *The Tour Guide: Walking and Talking New York*. Chicago: University of Chicago Press.

Zukin, Sharon. 1995. *The Culture of Cities*. Walden, MA, & Oxford, UK: Blackwell Publishing.

SUBJECT INDEX

accessibility: ethnic enclaves limit, 58–59; vs. exclusivity, 243; fosters heterotopia, 243; Gramercy Park vs. WSP in, 244–245; increases diversity, 243; limited by economics, gender, and social class, 112; of streets and squares, 59; to public places, 66, 67

acquaintances, 53, 92, 202, 260

affluence, 12, 25, 67; and banishment of the indigent, 120; in Greenwich Village, 25, 74; how affluent regard the homeless, 116; locales, 169; neighborhoods, 12, 19, 247; residencies, 4, 6, 8, 9, 44, 132, 218. *See also* segregation in cities

age, ix, 1, 30, 55, 175; about forty, 110; categories, 63; characteristics, 63; of violators, 96; of women, 26–35, 200. *See also* children; elderly, the; teenagers

agents of social control: act variably, 138; audiences as, 137, 140–141; challenge deviant sensibility, 54; define crimes, 121; formal, 13, 136, 150, 160, 234; not the only deviance-definers, 14; observe wrongfulness, 155; in Washington Square, 140. *See also* audiences; NYPD; PEP

alcohol abuse, 49; alcoholics, 68, 122, 123, 231. *See also* drinking alcohol

anomie, 48, 51, 127

anonymity: vs. accountability in a crowd, 38; darkness provides, 28; of interviews, 252, 256; large cities provide, 62

Arch, the: *Arch Conspirators* etching, 4; arch conspirators on top of, 4; building of, 7; line-of-sight through, 10

arrests: crime results in, 121; crime that doesn't lead to, 128; decline in, 123; homeless as harassment, 121; keep a lid on crime, 111; as a measure of deviance, 86; as a measure of where crime occurs, 124; most recent, 34; unable to stop illegal activity, 33

assault in WSP, 44, 128, 161, 178; vs. Bryant Park, 126; as a felonious crime, 43–44; in NYC's public parks, 128; as a predatory crime, 23; sexual, 147, 160; in Tompkins Square, 126; vs. Union Square, 126

assembly, patterns and rules of, 39–42, 220

audience/s: adjusting behavior, 56; avoidance of, 18, 141; deviance defined by, xii, 13, 39, 56, 57, 80, 82–83, 86–87, 89, 94; everyone as, 89, 141; in informal social control, 158; react to violations of moral code, 86, 89, 99, 101; in social interaction, 231; taking heed of, 101; withdrawal of, 85, 100, 102, 106, 135–138, 141, 146, 153, 158, 199, 230, 241

banishment: from affluent neighborhoods, 120; a common practice, 231; in controlling vagrancy, 113; rare in WSP, 231; stifles the heterotopia, 243

begging, 114–115; attitudes toward, 120–121; prohibited, 91, 120; questions of park rules-plus, 93; WSP attracts, 18

AUTHOR INDEX

ABOUT THE AUTHOR

Erich Goode is Professor Emeritus of Sociology at Stony Brook University. He is the author of eleven books, including *Deviant Behavior*, now in its eleventh edition, and *Drugs in American Society*, currently in its ninth edition, and the editor of *The Handbook of Deviance*.